Troubles of the past?

Manchester University Press

Troubles of the past?

History, identity and collective memory in Northern Ireland

Editors:

James W. McAuley, Máire Braniff and Graham Spencer

MANCHESTER UNIVERSITY PRESS

Copyright © Manchester University Press 2023

While copyright in the volume as a whole is vested in Manchester University Press, copyright in individual chapters belongs to their respective authors, and no chapter may be reproduced wholly or in part without the express permission in writing of both author and publisher.

Published by Manchester University Press
Oxford Road, Manchester M13 9PL

www.manchesteruniversitypress.co.uk

British Library Cataloguing-in-Publication Data
A catalogue record for this book is available from the British Library

ISBN 978 1 5261 5419 4   hardback
ISBN 978 1 5261 9127 4   paperback

First published 2023
Paperback published 2025

The publisher has no responsibility for the persistence or accuracy of URLs for any external or third-party internet websites referred to in this book, and does not guarantee that any content on such websites is, or will remain, accurate or appropriate.

EU authorised representative for GPSR:
Easy Access System Europe – Mustamäe tee 50,
10621 Tallinn, Estonia
gpsr.requests@easproject.com

Typeset
by New Best-set Typesetters Ltd

Contents

List of figures	*page* vii
List of contributors	viii
Preface	xi
List of abbreviations	xiii

	Through a single lens? Understanding the Troubles of the past, present and future – *James W. McAuley, Máire Braniff and Graham Spencer*	1
1	Agonistic remembering and Northern Ireland's 1968 @ 50 – *Chris Reynolds*	14
2	Pogroms, presence, myth and memory: August 1969 and the outbreak of the Northern Ireland conflict – *Shaun McDaid*	37
3	'Touching the third rail?' The problems of dealing with the past in Northern Ireland – *Eamonn O'Kane*	56
4	Collective memory, ethno-national forgetting and the limits of history in misremembering the past – *Aaron Edwards*	78
5	Irish republicanisms and radical nostalgia – *Stephen Hopkins*	97
6	Irish republican commemoration and narratives of legitimacy – *Kris Brown*	118
7	Ulster loyalism, memory and commemoration – *James W. McAuley and Neil Ferguson*	143
8	'Remember the women': memory-making within loyalism – *Lisa Faulkner-Byrne, John Bell and Philip McCready*	165

9 Visual memory at sites of troubles past: participatory and collective memories in Croatia and Argentina – *Máire Braniff*   183

10 The tears of the mothers: conflict and memory in comparison – *Catherine McGlynn*   204

11 The problem of legacy and remembering the past in Northern Ireland – *Graham Spencer*   222

Index   243

Figures

7.1	Carson's Volunteers Mural – East Belfast, May 2018. Author's photo.	page 152
7.2	Somme/Ulster Volunteer Force Mural – East Belfast, May 2018. Author's photo.	154
9.1	Walsh memorial at Perrin's studio, 2015. Author's photo.	184
9.2	Mural of Julio López, disappeared, at the former ESMA, 2015. Author's photo.	190
9.3	Former ESMA swimming pool windows adorned with faces and names of the disappeared, 2015. Author's photo.	192

Contributors

Dr John Bell is a Lecturer in Public Services and Security at Ulster University. He completed his doctoral dissertation in 2017 at Ulster University, with his PhD research focusing upon the football fan culture surrounding the Northern Irish international football team. Prior to joining Ulster University in 2013, John spent eight years working as a research associate for the Institute for Conflict Research in Belfast.

Máire Braniff is a senior lecturer in politics at Ulster University. Her research interests include the politics of memory, victimhood and peacebuilding, and her primary research focuses comparatively on Latin America, Northern Ireland and the Balkans. Máire is a board member of the Northern Ireland Community Relations Council.

Kris Brown lectures in politics at Ulster University, and is a researcher in the Transitional Justice Institute. Kris's research interests focus on the politics of commemoration in deeply divided societies, especially its interaction with transitional justice, conflict narratives, political symbols and national identities. Other research interests include ethno-nationalism, Ulster loyalism and modern Irish republicanism.

Aaron Edwards is a senior lecturer in defence and international affairs at the Royal Military Academy Sandhurst and an honorary research fellow in the School of History, Politics and International Relations at the University of Leicester. He is the author of several critically acclaimed books, including *Mad Mitch's Tribal Law: Aden and the End of Empire* (Mainstream/Transworld Books, 2014; 2015) and *UVF: Behind the Mask* (Merrion Press, 2017).

Lisa Faulkner-Byrne is an activist and academic. She has worked with young people, women, minority ethnic groups, ex-political prisoners and former combatants across a range of social and political issues including hate crime, reconciliation, physical transformation and social welfare issues.

Neil Ferguson is Professor of Political Psychology at Liverpool Hope University, and a 2020/21 Fulbright Scholar working with START at the University of Maryland. He recently held the position of visiting research fellow at the 'Changing Character of War Programme' at Pembroke College, Oxford.

Stephen Hopkins is a lecturer in politics in the School of History, Politics and International Relations at the University of Leicester. His book *The Politics of Memoir and the Northern Ireland Conflict* was published in 2017 by Liverpool University Press. He is author of several articles, including 'Narratives of Irish Republican hunger strikes: the politics of memoir and the "Republican family", 1923 and 1981' in the *Irish Review* (2020), and in 2018 'The life history of an exemplary Provisional republican: Gerry Adams and the politics of biography' in *Irish Political Studies* 33 (2).

James W. McAuley is Emeritus Professor of Political Sociology and Irish Studies at the University of Huddersfield. He has been active in, and written extensively about, Northern Ireland politics and society for many years. His current research surrounds the long-term legacies of historical violence on present-day political attitudes and behaviour, the construction and uses of narrative and collective memory in Northern Ireland, dynamics of radicalisation, and the politics of commemoration in conflict and post-conflict societies, including Kenya, Somalia and Ukraine.

Philip McCready is a lecturer and research associate at Ulster University. Lecturing and research interests include theories of crime and deviance, young people in conflict with law and justice, restorative justice and the role of restorative practices in response to legacy issues of hegemonic and patriarchal control by the state and paramilitaries in post-conflict societies.

Shaun McDaid is a senior lecturer in Criminology at Leeds Trinity University. His research focuses on political violence and its prevention, and he has published widely on the Northern Ireland conflict.

He is author of *Template for Peace: Northern Ireland, 1972–75* (Manchester University Press, 2013), and a Fellow of the Royal Historical Society.

Catherine McGlynn is a civil servant. She has held positions as a senior lecturer in politics at the University of Huddersfield and has previously worked at the American University of Central Asia in Kyrgyzstan. Her research focuses on conflict and radicalisation and her latest book (with Shaun McDaid) is *Radicalisation and Counter-Radicalisation in Higher Education* (Emerald, 2019).

Eamonn O'Kane is Reader in Conflict Studies at the University of Wolverhampton. He is the author of *The Northern Ireland Peace Process: From Armed conflict to Brexit* (Manchester University Press, 2021) and co-author (with Paul Dixon) of *Northern Ireland Since 1969* (Routledge, 2011), as well as numerous articles and book chapters on the Northern Ireland conflict.

Chris Reynolds is Professor of Contemporary European History and Memory Studies, at Nottingham Trent University. His main research interests initially focused on events in France during Mai 68. He has widened his analysis of this period and more recently has been deeply involved in research surrounding the events and memories of 1968 in Northern Ireland. His is author of *Sous les pavés … The Troubles: France, Northern Ireland and the European Collective memory of 1968* (Peter Lang, 2014).

Graham Spencer is Emeritus Professor of Social and Political Conflict at the University of Portsmouth, Distinguished Senior Research Fellow at the Edward M. Kennedy Institute for Conflict Intervention, Maynooth and Visiting Fellow at the John McCormack Graduate School of Policy and Global Studies, University of Massachusetts, Boston. His publications include a two-volume study *Inside Accounts: The Irish Government and the Northern Ireland Peace Process* (Manchester University Press, 2019).

Preface

The origins of this book rest in a seminar series 'Northern Ireland: memory, commemoration and public symbolism', which ran between 2015 and 2017. It was funded by the Economic and Social Research Council (ESRC, award no. RES-000–23–1614, coordinated by James W. McAuley, co-applicants Máire Braniff, Jon Tonge and Graham Spencer). We wish to record our sincere thanks to the ESRC for funding the project and also put on record our thanks to those universities across the United Kingdom that hosted events, and to our own institutions for the support they gave in making the seminar series such a success.

During the time the seminar was in formal existence, over sixty papers were presented and discussed by academics and practitioners, and the feedback and contributions made freely available to a public audience. We wish to record our gratitude to all involved for their commitment to the project, and to note especially the collegiate spirit in which the seminar was conducted.

Many of the contributions in this book directly reflect the engagement in that seminar, and the issues and ideas raised within it, including: the analysis of current research trends and methodologies of memory; symbols of commemoration and sites of memory, both physical and intellectual; collective memory and forgetting, the recall and re-memorising of the 'great events' of Irish history; conflicts of culture, the politics of commemoration and socialisation; memory and reconciliation; and the politics of collective memory in comparative contexts.

This proved a rich field for research, and during the seminar series we were fortunate to explore a variety of multi- and interdisciplinary approaches to the construction and politics of memory, as well as the opportunity to explore comparative and empirical examples in the area of memory and conflict. In the spirit of these multi- and interdisciplinary approaches, we have throughout the book reproduced sometime contentious terms, such as Northern Ireland/the North of Ireland, Derry/Londonderry, the province and Ulster, as originally used by the authors.

Finally, we would like to express our appreciation and thanks to Mr Jason Diamon of F. E. McWilliams Studio and Gallery and Mr Sean Barden of Armagh County Museum for their kind assistance in reproducing the cover image of 'Women of Belfast 5' by F. E. McWilliams.

Abbreviations

DUP	Democratic Unionist Party
CIRA	Continuity Irish Republican Army
CGP	Consultative Group on the Past
CRC	Community Relations Commission
DPP	Director of Public Prosecutions
EPIC	Ex-Prisoners Interpretative Centre
ESMA	Escuela Superior de Mechanical de la Armada – Higher School of Mechanics of the Navy
FICT	Flags, Identity, Culture and Tradition commission
GFA	Good Friday Agreement
GPO	General Post Office, Dublin
HET	Historical Enquiries team (Police Service of Northern Ireland)
HIU	Historical Investigations Unit
ICIR	Independent Commission on Information Recovery
ICTY	International Criminal Tribunal for the former Yugoslavia
INLA	Irish National Liberation Army
IRA	Irish Republican Army
IRG	Implementation and Reconciliation Group
IRSP	Irish Republican Socialist Party
NIO	Northern Ireland Office
NIOD	Netherlands Institute for War Documentation – since 2010 NIOD Institute for War, Holocaust and Genocide Studies
NMNI	National Museums Northern Ireland

OHA	oral history archive
PIRA	Provisional Irish Republican Army – created following split within Republicanism in 1969–70
RSF	Republican Sinn Féin
RUC	Royal Ulster Constabulary
SHA	Stormont House Agreement
The Troubles	A colloquial term for the conflict in Northern Ireland from 1968–98
UDA	Ulster Defence Association
UVF	Ulster Volunteer Force

Through a single lens? Understanding the Troubles of the past, present and future

James W. McAuley, Máire Braniff and Graham Spencer

When the Consultative Group on the Past (CGP) published its report in 2009 addressing the legacy of the Troubles, based on extensive public meetings across Northern Ireland, it recommended four main strands of action. First, conceptualisation of addressing the past should support a 'shared and reconciled future'. Second, reviewing and investigating historical cases would be a necessary part of that process. Third, integral to inclusive and expansive understanding would be a formal 'information recovery' mechanism. And fourth, there should be examination of 'linked or themed cases emerging from the conflict' (CGP, 2009: 7).

Interestingly, the report also stressed that a legacy process should prioritise 'promoting remembering across society as a means of achieving reconciliation' (CGP, 2009: 9), and that to help create this outcome there would need to be 'mutual forgiveness' and 'mutual recognition of wrongs committed on both sides' (CGP, 2009: 15). In its overall emphasis, the report appeared to propose engagement with the past through mechanisms that support reparation in a context of shared suffering. Though there was acknowledgement of the need for some judicial mechanism to deal with unresolved conflict-related crimes, it remained clear that, for the CGP, any attempt to formally engage with the past should be seen in relation to a future that is recognisably different from the divisions, antagonisms and humiliations that sustained conflict.

Unsurprisingly, therefore, the tone is one that wants us to reflect on the past less in terms of difference (blame and agency) and more in terms of similarity (suffering and society), with the aim of encouraging us to consider in depth some of the consequences of understanding the past, in particular how what we choose to remember and how the way we do so informs relations with that past. On that the message is clear: to escape from the suffering of the past we need to remember it differently and that difference is the basis for a new future.

In 2009 the CGP report was sidelined. Subsequently, there has been much work and noise about legacy, much of it divisive and driven by ideological and political motivation as well as pursuit of accountability and justice by the families of victims. In this context the imposition of suffering and so the responsibility for it is attributed to others, with demands for justice supplanting the needs of the individual to secure communal or organisational advantage. In this context, suffering is often used to reinforce victim and perpetrator narratives, both of which reflect party-political and communal divisions rather than address individual needs. What unites the positions of political parties in relation to this approach is the expectation of justice.

Contemporary developments have seen the British Secretary of State Brandon Lewis, some twelve years after the CGP report, conclude in 2021 that a justice-focused legacy process would be too divisive to pursue (Lewis, 2021). In a statement to the House of Commons in July of that year, Lewis declared:

> It is now a difficult painful truth that the focus on criminal investigations is increasingly unlikely to deliver successful criminal justice outcomes, but all the while it continues to divide communities and fails to obtain answers for a majority of victims and families.

Lewis expands the point as follows:

> If we fail to act now to properly address, acknowledge and account for the legacy of the Troubles, we will be condemning both current and future generations to further division, preventing reconciliation at both the individual and societal level.

The impact of this is that the British government would continue to pursue information and testimony from all sections of society but would not pursue perpetrators through the courts. The expectation of a legacy process being determined by legalistic procedures was effectively ended with legacy repurposed entirely as an oral and narrative process, since a

> focus on information would offer the best chance of giving more families some sense of justice through acknowledgement, accountability and restorative means.

As an acknowledgement that the CGP report had not lost its value, Lewis cited it directly in the conclusions to his statement, saying: 'To look backward for a while is to refresh the eye, to restore it, and to render it more fit for its prime function of looking forward.'

The emphasis on remembering and providing testimony about the Troubles has generated attention and focus on the experiences of individual suffering. As a result, this has established a new context on the basis of commonality and sameness rather than division and difference. As Lewis has stressed, the legacy process has now moved from the selective emphasis on justice and revenge to one that prioritises the collation of public and personal memories. As such, it allows those who do not seek recourse through justice the same opportunities to be heard as those who do.

Lewis's statement was not well received by any of the political parties in Northern Ireland and it is important to recognise those who do not feel that his approach is enough. But one notable potential is that this approach of offering the same opportunity for all to record and present their experience of suffering is more inclusive than the justice model. Whether it will lead to reconciliation (however defined) is another question entirely.

This volume takes the above context and examines further the implications of remembering (and forgetting) the past and what the possible social and political consequences emerging from various forms of recall and recollection might be for Northern Ireland. It may seem to some that this ground calls for a historical approach. Such an approach only takes us so far, however, and important though history is, we need to appreciate how memory operates outside of historical boundaries and functions as an expression of individual experience and community expectation.

In this book, we focus on how and why people recall particular events and the impact this has on the present and the future. Memory is active and continually fashioned. It is constructed and reconstructed, interpreted and reinterpreted to become part of now and a determinant for what lies ahead. Unlike historical analysis, memory offers a way to discuss the future and, in turn, how we might live better.

Memories of past events are relayed in several ways, for example through popular culture, the media, in demonstrations in the public sphere, political speeches and pamphlets, as well as in narratives, folk tales, stories and popular histories, and local history events. It is through such mechanisms that existing memories are often transmitted across generations in ways that are distorted and shaped to meet the present needs, political concerns and purposes of a particular group. Here, they tend to rely on a pregiven and 'common-sense' narrative, to ensure coherence and commitment among group members. Thus, perceptions of the individual, the self, others and collectives are created through struggles with identity and belonging, both of which are used to support a selective and reconstructed past.

One illustration of the treatment of memory can be found in the work of the Nobel Prize-winning Columbian writer Gabriel Garcia Márquez, in his superb novel *One Hundred Years of Solitude: Memories and Genocide* (2014 [1970]). The novel is set in the fictional village of Macondo and the tale contains a matrix of narratives that draw from memories and stories as told by inhabitants of the village. In one of the later passages, Columbian military forces open fire on a group of unarmed striking workers, killing several thousand. The workers were from the local American-owned banana plantation, which provided the bulk of employment in the region and upon which almost all inhabitants were dependent for their livelihoods. (The events mirror an actual incident from Márquez's own life history that took place not far from his birthplace in 1928, when many civilians were brutally murdered.)

In the novel, the bodies of the murdered workers are bundled onto freight trains and taken away by the army before being dumped in the sea. A tropical storm, seemingly conjured up in mysterious circumstances by one of the company's directors and lasting nearly five years, all but destroys any traces of the village, washing away not only the remaining inhabitants but also the physical space that the village occupied. One consequence is that all knowledge of the massacre is lost from history, and all memories of Macondo as a place, along with all recollections of social and political relationships, are lost too.

As a result, subsequent generations possess no knowledge of Macondo as a place and so have no understanding of its history. Indeed, they are taught in school textbooks that that there never was a place called Macondo and no banana plantation, and they find no reference to any widespread murder by the forces of the state. This narrative became so dominant and powerful in its telling and retelling that the only survivor of the massacre (who to this point had been in the background) is unable to convince anyone of the validity of his story, or that mass murder ever took place.

In the novel's closing scenes, we learn that despite attempts to erase the events of Macondo from history and memory, counter-narratives and memories are still active in the present (largely due to the efforts of the sole survivor of the massacre), supported by a manuscript recounting what happened. Much of the strength of these counter-narratives rests with the mysterious individual from the past who is determined to keep the 'truth' of the past alive. We learn at the end of the book that this person is the narrator.

A magic-realist novel set in South America may seem a strange starting point for an academic book about Northern Ireland, but Márquez's book, while fictional (although parts are semi-biographical), provides many parallels when considering the role of memory and narrative in contemporary society. Notions of truth and concerns about who can be seen to legitimately recall past events have become central to contemporary political discourses in Northern Ireland. Moreover, questions of how and why parts of the past are kept alive, while other events in history are forgotten, are of crucial importance in assessing how contemporary identities are made and used to shape political agendas. This brings us back to the inclusivity (or not) of commemorative and memorial practices, and how these manifest in the everyday roles of memory and collective memory.

Questions of memory

Central to this book are important questions about the role of memory, how it is constructed, who performs the acts of defining and reproducing the past, and the consequences of groups understanding that past in particular ways. Albeit from different perspectives, the contributors raise important questions about why certain individuals and memories hold attention and are commemorated, while others do not and are forgotten. Of central concern for many of the authors is the role of memory in understanding and presenting senses of the past that are accepted or defended as a matter of great importance in the everyday lives of people in Northern Ireland.

Contributors to the book explore and explain how selective narratives influence the present and consider how historical events are used in everyday conversations or commemorated as vital to community life and belonging. They present numerous examples of how constructions of the past are clearly bounded by, and intertwined with, issues of memory, giving rise to questions about inclusion or exclusion, and the seemingly intractable positions (which are more often monologues than dialogues) being forwarded about how to deal with the past in Northern Ireland. None of this is to say that recalling what has gone before is in any way straightforward, or that what is remembered (or sometimes forgotten) is agreed, uniform or homogenous in nature. Indeed, questions surrounding what and how earlier periods are depicted, and how particular events in the past are featured, or neglected, are a core focus for political consciousness and seen as such here.

Collective memory and Northern Ireland

The 'boom' in research of the concept of collective memory, pointed to by Jay Winter (2000) and Chris Reynolds in this volume, has led to the emergence of a huge interdisciplinary field of research that shows no signs of slowing down or having reached its peak. Research in this area has gathered much interest since the late 1990s, and has formed the basis for a multitude of writings on the subject across several disciplines. This is reflected in the contributions to this volume that draw on the concept in slightly different ways (see, for example, the chapters by Spencer, McGlynn, Braniff, McAuley and Ferguson, O'Kane); however, all display an interdisciplinary approach and ethos.

We can think of collective memory as a shared body of knowledge – which is based on processes – that draws on constructed narratives, discourses and images to reinforce the ideas and values of a group, both now and in the future. Shaun McDaid, for example, clearly demonstrates in Chapter 2 how explanations of the outbreak of the 1969 disturbances have been reconsituted in the context of the memory of previous violence of 1920, to assume a continuity that provides important explanatory power among contemporary republicans. Collective memory is utilised at different levels and by various groups to influence how community, regional identity and nationhood are seen, represented and reproduced. This volume makes clear how those processes of inclusion and exclusion operate.

Several writers turn their attention to how collective memory manifests in the everyday life of those who self-identify as republicans, British, Irish, loyalists, nationalists, combatants, soldiers or none of these (see the chapters by Hopkins, Edwards, McAuley and Ferguson, Brown, Faulkner-Byrne *et al.*). Particular attention is given to how such memories shape and give meaning to commonplace discourse, or influence the dynamic of everyday conversation. Others, meanwhile, turn to the role collective memory plays in more official accounts of history, and how this is reflected in the political positioning of both the British and Irish governments (see the chapters by McDaid, Spencer, Reynolds). In so doing, the authors consider not just the shape and form of the resultant narratives, but how these narratives influence relationships and guide contemporary political decision-making.

Identity, memory and belonging

The production of collective memories, and their subsequent ownership and use, is core to the formation of social identity. In this book, although we encounter collective memory as a process of shared knowledge about the past, we also look at how that shared knowledge provides meaning in the present and interrogate the role of conflicting identities as an influence on memory. We also encounter how a solidifying of identity and belonging takes place, not through historical consistency or facts about history, but through an interpretive process whereby certain events are remembered, explained, and relentlessly articulated, transmitted and filtered to form patterns of continuity and consistency for group purposes. In Chapter 4, for example, Aaron Edwards demonstrates the role of collective memory in constructing senses of belonging and a strong community identity to form powerful sociopolitical bonds.

It is through the consideration of much of the above that this book aims to shed light on processes of remembering, disremembering, recall and forgetting, including sometimes deliberate amnesia, and how these relate to, and are found in, contemporary issues of identity and politics in Northern Ireland. Many of the contributors refer to the multifaceted political, social and psychological processes and practices involved and the role they played in shaping identity and senses of the past for both the individual and the group (see Reynolds, Faulkner-Byrne *et al.*, Brown and Edwards for examples).

Each chapter investigates, in its own way, and from a variety of disciplinary perspectives, the processes through which collective memory provides a point of reference to make sense of events and current group identities. Such processes are of relevance not only in Northern Ireland but also far beyond; in their chapters, taken together, Máire Braniff, Shaun McDaid and Catherine McGlynn provide a comparative background to demonstrate more widely how identity is used to sustain expectations about community life.

In considering the ability of memory to separate and divide, it is always important to deliberate how, and by whom, such recollections are created and reproduced. Throughout the book, we find that various groups, including state and non-state actors, memory hosts and entrepreneurs, families, peer groups, local communities and nations, all play a role in this. Memories are constructed by these groups to become a locus for making sense of the present, and core to this book is understanding how issues of memory are used to bridge the past with the present. As Graham Spencer points out in Chapter 11, the issue of victimhood has been pushed to the forefront of contemporary political debates and arguments in Northern Ireland, the definition of which, for many, rests in a very different understanding and remembering of the past.

The consequences of such remembering reflect different notions of identity and collectively serve to mobilise opposing and competing understandings of the past. People are not inactive in constructing their sense of identity, which is formulated and reinforced through the continuous reformatting of biographical, autobiographical and group experiences. By drawing on history in a collective way, common narratives are formed and communal interpretations of the past allow people to form affiliations and relations with that past that become central to communal identity. It is, therefore, apparent that the production of memories and their subsequent ownership is core to the formation of identity as memories provide a coherent sense of meaning and belonging that uses the past to make sense of the here and now.

Reproducing memory through symbolism and narrative

Memory is often reproduced and communicated across generations through an easily accessible and common-sense narrative, albeit one that is subject to change to suit the needs of the present, with collective memory often transmitted through recognisable symbolism that serves to enhance group coherence. Thus, perceptions of the self and of others are intertwined, forged in debates and struggles around identity and the finding of an appropriate story that gives meaning and context to that which has gone before.

In this sense, the memory that is reproduced is always social, shaped through interactions between people and groups and developed within specific political and social circumstances. In considering this, due attention must be given to the role of public symbolism, and the 'social and cultural patternings of public and personal memory' (Olick, 1999: 333). Much of the focus of this volume is on how remembering operates to validate collective representations of the past. Throughout the book we encounter many examples of how, by privileging one particular set of readings and understandings of the past over others, social identities are constructed to complement meaning and the self-image of certain groups.

In addressing these issues, some of the authors in this volume examine how cultural tools, such as texts, songs and stories, are used to frame people's understanding of and relationships to the past. They also consider how these cultural tools influence the shape of contemporary discourses, symbolism and public debate in Northern Ireland. This is notable in Kris Brown's chapter, which clearly demonstrates the ways in which symbolism supplies a powerful tool to allow political actors to promote particular stories in order to evoke imagined and emotion attachment.

Commemoration and the theatre of memory

In creating narratives and symbolism, collective memory remains a crucial component in the reproduction of communal memories and identities. For Connerton, such commemorative ceremonies constitute a 'theatre of memory', where performances remind a community of its collective identity (Connerton, 1989: 70). The focus here, is on active remembering. It is this which distinguishes those commemorative events, which are typically planned with the purpose of enthusiastically affirming and reinforcing particular happenings or individuals from the past (see Brown, Hopkins, McAuley and Ferguson). These events seek to highlight and restate collective values and interpretations of the past, often emphasising that to which people are emotionally attached, and seeking to preserve such values and interpretations for future generations.

Remembering triggers the desire for ritual and ceremony, and this finds expression through most of the commemorative events encountered in this book. Some events are specifically staged so that the wider society are forced to remember and reflect upon meanings in relation to today's politics and society (see, for example, Brown, McAuley and Ferguson, McDaid, Reynolds). In form and organisation, commemorative events usually share similarities across a wide range of other types of planned events, festivals and commemorations. Commemorative dates provide powerful centrepieces for the presentation and communication of identity. As Connerton (1989) argues, such dates are imbued with special privilege and power, and are chosen for their perceived legitimacy and credibility. Hence, annual commemorative events, such as 12 July or the anniversary of the death of Bobby Sands, provide a focus and context for portrayals that reinforce social authenticity and reaffirm political views and expectations.

Some of the many commemorative events in Northern Ireland today involve still-living participants and those who were involved, or at least around, at the time of the original incident. By contrast, commemorations of events longer in the past (for example, centenaries) obviously do not draw directly on living memories. Rather, they are derived from the imagination to produce memories and interpretations of the past as determined by contemporary groups. This rests on collective memory to restate the importance of a coherent and constrained view of the past.

Commemoration works to directly shorten time and to flatten the collective memories of individuals and their community. One central theme that emerges throughout the book is linking issues of collective remembering and forgetting, memorialisation and commemoration. Contributors seek to identify how, in the Northern Irish context, collective memory is used in the construction of oppositional identities, which still operate at the core of that society. Importantly, this has less to do with reviving details of historical account, and more to do with what people think happened and how they see this as having an effect on their everyday lives.

Memory use and mobilisation in Northern Ireland

A further consideration in the book is how collective memory serves the interests of political movements and groups by helping to encourage mobilisation and activities to support these movements and groups. As we have seen, people are far from passive in the construction of their identity. Memory fulfils several crucial roles; importantly, one of these is to connect and unite people. Various authors in this volume (see Hopkins, Brown, McAuley and Ferguson, McGlynn, Braniff) consider not only how the past is constructed, reconstructed, understood and commemorated, but also the ways in which these processes are harnessed and mobilised to political and social effect.

Interpretations of collective memory can be, and are, used to bring about political action. In part, this is determined by how individuals and groups use – perhaps manipulate – collective memory to underpin a moral or political position and subsequent expectations of political action. The chapters by Máire Braniff, Catherine McGlynn, Lisa Faulkner-Byrne et al. and Shaun McDaid also explore issues surrounding the processes of what people recall of the past and what they do not. Collectively, they question why some individuals remember events from yesteryear in great detail, even if they have not directly experienced them, yet forget others, even if they happened in their lifetimes.

Culture and memory wars

The answer to questions surrounding why and how particular events are recalled and recorded almost without question, while the remembering of others is highly contested, or seemingly ignored, remain central to anyone undertaking a serious study on the role of collective memory. In examining the manner in which memories are continually and constantly fashioned, constructed and reconstructed, and the past interpreted, reinterpreted and represented, several other contributors focus on how collective memories and commemorative narratives are often adjusted and embedded in the public sphere. This occurs through vehicles such as popular culture, cartoons, stories, songs, school curricula, theatrical presentations, local histories, commemorations, celebrations, film, the print and electronic media, memorials and even tattoos and gravestones. All are used to provide reference points to construct and reinforce political and social identities and differences that reinforce group belonging.

In Northern Ireland, the overt face of politics has changed. Large-scale open conflict has receded, to be replaced by a fractious society, still interspersed with outbreaks of sectarian violence and a public arena best characterised by a widespread state of social and political distrust. For some, this has resulted in a culture of conflict involving violence being transformed into a culture of conflict that is serviced by oppositional narratives and debates about the past.

Large sections of civil society are now fully engaged with these narratives. They are constantly and consistently used to represent the present as well as help cement political and cultural differences, particularly between the republican and loyalist communities (see Brown, Edwards, McAuley and Ferguson, Faulkner-Byrne *et al.*). In their chapters, Stephen Hopkins and Graham Spencer point to the continual and ongoing debates surrounding how Northern Ireland should account for its past – whether, for example, the best way to deal with this is through some organised practice of collective remembering, perhaps in the form of a truth commission, or perhaps simply to draw a line under the Troubles and move on. The choice is far from straightforward or uncontested. As Spencer points out, underpinning all of this are other concerns; for example, can all those who see themselves as victims be deemed legitimate, or deserving of reparations? Or indeed, are all those who claim such status worthy of being called victims, if they were engaged in illegal activity at the time?

Structure of the book

Alongside the broad engagement by all the authors with the social and political implications emerging from the use of collective memory, commemoration and forgetting, there are four substantive areas covered in this book. Chapters 1 and 2, by Chris Reynolds and

Shaun McDaid, respectively, consider the role of remembering in the outbreak of conflict and the early Troubles. Chapters 3 and 4, by Eamonn O'Kane and Aaron Edwards, respectively, examine how remembering and forgetting have been and are used to make sense of the past, not just at the everyday level but also through official and governmental constructs, which are often directly reflected in policy. Steven Hopkins (Chapter 5), Kris Brown (Chapter 6), James W. McAuley and Neil Ferguson (Chapter 7), and Lisa Faulkner-Byrne, John Bell and Phillip McCready (Chapter 8), all in differing ways, outline how memory, identity and senses of belonging are used not just to consider what has gone before but also to shape narratives that directly influence contemporary political life and action. Chapters 9 and 10 by Máire Braniff and Catherine McGlynn, respectively, deal with the international dimension, reflecting on the uses of memory and commemoration in other conflict and post-conflict societies and offering us comparative perspectives to help us better reflect on the tensions between memory and forgetting in Northern Ireland. Finally, the book is brought to its conclusion by Graham Spencer's Chapter 11, which considers some of the main problems encountered in dealing with issues of legacy and remembering in Northern Ireland.

References

CGP (Consultative Group on the Past) (2009) *Report: Executive Summary*. Belfast: CGP. Available at: https://cain.ulster.ac.uk/victims/docs/consultative_group/cgp_230109_report.pdf (accessed 7 July 2022).

Connerton, P. (1989) *How Societies Remember*. Cambridge: Cambridge University Press.

Lewis, B. (2021) 'Secretary of State for Northern Ireland, Brandon Lewis MP, oral statement: Wednesday 14th July 2021: addressing the legacy of Northern Ireland's past'. London: Northern Ireland Office. Available at: https://bit.ly/3nnzOAI (accessed 15 December 2021).

Márquez, G. G. (2014 [1970]) *One Hundred Years of Solitude: Memories and Genocide*, trans. Gregory Rabassa. London: Penguin.

Olick, J. K. (1999) 'Collective memory: the two cultures', *Sociological Theory*, 17: 333–48.

Winter, J. (2000) 'The generation of memory: reflections on the "memory boom"', *Contemporary Historical Studies, Bulletin of the German Historical Institute*, 27: 69–92.

1

Agonistic remembering and Northern Ireland's 1968 @ 50

Chris Reynolds

Of all the issues facing the political institutions in Northern Ireland that could help explain the turbulence since around 2016, that concerning the question of 'legacy' is unquestionably one of the most challenging. While there is broad agreement that carefully developed and considered mechanisms need to be established in order to manage this highly sensitive aspect of the peace process, there is little consensus on how this should actually be done. The scattergun approach taken so far has seen the emergence of some broadly agreed principles, but the time has come for a more defined, strategic approach.

This chapter draws on the example of a collaborative project between the author and National Museums Northern Ireland (NMNI) on the question of Northern Ireland's 1968 to propose a potentially fruitful approach to confronting the legacy issue head-on. Starting with an overview of the difficulties of managing the past in Northern Ireland, the chapter then moves to set out the context of the theoretical field of memory studies with a specific focus on defining the notion of agonistic memory.

There then follows a discussion of how the antagonistic–cosmopolitan–agonistic paradigm can be applied to the context of the province as it has moved from violence to peace. The example of the civil rights struggle of 1968–69 and the memory politics surrounding this pivotal moment is then used to demonstrate the difficulties and a potential way through them. It will be argued that the expansion and effectiveness of the NMNI collaboration provides potentially applicable lessons beyond the case of Northern Ireland's 1968.

Managing the difficult legacy of the past

The signing of the Good Friday Agreement (GFA) in 1998 has gone down in history as a momentous and pivotal moment in the history of Northern Ireland. Following a long period of negotiation, this accord paved the way for the end of structured violence and the onset of peace. In the years since, life in Northern Ireland has changed dramatically (Byrne, 2014; Tonge, 2013: 92–93). This is most obviously evident in the absence of the daily violence which provided the depressing backdrop to life during the Troubles of 1968–98. As the years have passed and the province has sought to extricate itself from the conflict, the benefits of transitioning towards peace have been identifiable in many other areas.

So, for example, the economic rewards of peace have been remarkable. One only has to look at the infrastructure developments and general modernisation of the economy to see that peace has enabled investment that previously stayed away. Surfing the wave of positivity captured by sporting successes and the blooming film industry, tourism has boomed and is now a staple of the Northern Irish economy (Bairner, 2008; Boyd, 2019). Generally speaking, a sense of hope and positivity hangs in the air where once one could only really sense fear and suspicion. This, of course, is not to suggest that the post-1998 era has been without its difficulties.

The Northern Ireland peace process is precisely that, a process. Peace may well have been won with the signing of the GFA but it is an imperfect peace and one that requires management so as to prevent any risk of a return to the dark days of the Troubles (Armstrong et al., 2019). Such imperfection stems from the fact that the Belfast Agreement did not really solve any of the fundamental issues that underpinned the conflict and have remained in place since. The divisions that pitted communities against each other are still present and help explain the various challenges that have had to be overcome in the process to date. These issues have included delicate questions related to the decommissioning of weapons, the role of the police, how to deal with prisoners and the establishment of political institutions (Cochrane, 2013; Power, 2011).

The ongoing nature of division that defines Northern Irish society explains why such questions have been the source of such intense debate and tension. However, despite the great difficulties, these issues have been overcome as the peace process has bedded in and plotted its course. That is not say that no challenges remain. One only has to consider the ongoing political instability of the Stormont Assembly to take stock of the fact that much work is required before we can talk of any genuine sense of normalcy.

There are many reasons to explain why, since 2016, the political institutions in Northern Ireland have been in such turmoil. The Renewable Heat Incentive scandal may well have been the issue that brought Stormont down, but one must also be mindful of the broader context of Brexit and simmering tensions around debates on the Irish Language Act and rights issues (Fenton, 2019; Savage, 2019; Tonge, 2016; Walker and Carrol, 2019). Perhaps even more important was the question of legacy. Much of the discussion that had been at the core of tensions leading up to 2016 concerned the thorny issue of how the past was to be handled as part of the peace process (McEvoy and Bryson, 2016; McGrattan and Hopkins, 2017). Over the years, it has been clear that this was an element of the peace process that was going to create serious difficulties but one that needed to be tackled. It may well have been the case that the process needed a certain level of maturity before these questions could be addressed.

When one considers the progressively marked prominence this question has attained thanks to the increasing number of initiatives announced over the years, it is obvious that governments in London, Dublin and Belfast have come to accept that it is a question that requires careful management. We find clear examples of this approach in initiatives such as the 2014 Stormont House Agreement (NIO, 2014), the formation of the Flags, Identity, Culture and Tradition (FICT) commission in 2016 and the 2018 Northern Ireland Office public consultation on 'Addressing the legacy of Northern Ireland's past' (NIO, 2018).

However, despite the various attempts and initiatives aimed at tackling the legacy issue, it would be wrong to suggest that any have been successful enough to make any real progress. Indeed, it would be fair to argue that there has been a genuine inability to come up with an agreed roadmap that has been backed by political representatives and received the support of the general public (McEvoy and Bryson, 2016: 70–74). Indeed, the legacy issue remains perhaps the greatest stumbling block facing the peace process at the beginning of the 2020s, and it is not one that can simply be brushed aside. The reason why the past poses such difficulties is to be found in the very nature of the process itself.

As mentioned previously, the GFA may well have ended much of the violence, but it did not solve the issues that underpinned the conflict. As a result, there are no obvious winners or losers; debates over responsibility and accountability are mired in controversy and conjecture in a context where there is no clear line between who should be considered the victims and who were the perpetrators (Lawther, 2014). Constructive ambiguity may well have been an important ingredient in arriving at some sort of agreement in 1998 but it is also one of the greatest weaknesses of the peace process (Dingley, 2005).

More an accommodation than an accord, the GFA has enabled a sharing of the spoils of peace that has been vital to its maintenance since. However, while it has been possible to spread the economic and social benefits of the ending of the conflict across the divides, it is not so easy to do the same with how the past is remembered (Beiner, 2018; Brown and Grant, 2016). Each community looks back on the past through its own prism and based on its own needs and identity (McDowell and Braniff, 2014; Smyth, 2017; Viggiani, 2014). Right across the divides, the past is very present and at the heart of how communities make sense of themselves and their predicaments.

Frequent mobilisation of the past is part and parcel of Northern Irish culture; it is a central aspect of life there and often the source of much tension (Lundy and McGovern, 2001; McAuley, 2016). Furthermore, the fact that many people are still living with the consequences and fallout of the violent conflict of 1968–98 and have many questions that remain unanswered in terms of responsibility and accountability means that the population is by no means willing to draw a line under what happened and turn the page (Bell, 2003; Dawson, 2014).

These factors converge with the perpetuation of communal divisions to help explain why perspectives on the past have remained divided and such a source of intense debate. It is precisely this conundrum that explains the challenge that legacy presents. Before proposing one potentially fruitful response to this challenge via the example of a collaborative project with NMNI on the issue of the events of

1968, let us first of all outline the theoretical parameters that provide the scaffolding for this innovative project and its approach.

Memory modes

Since the 1980s we have witnessed the rise and rise of memory studies (Bell, 2008: 148; Winter, 2000: 69–92). This 'boom' has led to the emergence of a huge interdisciplinary field of research that shows no signs of slowing down or having reached its peak. This 'growth industry' has seen the question of memory become a central focus of a whole plethora of research projects and increasingly intense, complex debates (Dutceac-Segesten and Wüstenberg, 2017). Such a surge in interest is to be understood as part and parcel of a more general turn to the past that has led to a much more critical, sophisticated and detailed examination of society's relationship to the past and the mechanisms that shape how it is remembered and passed on (Bell, 2008; Cubitt, 2007: 1–2; Phillips, 2004: 2; Radstone and Schwartz, 2010: 2).

As interest has grown and the reach of memory studies has spread, one of the logical consequences has been the complication of it as a field, as exemplified by the proliferation of memory modes that have come to define the various applications of memory theory (Wertsch, 2002: 30). These modes have included memory understood as 'collective', 'cultural', 'social', 'communicative' or 'multi-directional', to name but a few. This chapter takes as its focus one of the latest additions to the list of modes: agonistic memory.

The notion of agonistic memory was first discussed by Cento Bull and Hansen (2016) where they set out how the merits of agonism more generally – as advanced by Chantal Mouffe (2000; 2005) to help overcome the challenges faced by contemporary society – could be applied to approaches on how we deal with the past. Indeed, Mouffe's theory set out how the defining characteristics of modern-day politics and society had been on a journey that had moved from systems based on antagonism through to those focused on the notion of cosmopolitanism. Despite the benefits of such a transition, for Mouffe (2012), the time was ripe for a necessary change, one defined by agonism.

Mouffe argues that the era that brought the world to the brink, culminating in the Second World War, was one that was dominated by nationalism that defined predominant, antagonistic outlooks. The very nature of nationalism was one that saw the emergence of a clear 'Us vs Them' approach to managing social and political relations and dealings on the international stage. Nations defined themselves in opposition to each other and were set on a course that reached its inevitable conclusion with the global conflicts of the first half of the twentieth century (Mouffe, 1993; 2000; 2005). For Cento Bull and Hansen (2016), memory practices were equally defined by this divisive and antagonistic logic. History and the past were instrumentalised to feed into and bolster a sense of nationalism that inevitably saw perspectives pitted one against the other (Cento Bull and Hansen, 2016: 391).

It is the conclusion of the Second World War and the emergence of a desire to avoid any future such conflicts that paved the way for the rise of a new approach to replace the antagonistic model that had previously proved so damaging and costly. This new era is described as being defined by cosmopolitanism. Mouffe argues that in order to overcome the challenges exposed as responsible for bringing the world to the brink, a new mentality emerged that sought to focus on greater collaboration, particularly at a transnational level. This new mentality post-1945 explains the emergence of supranational bodies such as the North Atlantic Treaty Organization, the United Nations and the European Union (Mouffe, 2005; 2012).

Mouffe further explains that in order to replace the vicissitudes of antagonism, there was an explicit focus on finding consensus and agreement across previous divides. Just as was the case in the previous model, everything would become defined by such an approach, including mechanisms on how the past was treated. Cento Bull and Hansen outline how cosmopolitanism came to define memory practices and saw the emergence of a new approach to the past, one focused on reaching some sort of agreed narrative, often with a specific focus on issues of human rights and the place of victims (Cento Bull and Hansen, 2016: 391–92).

Despite the unquestionable merits of cosmopolitanism, Mouffe has argued that it has reached its limits and indeed is partly responsible for some of the difficulties of twenty-first-century Europe that have brought back a certain degree of antagonism (Mouffe, 2012). For example, Mouffe argues that the case of the European Union and the difficulties it has faced in terms of its political legitimacy is the result of cosmopolitanism. The explicit avoidance of certain issues and debates as a result of the quest for a more conciliatory, consensus-driven approach has meant that uncomfortable issues and truths have been marginalised and left to fester. The upshot has been that those elements opposed to the advancement of the European project have been able to pick up and instrumentalise such questions, claiming they have led to certain sectors of society being forgotten and neglected in order to present some sort of political alternative (Mouffe, 2012).

It is no surprise, it is argued, that populist politics has grown so fiercely in the first decades of the twenty-first century; this has been facilitated by the cosmopolitan approach that has reached its limits and is now providing the grounds for the antagonistic elements it seeks to eradicate to make a return. Cento Bull and Hansen point to how memory politics have been an importance feature of such developments as extreme political forces have sought to use the more contested and uncomfortable aspects of the past to stir up tensions and generate support for their own objectives (Cento Bull and Hansen, 2016: 393). The answer, they advance, follows that of Mouffe's more general conclusion that the time is ripe for an approach to memory that is based on agonism.

Instead of marginalising the more difficult issues and debates in the interest of reaching some sort of consensus, Mouffe argues that they should in fact be part of the approach so as to guarantee what she considers a vital element of democracy: conflict (Mouffe, 2012: 633). This friction, it is argued, is a necessary component of helping society advance and make progress. Its obfuscation may well help reach some sort of consensus but, eventually, by its very nature, such an approach will marginalise certain people, whose ideas and beliefs will go on to pose a serious risk to the democratic structures of our society.

Bringing the difficult elements into the conversation, confronting the discomforting issues and accepting that such conflict can be a constructive attribute is what the agonistic approach advocates. Cento Bull and Hansen (2016: 400) have argued that such ideas are equally applicable to the question of memory. As part of the cosmopolitan approach, efforts have been made to try to establish a consensual narrative on the past that has contributed to the generally conciliatory objectives. However, in so doing, certain memories of the past, deemed too difficult to confront or not in keeping with the dominant narrative, have inevitably been marginalised. It is precisely such sidelined memories that have been manipulated by opposition forces to help bolster their objectives. To combat this, it is argued that agonistic memory practices, which seek to make difficult pasts part and parcel of conversations, are the way forward. Only by engaging with the uncomfortable truths of our past are we able to negate their instrumentalisation by negative forces; only by making such problematic narratives part of the story is it possible to formulate a genuinely inclusive and constructive approach to our past.

This journey from antagonism to cosmopolitanism through to the advent of calls for agonism is, of course, only really applicable from a very broad perspective. One must be careful not to assume that a similar timeframe or speed of progression have been evident in all localities. However, in the case of Northern Ireland, even if the timeline is somewhat different, it is entirely possible to see how there has been a similar progression from antagonism through to cosmopolitanism that has arguably now reached the limits of what it can achieve. It will be argued that here too, and particularly in relation to issues linked to dealing with the past, agonism may well provide a way through the current impasse.

From antagonistic Troubles to cosmopolitan peace

The history of Northern Ireland is littered with what could be described as pivotal moments that have become essential building blocks of the province's divergent collective memories. It therefore follows that how such moments are remembered and discussed contain the potential to highlight and even perpetuate the tensions that continue to exist in what remains a divided society (Clancy, 2010). In order to demonstrate this via a specific example, the following focuses on the crucial events of October 1968 – February 1969, understood here as Northern Ireland's 1968 (see, for example, Prince, 2007; Purdie, 1990; Reynolds, 2015 for an overview of the events).

Following building tensions in the preceding years, 5 October 1968 saw what can be considered the spark that triggered the beginning of what would become a defining chapter of Northern Ireland's recent past. When the Royal Ulster Constabulary (RUC) attacked a banned but peaceful march for civil rights on Duke Street in Derry, the images were captured by a cameraman from Irish national broadcaster RTE whose footage would very quickly be beamed into households not only locally but also in the Republic of Ireland, Britain and around the world. From this point on, a mass movement built up – including, crucially, the creation of an influential student body at Queen's University Belfast, the People's Democracy (PD) – which went on to draw support from large swathes of the population. This movement, which included the participation and support of some elements of the Protestant community, soon forced Prime Minister Terence O'Neill to offer up concessions.

While moderate forces in the civil rights movement may have been inclined to accept such an offer, more radical elements were determined to push for more. This culminated in the infamous Burntollet Bridge episode on 4 January 1969 where a PD march was brutally ambushed on the outskirts of Derry by a group of unionist vigilantes. Having exposed the sectarian tensions that lay beneath the surface, this march – and the attack upon it – led to the end of street politics and opened the door to violence. When O'Neill decided to call an election as his response to what had happened, Northern Ireland's 1968 was over and the spiral towards the conflict known as the Troubles began. Given how crucial this moment was in relation to what was to follow, it provides a particularly pertinent example of the difficulties and challenges associated with memory politics both during a conflict and in its aftermath.

Both in the run-up to, and particularly during, the Troubles, the deep and dangerous divide that existed within the context of Northern Ireland unsurprisingly meant that the backdrop was defined, in Mouffean terms, by antagonism. Such was the nature of the conflict that this antagonism transcended most aspects of life, including how the past was to be framed. In the case of 1968, this, broadly speaking, led to the emergence of two very different narratives that were consolidated over the course of the three decades of violence (Campbell, 2018; Farrell, 1988; Kingsley, 1989).

One the one hand, the Catholic, nationalist, republican community memory of this period was one that interpreted the civil rights era as a peaceful and justified attempt to secure basic rights for the minority population who had suffered gross discrimination in housing, employment and voting. This narrative posits such attempts at being met with state brutality and violence, leaving protestors with no other choice than to respond in kind, explaining the emergence of the men of violence. The opposing narrative of the Protestant, unionist, loyalist community presents the civil rights movement as nothing more than a veiled attempt by republicans to advance their cause for a united Ireland under the cloak of non-violence and peaceful protest. Such an interpretation presents the civil rights movement as nothing more than a front for the IRA.

While it is perfectly possible to pick holes in and criticise both such simplistic readings of this crucial time, that is frankly not the issue at hand. What is important to understand is that the background of the Troubles and its inherent antagonism provided the grounds for the emergence of these two diametrically opposed perspectives that would become anchored within the opposing communities and be bolstered by the passage of time and the exacerbation of the conflict. Any hope of engendering a change that would see such divergent narratives take a different path would be predicated on a shift away from the defining backdrop of conflict. This is precisely what happened in 1998 and the onset of peace with the GFA (Reynolds, 2017).

As Northern Ireland moved away from the Troubles and into the post-1998 era, it could be argued that the previous backdrop of antagonism was replaced by one defined by a certain cosmopolitanism. The desire to consolidate peace and avoid any return to violence meant that great attempts were made to overcome differences in a bid to reach a consensus on a future based on peace. This was the approach exemplified in initiatives such as the 2013 Haass report and the 2014 Stormont House Agreement. Such a constructive and positive mindset swept across the vast majority of the population and inflected all sectors of society, including attitudes towards the very sensitive issue of managing the past. To again take the example of 1968, when one considers how the nature of the narrative surrounding this moment shifted and evolved with the advent of peace, it is possible to identify how the post-Troubles context paved the way for a certain shift; but it was one that, like the issue of the past more generally, reached its limits and has required a further shift in focus.

The first peacetime commemoration of 1968 in 2008 highlighted the potential of this new context to enable a change in how this period was discussed (Reynolds, 2018). The standout characteristics of this commemorative moment included the broadening of perspectives beyond the usual suspects to include voices that had hitherto remained silent concerning their experiences, as well as a focus on victims and the importance of human rights. One could also point to some efforts to include the Northern Irish experience within the exceptional global context of revolt and rebellion. However, despite such strides in helping forge a new, less-divisive narrative, the quest for some sort of consensual perspective meant that difficult issues, debates and voices were marginalised (Reynolds, 2015: 194–97). Herein lies the crux of the problem and explains why, both in the case of 1968 and the legacy issue more generally, the cosmopolitan approach has reached its limits.

The quest to recalibrate a new, consensual narrative of the civil rights era in a context of peace meant finding the lowest common denominator that would permit the recounting of this period that caused as little offence as possible and did not fan the flames of any potential conflict. This is, of course, very laudable. However, while such a race to the bottom may well have resulted in an improved, more accommodating narrative for some, it inevitably meant that certain difficult questions and numerous conflicting voices were marginalised. Just as Mouffe and Cento Bull and Hansen have argued, such a cosmopolitan approach inevitably provides the grounds for antagonism to re-emerge. By framing the new peacetime narrative of 1968 as was the case in 2008, it simplified the story.

By failing to address sensitive issues around the role of the IRA, tensions within the various factions of the civil rights movement, or the participation of the Protestant community, it paved the way for disaffected voices and opinions to feel marginalised. As a result, such voices were able to once again draw on the past to make an argument that this new era of peace was one that had no place for them. In other words, the desire to flee conflict via the calibration of a consensual view on the past had the opposite effect of actually provoking tension and making the past an issue to perpetuate divisions and expose the weaknesses of the peace process.

In many respects, one can understand why the consensual, cosmopolitan model took hold in the early days of the peace process. So hard-won and yet so fragile was the newly arrived peace that it is hardly surprising that the reflex to avoid anything conflictual was so dominant. However, as the violence has moved further and further away and peace has bedded in, it has become clear that the (undoubtedly necessary) consensual, conflict-adverse approach requires reconsideration.

It is argued here that the emergence of the potential disadvantages of this approach has converged with a certain maturity of the peace process and Northern Irish society that both necessitates and opens up a window for a new approach defined by agonism. Focusing in particular on the crucial issue of dealing with the legacy of the past, what follows is an overview of a collaboration between Reynolds and NMNI that deploys agonism in a bid to recalibrate the story of Northern Ireland's 1968 and offers a way through the challenges presented by the broader legacy conundrum.

68 @ 50 and the agonistic turn

The symbiotic relationship between the sensitivities of the legacy issue and the inherent weaknesses of the political institutions provides part of the explanation for the political vacuum in Northern Ireland since 2016. It has been interesting to note how in the absence of genuine leadership over this question, grassroots community activities aimed at dealing with the past have sprung up all over the province (Hamber and Kelly, 2016; McEvoy and Bryson, 2016). Such 'memory activism' has sought to fill the void left by the inability of the political elite to define an approach for dealing with a problem that communities recognise requires attention (Gutman, 2017).

This activism has unquestionably been of great use to respective communities in helping them come to terms with their pasts and develop mechanisms that are important for the definition of their identities as we move from conflict through peace and towards some form of normality. A vital component of many of these community initiatives is the use of oral history (Bryson, 2016; Crooke, 2008: 124–28). The effectiveness and importance of gathering and listening to testimonies has become a central plank of many projects across the province. The fact that oral history has also been cited as a vital element of the Stormont House proposals for managing the legacy of the past is an excellent example of how such bottom-up memory activism can and does shape state-led policies and initiatives (Wüstenberg, 2017).

However, while such work is to be applauded, there is some potential for it to create further difficulties. The fact that such activities are often based within their own specific communities with a singular focus on their own narratives and experiences of the conflict increases the risk of enhancing and perpetuating the differences that exist across the communal divides that remain at the heart of tensions in Northern Ireland. There are, of course, numerous projects and initiatives that seek to bring different perspectives together (see, for example, material at www.peaceinsight.org/conflicts/northern-ireland/). However, it could be argued that such work, despite being of unquestionable value, is wedded to the cosmopolitan predication of consensus and reconciliation and devoid of conflict. It is argued here that the time is ripe for the necessary bringing together of conflicted perspectives in a spirit of agonism.

One can point to a number of specific examples where agonistic credentials are seeping through and provide evidence of the readiness of Northern Irish society to face up to the discomforting conversations this entails. For example, the controversial Ed Moloney book *Voices from the Grave* (2010) is an excellent illustration of the benefits of the juxtaposition of two different perspectives without any sense of the need for there to be agreement. The divergent narratives of the former IRA volunteer Brendan Hughes and former loyalist David Ervine of their personal experiences of the same period of conflict is a potent encounter that helps us get to a closer understanding of how and why such important figures made the decisions they did. The upshot, whether you sympathise or disagree with the narratives presented, is an unquestionably enhanced understanding of how the province found itself caught up in the spiral of violence that was the Troubles.

Another such example of agonism in action is a walking tour in Belfast entitled 'Conflicting Stories' (see www.belfastpoliticaltour.com/

conflicting-stories-walking-tour). During this tour, visitors are taken across the divide in Belfast and told the story of the conflict by former prisoners from both the loyalist and the republican communities. The existence of such an activity is recognition that single-narrative perspectives on the past are both incomplete and unhelpful. It is also a sign of the times that the peace process has reached this level of maturity to enable such a coming together that would have been unthinkable during the conflict or in the early years of the peace process.

Equally indicative of this evolving maturity, and turning our attentions back to the case of Northern Ireland's 1968, was the approach of the 50th Anniversary Civil Rights Commemoration Committee in its plans for marking this milestone in 2018. In addition to a plethora of activities that unquestionably sought to move more towards a plurality of views and perspectives, one only has to consider the following line from its stated objectives as evidence of its agonistic credentials: 'The Civil Rights Committee will be engaging in constructive dialogue with those who did not, or do not, share the views of the Civil Rights movement' (50th Anniversary Civil Rights Commemoration Committee, 2018).

While the three examples above are indisputably agonistic in some elements of their approach, what follows is a brief overview of a project that explicitly embedded agonism at its core and proved to be a very effective and constructive means for dealing with a potentially very problematic chapter of Northern Ireland's past (Reynolds and Blair, 2018). Following the 2015 publication of *Sous les pavés ... The Troubles*, Reynolds entered into contact with NMNI to discuss the translation of the study's findings into how this crucial period was to be presented at Belfast's Ulster Museum. The subsequent collaboration developed in four clear stages. Starting with an initial minor intervention it then led to a complete overhaul of the gallery space dedicated to 1968.

The next stage saw the development of an expanded temporary and travelling exhibition entitled *Voices of 68* that coincided with the fiftieth anniversary of the events (see NMNI, 2018). The final stage saw the incorporation of an adapted version of *Voices of 68* into the permanent gallery of the Ulster Museum where it stands adjacent to the newly developed *Troubles and Beyond* gallery. Alongside these developments, the project spawned a diverse range of activities that included a series of public-facing events (in locations including Liverpool and Luton), as well as its presentation through an exhibition tour at national and international venues. Supporting materials were also published online, and an influential education programme was developed that includes bespoke online resources and GCSE study days (Black and Reynolds, 2020; see also Campbell, 2017; NMNI, n.d.).

Vital to the expansion and success of this collaborative project was the centrality of agonism and oral history. The inherent capacity of the oral history approach was used to ensure that, in the collection of testimonies related to the events of 1968 in Northern Ireland, this project went beyond the 'usual suspects' who had come to define how the story of this pivotal moment had been constructed over the years. That is not to say that these prominent voices were ignored. Instead, they were joined by a range of perspectives that had hitherto been marginalised and were not afraid to offer up a different, often conflicting, viewpoints.

This agonistic encounter ran through the integrated tapestry of material produced for this project. In exhibition panels, conflicting perspectives on similar moments were presented in direct opposition to each other. In video extracts embedded within the various exhibitions, visitors were presented with directly contrasted narratives that clashed over similar moments or questions. Such agonism was equally apparent in the online material as well as the range of public-facing activities where explicit attempts were made to ensure that the polyvocality of the project was brought to life in live debates and discussions.

This was and remains particularly the case with the range of study days hosted at the Ulster Museum that presented the more than two hundred pupils in attendance with the often-tense exchanges of speakers representing very different viewpoints and understandings. That the project expanded and grew as it did is in itself evidence of its effectiveness. However, one is able to highlight other sources that underscore the impact of its central approach and how it offers potential broader lessons for the challenge of dealing with the legacy of the past.

It would be incorrect to suggest that everyone who encountered some iteration of the project was enamoured with what they saw. Indeed, there were some who indicated their discomfort with the material they were faced with. However, as exemplified by the testimonies below, the vast majority of feedback garnered was not only positive but also spoke to the widespread readiness and willingness of Northern Irish society to face up to the challenges presented by the past, however uncomfortable. Declan White, a GCSE history teacher, and study day participant expressed the following views, in a testimony letter:

> Projects such as this underscore just how important it is for our young people to make sense of our past and understand how it is that we find ourselves in our current predicament. The 1968 project goes a long way towards helping enhance the level of understanding of what was such pivotally important moment. ... The wide range of often opposing perspectives that are presented in the various facets of this project has had an immeasurable impact on our pupils. It is so vitally important that our young people improve their understanding of all sides in the debate.

David Lewis, from one of Northern Ireland's major creative media arts organisations, the Nerve Centre in Derry, shared the following perspective in a testimony letter:

> *Voices of '68* has made a valuable contribution to increasing understanding of the crucial time period leading into the Troubles. Opening up multiple narratives through video interviews was an extremely effective model of encouraging audiences to engage with perspectives that may have been far from their own. The more marginalised and 'lesser known' voices were, in particular, interesting and enlightening to hear.

Another visitor to the exhibition said on a feedback form:

> The exhibition at the Ulster Museum is unsettling – being confronted by some narratives about '68 that you believe are wrong. But that is the point and it is quite discomforting. ... One has to be prepared to listen to other viewpoints. I think that the material should be the start of a critical debate as to what did happen.

The following view was expressed in a testimony letter by the director of the Institute of Irish Studies at the University of Liverpool:

> It is a reminder of how present political actions must embed civic participation and democracy so as to ensure violence does not return. It presents a set of novel views of this critical year on the life of

Northern Ireland and indeed Ireland and does so through capturing voices and also the social dynamics of civil rights. ... The exhibition is dignified and stimulated a series of important inter-community conversations at the University of Liverpool that concern misreading of the past, forgotten social memories and the centrality of peacebuilding through human rights and reform. At Liverpool, it also permitted ex-members of the British Army to look at this period and share their memories and experiences with those who would have been opposed to them. This aided broader and more sympathetic readings of each.

Gemma Attwood, Policy Development Officer at the Northern Ireland Community Relations Council, had this to say in her testimony letter:

> The work carried out by this project was both timely and significant as it fed into discussions around important areas for us such as the Decade of Commemorations, ongoing debates on the legacy of the conflict, as well as issues around ethical and shared remembering. Through its multifaceted outputs and reach, the project has provided a new platform for debate and discussion on this vital period. It has demonstrated how such difficult moments can be the focus of attention and debate and how they can be explored from an academic and factual framework via personal recollections and perspectives. It is an example of what can be achieved with joint societal responses to such challenges; the presentation of realities over myths through conversations and debates in safe spaced where the focus is on respect for different opinions but a determination to have such discussions.

Further evidence of the effectiveness of the approach deployed is to be found in the reflections of NMNI partners on how the 1968 project has informed their thinking in relation to their central role as an important vector on the challenge of overcoming the difficulties of the past. As the testimony extracts below highlight, the 1968 project has proved to be hugely influential in a number of domains of this institution's valuable work.

> This collaboration has been significantly influential in terms of the approach of National Museums Northern Ireland. ... The project and its approach have provided an opportunity for better understanding of our history, and a platform for the public to be able to listen and talk to those who were involved and their reasons for their actions. (Fiona Baird, history education officer, Ulster Museum, testimony letter)

Agonistic remembering 31

The multi-perspective approach that has underpinned [this] collaborative project has been a perfect fit for us here at NMNI as it very much aligns with our own desire to challenge the existence of single narratives when treating historical events – particularly sensitive periods such as that of 1968. This multi-perspective approach, with an adherence to the notion of ethical remembering, is part of our objective of creating a safe space for sensitive and difficult histories to be confronted in a constructive manner. (Hannah Crowdy, Head of Curatorial, NMNI, testimony letter)

From an institutional perspective, this has been a hugely valuable project for NMNI. Its various strands have provided a range of lessons that we can apply to our more general approach to dealing with the challenge of the past in Northern Ireland. The 1968 collaboration in many respects has become a model we can now apply to how we treat other such topics. (Karen Logan, Senior Curator of History, NMNI, testimony letter)

The impact of this collaborative project has been radical for us at NMNI. Given our role in dealing with the challenge of managing Northern Ireland's contested past, this venture has been groundbreaking in that it defined a whole new methodology to how we might research and interpret that part of our past. (Kathryn Thomson, Director and CEO, NMNI, testimony letter)

This collaboration has provided a successful example of how we can deploy our collection in the future especially in terms of the interpretative output of the museum in the public arena. Its multifaceted, integrated approach that used the collection to then produce outputs that included exhibitions, travelling exhibitions, digital content, programming, and schools' events, all demonstrate what a successful project can achieve with oral history at its core. ...

More generally, state-led initiatives such as the Stormont House Agreement have placed great emphasis on the need for a similar type of approach with oral history consistently front and centre. However, such proposals are devoid of detail and examples of just how and why this approach can be applied; the 1968 project provides an excellent example of just what can be achieved and has inevitably influenced conversations in this discussion. (William Blair, Director of Collections, NMNI, testimony letter)

Finally, one can point to how the 1968 project has not been without influence in very important policy-level discussions on the legacy issue highlighted by Blair above. For example, the NMNI submission to the 2018 public consultation launched by the government on 'Addressing the legacy of Northern Ireland's past' places the 1968 project front and centre as a successful example of the possibilities of confronting this challenge in a constructive and positive manner.

Furthermore, as highlighted in the following testimony extract, the collaboration and its approach have featured in discussions of the FICT commission, with specific attention being paid to the benefits of the educational strand of the project:

> Its balanced, inclusive, constructive and innovative approach has proved to be welcomed by both teachers and pupils across a range of schools in the province. Its popularity and effectiveness certainly suggests that it could provide a framework to be emulated beyond the case of the 1968 period to establish a considered, strategic and proactive approach to help ensure that future generations are provided with the tools that will enable them to avoid the contested past from perpetuating the divisions that continue to provide such a challenge in Northern Ireland. (FICT commissioner, testimony letter)

Conclusion

The approach of this collaborative venture that places agonism at its heart has unquestionably had some identifiable impact in helping shape attitudes and understandings of the specific case of Northern Ireland's 1968. However, given the importance of this crucial moment and the fact that it has been the source of such contested perspectives, there is some merit to the argument that such an approach could provide lessons beyond this specific period. It is argued here that an agonistic approach to confronting the difficulties of the past more broadly is potentially one fruitful mechanism to overcome the challenge that this issue poses.

The effectiveness of the approach is evidenced in how the project has grown across its iterative development. However, and perhaps even more importantly, the general feedback and response to the project and its various strands have demonstrated a real willingness and readiness to accept that difficult conversations need to be had in order for the past to no longer be an element that perpetuates divisions with the potential to bring back the days of violence.

A more general deployment of this approach could provide a blueprint to help overcome one of the most important obstacles facing the Northern Ireland peace process. The importance of devising a carefully considered strategy for dealing with the past has never been more pressing. As the fiftieth anniversaries of the defining moments of the Troubles line up on the commemorative horizon, it is imperative that the potential challenges these represent are met head-on and in a constructive manner. This chapter argues that doing so by drawing on approaches defined by agonistic credentials as effectively piloted by the 1968 NMNI collaboration is certainly an avenue worth exploring.

References

50th Anniversary Civil Rights Commemoration Committee (2018) Pamphlet produced and distributed at their launch of the fiftieth anniversary event on 25 January in First Presbyterian Church, Belfast.

Armstrong, C. I., Herbert, D., Mustad, J. E. (2019) *The Legacy of the Good Friday Agreement: Northern Irish Politics, Culture and Art after 1998*. Cham: Springer.

Bairner, A. (2008) 'Still taking sides: sport, leisure and identity', in C. Coulter and M. Murray (eds), *Northern Ireland after the Troubles: A Society in Transition*, pp. 215–31. Manchester: Manchester University Press.

Beiner, G. (2018) *Forgetful Remembrance: Social Forgetting and Vernacular Historiography of a Rebellion in Ulster*. Oxford: Oxford University Press.

Bell, C. (2003) 'Dealing with the past in Northern Ireland', *Fordham International Law Journal*, 26 (4): 1095–2003.

Bell, D. (2008) 'Agonistic democracy and the politics of memory', *Constellations*, 15 (1): 148–66.

Black, G. and Reynolds, C. (2020) 'Engaging audiences with difficult pasts: the Voices of '68 project at the Ulster Museum, Belfast', *Curator: The Museum Journal*, 63 (1): 21–38.

Boyd, S. W. (2019) 'Post-conflict tourism development in Northern Ireland: moving beyond murals and dark sites associated with its past', in R. K. Isaac, E. Çakmak and R. Butler (eds), *Tourism and Hospitality in Conflict-Ridden Destinations*, pp. 226–39. Abingdon: Routledge.

Brown, K. and Grant, A. (2016) 'A lens over conflicted memory: surveying 'Troubles' commemoration in Northern Ireland', *Irish Political Studies*, 31 (1): 139–62.

Bryson, A. (2016) 'Victims, violence and voice: transitional justice, oral history and dealing with the past', *Hastings International and Comparative Law Review*, 39 (2): 299–353.

Byrne, J. (2014) *Flags and Protests: Exploring the Views, Perceptions and Experiences of People Directly and Indirectly Affected by the Flag Protests*. Available at: https://pure.ulster.ac.uk/ws/files/11420617/Report.pdf (accessed 28 June 2018).

Campbell, C. (2017) '1968. An opportunity missed?' [blog post], St. Malachy's College (24 March). Available at: www.stmalachyscollege.com/post/2017/03/24/-1968-an-opportunity-missed (accessed 28 June 2018).

Campbell, S. (2018) '"We shall overcome"? The Good Friday/Belfast Agreement and the memory of the civil rights movement', *Open Library of Humanities*, 24 (1): 1–25.

Cento Bull, A. and Hansen, H. L. (2016) 'On agonistic memory', *Memory Studies*, 9 (4): 390–404.

Clancy, M. A. C. (2010) *Peace Without Consensus: Power Sharing Politics in Northern Ireland*. Farnham: Ashgate.

Cochrane, F. (2013) *Northern Ireland: The Reluctant Peace*. New Haven, CT: Yale University Press.

Crooke, E. (2008) *Museums and Community: Ideas, Issues, and Challenges*. Abingdon: Routledge.

Cubitt, G. (2007) *History and Memory*. Manchester: Manchester University Press.

Dawson, G. (2014) 'The desire for justice, psychic reparation and the politics of memory in "post-conflict" Northern Ireland', *Rethinking History*, 18 (2): 265–88.

Dingley, J. (2005) 'Constructive ambiguity and the peace process in Northern Ireland', *Low Intensity Conflict & Law Enforcement*, 13 (1): 1–23.

Dutceac-Segesten, A. and Wüstenberg, J. (2017) 'Memory studies – the state of the field', *Memory Studies*, 10 (4): 474–89.

Farrell, M. (ed.) (1988) *Twenty Years On*. Dingle: Mount Eagle Publications.

Fenton, S. (2019) 'How the Irish language became a pawn in a culture war', *New Statesman* (5 July). Available at: www.newstatesman.com/politics/northern-ireland/2019/07/how-irish-language-became-pawn-culture-war (accessed 19 September 2019).

Gutman, Y. (2017) *Memory Activism: Reimagining the Past for the Future in Israel–Palestine*. Nashville, TN: Vanderbilt University Press.

Hamber, B. and Kelly, G. (2016) 'Practice, power and inertia: personal narrative, archives and dealing with the past in Northern Ireland', *Journal of Human Rights Practice*, 8 (1): 25–44.

Kingsley, P. (1989) *Londonderry Revisited: A Loyalist Analysis of the Civil Rights Controversy*. Belfast: Belfast Publications.

Lawther, C. (2014) *Truth, Denial and Transition: Northern Ireland and the Contested Past*. Abingdon: Routledge.

Lundy, P. and McGovern, M. (2001) 'The politics of memory in post-conflict Northern Ireland', *Peace Review. A Journal of Social Justice*, 13 (1): 27–33.

McAuley, J. W. (2016) 'Memory and belonging in Ulster loyalist identity', *Irish Political Studies*, 31 (1): 122–38.

McDowell, S. and Braniff, M. (2014) *Commemoration as Conflict: Space, Memory and Identity in Peace Processes*. Basingstoke: Palgrave Macmillan.

McEvoy, K. and Bryson, A. (2016) 'Justice, truth and oral history: legislating the past "from below" in Northern Ireland', *Northern Ireland Legal Quarterly*, 67 (1): 67–90.

McGrattan, C. and Hopkins, S. (2017) 'Memory in post-conflict societies: from contestation to integration?', *Ethnopolitics*, 16 (5): 488–99.

Moloney, E. (2010) *Voices from the Grave. Two Men's War in Ireland*. London: Faber and Faber.

Mouffe, C. (1993) *The Return of the Political*. London: Verso.

Mouffe, C. (2000) *The Democratic Paradox*. London: Verso.

Mouffe, C. (2005) *On the Political*. London: Routledge.

Mouffe, C. (2012) 'An agonistic approach to the future of Europe', *New Literary History*, 43: 629–40.

NIO (Northern Ireland Office) (2014) *The Stormont House Agreement*. Available at: www.gov.uk/government/publications/the-stormont-house-agreement (accessed 28 June 2018).

NIO (2018) *Addressing the Legacy of Northern Ireland's Past* (consultation paper, 11 May). Available at: www.gov.uk/government/consultations/addressing-the-legacy-of-northern-irelands-past (accessed 28 June 2018).

NMNI (National Museums Northern Ireland) (n.d.) 'Changing relations: Northern Ireland and its neighbours, 1965–1998', Ulster Museum learning resource: CCEA GCSE History. Available at: www.nmni.com/learn/1968-history-resource/Home.aspx (accessed 12 July 2022).

NMNI (2018) 'Voices of '68 exhibit launches' (17 September). Available at: www.nmni.com/news/voices-of-68-exhibition (accessed 12 July 2022).

Phillips, K. R. (2004) *Framing Public Memory*. Tuscaloosa, AL: University of Alabama Press.

Power, M. (2011) *Building Peace in Northern Ireland*. Liverpool: Liverpool University Press.

Prince, S. (2007) *Northern Ireland's '68: Civil Rights, Global Revolt and the Origins of the Troubles*. Dublin: Irish Academic Press.

Purdie, B. (1990) *Politics in the Streets: Origins of the Civil Rights Movement in Northern Ireland*. Belfast: Blackstaff Press.

Radstone, S. and Schwartz, B. (2010) *Memory: Histories, Theories, Debates*. New York, NY: Fordham University Press.

Reynolds, C. and Blair, W. (2018) 'Museums and "difficult pasts": Northern Ireland's 1968', *Museum International*, 70 (3–4): 12–25.

Reynolds, C. (2018) 'Beneath the Troubles, the cobblestones: recovering the "buried" memory of Northern Ireland's 1968', *American Historical Review*, 123 (3): 744–8.

Reynolds, C. (2017) 'Northern Ireland's 1968 in a post-Troubles context', *Interventions*, 19 (5): 631–45.

Reynolds, C. (2015) *Sous les pavés… the Troubles: Northern Ireland, France and the European Collective Memory of 1968*. Bern: Peter Lang.

Savage, R. (2019) '"New culture war": Northern Ireland's LGBT+ community fights for gay marriage', *Thomson Reuters Foundation News* (27 March). Available at: https://news.trust.org/item/20190327074742-yyrq6 (accessed 19 September 2019).

Smyth, J. (ed.) (2017) *Remembering the Troubles: Contesting the Recent Past in Northern Ireland*. Notre Dame, IN: University of Notre Dame Press.

Tonge, J. (2016) 'The impact of withdrawal from the European Union upon Northern Ireland', *Political Quarterly*, 87 (3): 338–42.

Tonge, J. (2013) *Northern Ireland: Conflict and Change*. Abingdon: Routledge.

Viggiani, E. (2014) *Talking Stones: The Politics of Memorialization in Post-Conflict Northern Ireland*. New York, NY, and Oxford: Berghahn Books.

Walker, P. and Carroll, R. (2019) 'MPs vote to extend abortion and same-sex marriage rights to Northern Ireland', *Guardian* (9 July). Available at: www.theguardian.com/uk-news/2019/jul/09/mps-vote-to-extend-same-sex-marriage-to-northern-ireland (accessed 19 September 2019).

Wertsch, J. V. (2002) *Voices of Collective Remembering*. Cambridge: Cambridge University Press.

Winter, J. (2000) 'The generation of memory: reflections on the "memory boom"', *Contemporary Historical Studies, Bulletin of the German Historical Institute*, 27: 69–92.

Wüstenberg, J. (2017) *Civil Society and Memory in Postwar Germany*. Cambridge: Cambridge University Press.

2

Pogroms, presence, myth and memory: August 1969 and the outbreak of the Northern Ireland conflict

Shaun McDaid

The period between 12 and 16 August 1969 is often taken as the real starting point for the violent conflict in Northern Ireland known colloquially as the Troubles. While 1968 saw the beginnings of rioting in both Belfast and Derry, the levels of violence worsened considerably the following summer. In particular, the first death of the period due to political violence occurred in July of this year. As the disorder spread to Belfast, eight people, of which six were civilians (including a child), died as a consequence of the violence.

The tragic events of the early period of the conflict have been covered extensively by scholars, from a range of different perspectives (see Hennessey, 2005; Kennedy-Pipe, 1997). The memory of republican violence has also been studied, including from the perspective of those who have attempted to categorise it as a form of 'ethnic cleansing', a term more usually associated with the Balkan wars of the 1990s (Lewis and McDaid, 2017). What is perhaps less well studied is how the events at the outbreak of the conflict have come to be remembered collectively in nationalist and republican circles, especially the ways in which the events of 1969 are viewed diachronically through the prism of events from elsewhere. In particular, the violence of 1969 has often been remembered collectively, especially in nationalist or republican communities, through deploying the metaphor of a 'pogrom'. In this case, the events of August 1969 are seen as being part of a wider attempt by unionists or loyalists to eliminate or expel Catholics from particular areas.

This chapter seeks to explore these processes of collective memorialisation in relation to the violence of August 1969. In so doing, it will explore the speeches and statements of republican politicians as well as draw on historical theory to provide suggestions why these events were remembered in the way that they were, with a specific focus on the pogrom narrative. The use of the term was also associated with the violence, experienced particularly intensely in Catholic areas of Belfast, during the 1920s at the time of the partition of Ireland. This provides a clue as to why it also found resonance during the later period, which will be expanded upon in the discussion that follows.

The central argument of the essay is that the commemoration of '1969 as pogrom' is driven by what Runia (2006) has defined as 'parallel processing', which sees a 'remembering or subconscious re-enactment of past events' in a new context. In this case, the collective memory of the events of the 1920s 'stowed away' (Runia, 2004) into the then present, and provided a particular prism through which the events of 1969 came to be remembered. The essay concludes by considering the implications of this phenomenon for initiatives that attempt to deal with the legacies of past violence in Northern Ireland. But the lessons might equally apply in other international settings where the memory of ethnic violence is central to contemporary politics, such as the Balkans, which is discussed in the above-mentioned work of Runia.

Background to the events of August 1969

Although it is not the purpose of this essay to explore the events of the outbreak of the conflict in detail (see Hennessey, 2005; Prince, 2007; Dixon and O'Kane, 2014), some facts pertinent to the following discussion are worth recalling here. As mentioned, August 1969 is central to the chronology of the Northern Ireland conflict. While the first deaths due to political violence in 1969 occurred in July of that year, it was not until August that the violence intensified to the point where the security forces in Northern Ireland, led by the police (Royal Ulster Constabulary, RUC), were no longer able to contain it without external assistance.

During the early part of August, sectarian rioting was becoming more intense, especially in Belfast. The official investigation into the disturbances found that loyalist mobs had attacked mostly Catholic/nationalist residential areas in the west of the city. The previous month, an organisation styling itself the Shankill Defence Association, named after a loyalist area, had assisted Protestant families in leaving the Hooker Street area, and is said to have 'encouraged Catholic families to move out of Protestant streets south of the Ardoyne' in the northern part of the city (Government of Northern Ireland, 1972). In August, barricades were erected in Hooker Street, and other areas, and a process of enforced migration was initiated, which affected both sides of the community (although Catholics were affected in greater numbers). While the RUC had prevented some loyalist excesses during this time, its tactics were increasingly aggressive, and it was further losing the confidence of Catholics, insofar as it had ever enjoyed it. Loyalists, however, were also frustrated with the RUC, precisely because it had intervened to prevent a full-scale assault on nationalist properties (Farrell, 1976: 259–64; Prince and Warner, 2012: 148–49). Many loyalists, in fact, preferred the reserve police force to the regular RUC. The Ulster Special Constabulary (known as the 'B-Specials') had its roots in the partition of Ireland and was exclusively loyalist in character (Nelson, 1984: 89).

On 14 August, British soldiers were deployed at the request of the Northern Ireland government, led by the Ulster Unionist Party, which sat at Stormont in the eastern part of Belfast. Despite the temporary respite that the appearance of the British Army heralded, intense violence continued and community relations were irreparably damaged during this period. This was, in part, fuelled by the significant transfers of population that occurred as a consequence of the disorder.

In short, many Catholic and Protestant families left voluntarily, or were intimidated from, their homes, seeking sanctuary in areas with, from a communal perspective, more favourable demographics. Contemporary reports have claimed that there was even some highly instrumental inter-communal cooperation, to oversee property swaps among the communities (Prince and Warner, 2012: 149). Arson was one of the most challenging issues at the time: entire streets were set alight in some of the worst-affected areas. As Fergal Cochrane (2013: 35) has noted, the perception that the security forces permitted the torching of areas such as Bombay Street contributed to the notion that they had facilitated an 'anti-Catholic pogrom'.

While no side had the monopoly on suffering, it has been claimed that of the approximately 1,800 families that left their homes in Belfast in the summer of 1969, 1,500 were Catholic (83 per cent) (Cochrane, 2013: 55). It has been reported that this amounted to one of the biggest population transfers in Europe since the end of the Second World War, and was surpassed only by the break-up of the former Yugoslavia (O'Brien, 2000: 45).

At this point, it should be noted that the population transfers did not come to an end in 1969. In fact, further significant movement occurred soon afterwards, in August 1971. The context surrounding these transfers was the widespread disorder that occurred following the introduction, on 8 August 1971, of internment without trial for those suspected of paramilitary violence. Initially, only those with suspected links to republicanism were interned (McCleery, 2015). Like in 1969, the three-week period following the introduction of internment saw considerable numbers of households leave or move within the Belfast urban area (although the immediate imperative for moving was not necessarily identical in both periods). A report compiled by the Community Relations Commission (CRC) estimated that there were 2,069 moves during this period (CRC, 1971). These later events are worth recording, because it is plausible that they may have influenced the remembrance of the entire period after 1969 as one where members of the community were forcibly ejected from their homes, seeking solace with their co-religionists, as the result of a loyalist pogrom.

Such a narrative has also been constructed to explain the violence in Belfast in the 1920–22 period, following the partition of Ireland. Between 1920 and 1922, it is estimated that between 452 and 463 people were killed, and 1,100 injured. Around 650 properties were destroyed, many by arson (Lynch, 2008: 375). Several contemporary, or near contemporary, accounts of these disturbances deployed the term 'pogrom' to describe the nature of the violence. Often, the pogrom explanation (in either period) is accompanied by the suggestion that the forces of law and order were uninclined to intervene to prevent it (see Kenna, 1922; McCann, 2019).

In the case of the 1969 violence, the remembrance of the events of August is often framed through the prism of the 1920–22 period. But what is also interesting about the accounts of 1920–22 is how they were influenced by international events, which were then used as the reference point for what was happening in Belfast. The use of the term 'pogrom' itself was an obvious example, but analogies were also drawn between what was happening in Belfast and other places.

Pogroms: Ireland and the international dimension

As has been shown, the term 'pogrom' is often used in the discussion of the violence in Northern Ireland both of the 1920s and 1960s. Surprisingly little attention has been paid to actually defining what is meant by it, however. One exception is Peter Hart's study of the Irish Republican Army (IRA) during the 1916–23 period, which points out that the term was used to describe the communal attacks on Russian Jews in the latter part of the nineteenth and early decades of the twentieth century (Hart, 2003: 247). But a more detailed definitional discussion is often lacking.

Pogroms have been defined in a number of ways. Richard Arnold has contended that the pogrom can best be understood as a violent attack on a minority community, which is focused on their property. There is no particular rationale for the type of property targeted, apart from the fact it belongs to the target group. The occurrence of a pogrom demonstrates 'the unwillingness of the majority group to tolerate the presence of the minority any longer and so mark attempts to force them out'. The overriding message to the target group is that they should leave the area (Arnold, 2016: 10).

Ghassem-Fachandi (2012: 9) suggests that, for its successful execution, a pogrom requires 'logistical planning and preparation', as well as 'support from the state apparatus', especially the police. This definition suggests a significant overlap with the logic of ethnic cleansing, a term latterly associated with the disintegration of the former Yugoslavia. Ethnic cleansing can take many forms, from administrative measures against a target population, all the way through to mass killing. It is generally regarded to be a systematic process, either encouraged by the authorities or at least tolerated by them (see Petrovic, 1994).

It has been suggested that pogroms and genocide are 'twin concepts' (de Zayas, 2007). However, scholars (and international law) agree that the terminal logic of genocide is the elimination of the target population as such (Bloxham, 2009; United Nations, 1951). Helen Fein (1993) has identified four categories of genocidal motives, but what unites them is their eliminationist intent. It might be more accurate in some cases, therefore, to describe ethnic cleansing and pogroms as twin concepts, as the (abhorrent) motivation seems to centre on the acquisition of territory, howsoever violently achieved, rather than the elimination of the group per se. Though there have undoubtedly been some extreme examples of pogroms where the intent seems to have been eliminationist, especially (but not limited to) during the Second World War in areas which were under Nazi occupation or had local proxies in power.

Examples of collective violence defined as pogroms are abundant, especially throughout central and eastern Europe in the early part of the twentieth century. Massacres of and attacks on Jews were carried out at Kishinev in the Russian Empire (now Moldova) in 1903 (Penkower, 2004); in Lviv, then under Polish control, in 1918 (Hagen, 2005); and during the Second World War in Iaşi, Romania, Kaunas, Lithuania (Kallis, 2007) and Lviv again throughout 1941 (Himka, 2011). Pogroms, however, have also occurred outside Europe. The *Farhud* (pogrom), also in 1941, against the Jews of Baghdad during the Anglo-Iraq war is one striking example (Cohen, 1966).

The term pogrom has also been applied to violence that was not directed solely against Jewish peoples. For instance, there was targeted violence primarily directed against the Greek residents of Istanbul, Turkey, in 1955, in which Jewish and Armenian minorities were also affected (de Zayas, 2007). What links a number of these cases is both the intensity of the violence and the sense that, in many cases, the authorities were either orchestrating, complicit or at least indifferent to the outrages.

Notwithstanding the definitional discussion above, the violence in Belfast during the 1920–22 period was, indeed, as noted, classified by many at the time as a pogrom. The book *Facts and Figures of the Belfast Pogrom, 1920–22*, published under the pseudonym G. M. Kenna in 1922, which documents the events and attempts to situate them in a context of earlier 'pogroms' in the form of the violent expulsions of nationalist workers from the shipyards in 1912, is a prominent example (for discussion of the events in Parliament, see Hansard, HC vol. 41, cols 2088–149, 31 July 1912). Some, however, drew on international examples to explain the violence.

An article in the Dublin daily the *Irish Independent* of 5 June 1922 described the events in Belfast as a 'New Armenia', claiming that the 'pogrom goes on', with loyalists hunting Catholics in the city. Furthermore, it was claimed that the events were evidence of a 'plan for the extermination of Catholics' in the city.

The use of the Armenian analogy was particularly interesting. In 1915, the Ottoman Empire conducted a policy of mass execution and expulsion of Armenians from its territory. Hundreds of thousands were killed or died of starvation during the Armenian genocide, with a figure of one million often cited (de Waal, 2015: 35). In this context, the events in Belfast, even allowing for smaller population and geographical concentration, do not seem to neatly fit the pogrom categorisation. Robert Lynch has suggested that if the violence against Catholics in Belfast was a pogrom, it was a 'curiously disjointed and badly organised one' (Lynch, 2008: 378). It should also be noted that roughly a third of the victims of the violence in Belfast between 1920 and 1922 were Protestant, which adds a further problematic aspect to the pogrom narrative.

Despite the problematic nature of comparing the violence in Belfast to the systematic extermination of the Armenian case, and the benefit of several decades remove from the 1920s, the pogrom narrative returned strongly in the collective memory of the events of 1969. As Kieran Glennon has noted, 'evidently there was still at that stage a strong handed-down folk memory of the earlier period, even if very little of it had been committed to print' (Glennon, 2013: 12). There seems little doubt that the phenomenon described by Glennon has happened. Such folk memories have indeed been handed down, or absorbed, across generations, and different international reference points still used as a means to explain and interpret the past via the present, as the following section demonstrates.

The manifestation of pogrom narratives

As well as contemporary or near contemporary accounts of the 1969 disturbances which used the term pogrom, or drew parallels with the violence of the 1920s, there is evidence that the term has assumed an important explanatory power among contemporary republican politicians. In other words, the events of 1969 are collectively remembered as a pogrom against the nationalist community (sometimes with explicit harking back to the earlier 'pogrom' of the 1920s), and this narrative is promulgated by the political representatives of the republican movement. A few examples are indicative of the wider trend.

Former republican prisoner Sean Murray, writing on the fortieth anniversary of the outbreak of the conflict, attempted to portray the republican cause as a consistent struggle against discrimination from an 'Orange' (Protestant) state, which occasionally required the need for resistance by force. Such force was not, in this account, the favoured choice of republicans, rather portrayed as the only option in the face of the same tribulations as earlier generations of their co-religionists faced:

> As was the case in the 1920s, Clonard once again was on the receiving end of a loyalist backlash as revenge for nationalists having the audacity to challenge the Orange state. But our generation would not be cowed or intimidated ... Never again, unlike our parents' generation, would we accept discrimination and second-class citizenship. The death knell was sounded for the Orange state. When we looked around for a vehicle for change the only viable option, unlike today, was the ranks of militant republicanism, namely Fianna Éireann [youth wing of the IRA] or Óglaigh na hÉireann [the name used by the IRA to describe itself in the Irish language]. Many young men and women of my generation took that step. Out of the ashes of Bombay Street arose the Provisional IRA [PIRA] like the legendary phoenix of old, reborn and rejuvenated and, as they say, the rest is history. (Murray, 2009)

In the same year, Sinn Féin published an article on the party website, commemorating the 1969 violence. The article featured, in depth, a speech made by Murray at a public commemoration, which further articulated the perceived links between both periods in republican mythology:

> Forty years ago, this area, like the Falls and Ardoyne, was in a state of shock, trepidation and disbelief, at what had unfolded before our very eyes over the previous 48 hours. And of course, this was not the first time that this community had been subject to murder and terror. In July 1920, eight local residents were murdered by the British army, including Brother Michael Morgan from Clonard Monastery.

The rationale for the attacks in the 1920s was to coerce, intimidate and terrorise nationalists into tolerating partition and the establishment of the Orange state. In 1969, the loyalist pogrom across Belfast was the Orange state's response to our just demands for basic human and civil rights, for housing and the right to vote. 8 died, 750 were injured and 133 were treated for gunshot wounds. 1,505 nationalist families were driven from their homes through burning and intimidation. 179 homes and buildings were completely destroyed and almost 400 were damaged. But in 1969 a generation of young nationalists weren't for lying down. Mindful of other inspirational events worldwide the pogroms were a major watershed in their lives. No longer would they accept unionist discrimination and one party rule. The death knell was sounded for the Orange state. (*Irish Republican News*, 2009)

A 2013 article in *Irish Republican News* featured interviews with local people and collated their recollections of the August 1969 disturbances. Veteran republican Martin Meehan, in recalling the events of that year, drew on more recent international events to contextualise the experiences of those within his community:

> 'It was like something you would see in Kosovo,' says Martin, 'wave after wave of refugees fleeing to relative safety within Ardoyne and further afield to West Belfast.' Every classroom in the local school was sheltering families with their few belongings. (*An Phoblacht*, 1999)

Here, the reference point was one of the areas of conflict in the Balkans following the collapse of Yugoslavia. The case of the Kosovo war of 1998–99, which became eponymous with forced expulsions and intense ethnic violence, had resulted in approximately 13,500 deaths (Visoka, 2016). This may suggest that Meehan understood the events in Kosovo, usually categorised as ethnic cleansing (a term sometimes used by unionists in Northern Ireland to describe the PIRA campaign), as analogous with what many in his community regarded as a 'pogrom'.

More recently, initiatives by the Mid and East Antrim local authority to commemorate the foundation of Northern Ireland have met with considerable resistance from Sinn Féin, again referencing the term 'pogrom' to cement a narrative that the state's genesis was secured by violent repression and organised attacks on the Catholic/nationalist majority. Conor Murphy, a leading Sinn Féin politician, critiqued the proposal, drawing on the traditional republican narrative of the 1920s as a time of pogroms against Catholics and nationalists:

> This ... is an attempt to rewrite the history of the six county state. It is outrageous and typical of unionist-dominated councils where other perspectives and experiences are either ignored or treated with contempt. Ireland was torn apart under the threat of 'total war' from Britain. The democratically expressed will of the people of Ireland in the 1918 election was cast aside. An era of repression, gerrymandering, sectarianism, state violence, pogroms, domination and discrimination was ushered in. Nationalists were left in absolutely no doubt that they were neither wanted nor valued in the new state that we are now being asked to celebrate (Newry and Armagh Sinn Féin, 2019).

In this way, the pogrom narrative was utilised by Sinn Féin to make the case that those who engaged in contestation with the state were left with no option. If the state was, in this formulation, the facilitator (or worse, orchestrator) of violence against the minority community, then the implication is that resistance was justified as a means of communal defence. A 2014 speech in the Irish Parliament (Dáil Éireann) by former Sinn Féin president Gerry Adams made this point explicitly:

> The campaign of the Civil Rights Association in the late 1960s for equality in housing, education, employment and at elections, was met with a violent response by the Stormont regime. Savage attacks by the RUC and the B Specials, backed by loyalist mobs culminated in organised pogroms in August 1969 against Catholics in Belfast and Derry. The violence saw the biggest population movement in western Europe since the Second World War. As the Orange state began to crumble under the weight of democratic demands, British troops were deployed. Promised reforms from London turned out to be purely cosmetic and the British Army's guns were turned against the nationalist population. Following the introduction of internment without trial, many nationalists who had advocated reform within the Six County state, realised the state was not reformable ... The IRA that emerged in these years was one built by ordinary people out of sheer necessity because of the conditions in which they found themselves (*Sinn Féin* website, 5 February 2014).

The above examples are sufficient to illustrate the ways by which the pogrom narrative has been absorbed into the collective memory of some republicans, and how it has been deployed at particular junctures to provide ideological legitimacy for those narratives. The use of the term pogrom, and the tendency to draw on some of the worst excesses of conflicts in other international spheres, has also been a constant in the way the experiences of nationalists in Northern Ireland have been portrayed. The question is why this process has occurred in a similar manner concerning both the 1920s violence and that of the 1960s. The following section considers this question, positing that some of the literature in the discipline of historical theory can offer some useful insights.

Pogroms, presence and parallel processing

The work of Eelco Runia discusses the phenomenon of 'presence' in relation to how the past is remembered. Presence is defined as '"being in touch" – either literally or figuratively – with people, things, events, and feelings that made you into the person you are'. It is seen as the imperative behind all forms of commemoration and is expressed as 'a desire to share in the awesome reality of people, things, events, and feelings, coupled to a vertiginous urge to taste the fact that awesomely real people, things, events, and feelings can awesomely suddenly cease to exist' (Runia, 2006: 5).

One of the key discussions in Runia's essay centres on memorialisation. Modern commemoration, in this view, is notable for being more denotative than connotative. In other words, monuments make 'past events present on the plane of the present, fistulae that connect and juxtapose those events to the here and now' (Runia, 2006: 17). While Runia's discussion centres on physical memorials, similar features might be ascertained in collective forms of remembrance. The past events, in the context of our discussion, are the traumatic incidents from elsewhere, used to decode and make sense of what happened in the (then) present – or what is now the past. This may result in the local contexts being reproduced through the prism of the external events. In this case, it could be that the remembrance of the Northern Ireland conflict at partition as being comparable with events in Armenia, or the violence of 1969 as a 'pogrom' akin to that of the 1920s. This may not be intentional, but the result is a metonymical 'presence in absence': the events are remembered as much for what they were not (or what was absent) as for what they were.

The ideas of Runia were further developed by Frank Ankersmit, who suggested that the concept of presence may shed more light on the notion of myth, which he argued was more present in contemporary historical writing than had hitherto been appreciated (Ankersmit, 2006: 329). Ankersmit's argument focused on historical writing in the professional sense, but it could be argued that similar trends of this phenomenon exist in the collective memories and commemorations of the past, and the case of Northern Ireland provides a good example of this. But why might there have been a tendency to repeat what happened in the memorialisation of the 1920–22 period in later years? Here, Runia's compelling, and at times provocative, discussion of 'parallel processing' may be instructive.

The concept of a parallel process originates in psychoanalytic psychology, and can be broadly understood as when 'difficulties experienced in a particular environment are replicated in another environment', which can manifest as 'subconscious re-enactments of past events' (Runia, 2004: 297–98). Runia uses the example of the 'official report' by the Netherlands Institute for War Documentation (NIOD, since 2010 NIOD Institute for War, Holocaust and Genocide Studies) into the actions of the Dutch battalion ('Dutchbat') leading up to the genocide at Srebrenica in Bosnia and Herzegovina in 1995 to explain how parallel processing works in practice. Dutchbat, as part of the United Nations peacekeeping force, had been tasked with protecting the so-called 'safe zone' in Eastern Bosnia, but was ill-equipped and under-prepared for the task, and quickly over-run by Bosnian Serb forces under the command of General Ratko Mladic. It was also denied air support by mission command, and offered no effective resistance as Mladic's forces organised a systematic massacre of civilians.

In the article, Runia argues that NIOD subconsciously 'paralleled', at surface level, some of the circumstances of the events it was tasked to investigate. This included taking what he calls 'the same moral high ground as the one from which the Dutch Srebrenica policy had been conducted' (Runia, 2004: 303). But, according to him, it was not only in attitudes that the NIOD report mirrored the circumstances of the events. He also argues that the researchers copied the mode of operation of the military deployment. This Runia characterises as 'a combination of wilful unpreparedness, lack of interest in the big picture, improvisation and a hands-on approach'. This was evidenced by the fact that neither NIOD nor the lead investigator 'had any expertise in the subject when they grabbed the opportunity to study it'. Among other uncanny parallels traced by Runia is the fact that the research team replicated the 'logistic predicament' of Dutchbat by being dependent on the Dutch government for access to sources, in the same way Dutchbat was dependent on the caprices of the Bosnian Serb forces who had surrounded the enclave for access and egress (Runia, 2004: 304–5). In these circumstances, too harsh a critique of the authorities on whom they depended for access was always going to be challenging.

The NIOD approach to the project, Runia (2004: 306–7) contends, also echoed the political class in the sense that they replicated the style of decision-making in the Dutch government, where collective responsibility holds and all ministers must defend the common policy. The end result of NIOD's deliberations was a huge, multi-volume report, which was heavy on detail but light on analysis, and lighter still on allocation of blame for the fiasco.

In his discussion of these events, and Runia's article, Ankersmit suggests that the NIOD researchers inadvertently (and unintentionally) perpetuated a national myth about what the Dutch and the Dutch nation itself is like: 'decent, nice, cooperative, and without prejudice against Jews, Muslims, or whatever theological or racial denominations you may have'. He says: '*That* was the *action* performed by the NIOD researchers that they copied from their principals in a "parallel process." The NIOD Report historicised everything that could be historicised about the Srebrenica drama except this, except this *myth*' (Ankersmit, 2006: 334, original emphasis).

Might parallel processing help us explain the 'stowing away' of the pogrom or genocide narrative in twentieth-century Irish history, and particularly the collective memory of such traumatic events? Confino (1997: 1403) writes that the 'first task of the history of memory is to historicize memory'. While it is not the intention here to exhaustively track the development of the internalisation of the pogrom narrative in its totality, a few outline observations may be possible.

Firstly, like the discussion referred to by Ankersmit and Runia, the commemoration of 1969 as pogrom, in a manner similar to the ways in which the 1920–22 period has been remembered, fits rather neatly with an Irish nationalist myth of an almost unbroken history of occupation, oppression, starvation and eliminationist colonialism (although not all nationalists subscribe to this version of the past). Crucially, this narrative underpins in (some) Irish nationalist collective memory of the past what Liam Kennedy (2016) has described as 'MOPE' syndrome – 'most oppressed people ever'. Undoubtedly, many of the above-mentioned grievances, particularly the worst excesses of British rule, are entirely legitimate and well evidenced. But, in the above metonymical formulation, the part is substituted for the whole (see White, 2014: 12).

Secondly, and because of this, there has been a tendency in Ireland to both equate and relate more contemporary events to those of a more traumatic past. This has also seen the tendency to explain events in Ireland through the prism of contemporary international events and conflicts, even where such comparison is historically questionable. This tendency was evident in the 1920s, with the importation of the notion that the Belfast violence could be equated with the Armenian genocide or pogroms, and was, in a parallel process, repeated when the conflict broke out in 1969. Just like the NIOD report on the massacre of Srebrenica, for some Irish nationalists this served the notion of what their historical experience was: being oppressed, despised and unwanted.

Such instances, however, are by no means confined to Irish republicans. We have seen, for example, how some unionists in Northern Ireland, in the aftermath of the Balkan wars, have equated the IRA's campaign of violence, especially in frontier areas, as being akin to a form of ethnic cleansing. This, too, is indicative of how many such unionists saw their historical experience on the island: being oppressed, despised and unwanted.

Conclusion

This essay has explored the collective memory of the outbreak of the modern conflict in Northern Ireland, from August 1969 onwards. By exploring a sample of the recorded speeches and statements of prominent republican political actors, it has highlighted how the immediate events of the time, especially in Belfast, have been interpreted in nationalist and republican folklore as a 'pogrom', which had the express intent of cleansing nationalists from particular parts of the city. However, 1969 is also seen as a turning point, a time when republicans 'took back control', so to speak, and began fighting back against what they regarded as the oppression of the unionist government in Northern Ireland. In this narrative, the IRA (re-)emerged as a fighting force not because it wished to engage in conflict, but out of necessity. It should be noted, however, that not all of those who interpret the events of 1969 as a pogrom against nationalists subscribe to or promote that view of the IRA campaign.

Furthermore, the essay has explored how the pogrom narrative was by no means a new one in nationalist and republican collective memory. The often-intense violence around the time of the partition of Ireland, 1920–22, was regarded as such at the time by many, and collectively remembered in a similar way. Thus, it has been argued that the collective memory of 1969 can be regarded as a form of parallel processing, where past events have stowed away, to re-emerge at a later juncture as part of a tendency to remember or re-enact the past in a certain way. This is regardless of whether or not there is sufficient justification for the importation of a term, or on the appropriateness of its use in a context outside of which it was originally intended. The comparison of 1920s Belfast to 1915 Armenia, or the border regions of Ireland in the 1970s and 1980s to the former Yugoslavia during the 1992–95 period are the most prominent examples.

It has been further argued that this approach has displayed a tendency to remember historical events in a way that focuses on the worst excesses of the Irish past – of which there were undoubtedly many. However, what is at issue is not that such excesses occurred, but the tendency to see and interpret all subsequent events through the prism of these most traumatic cases. In this formulation, to borrow a phrase from Hayden White, the part has been taken for the whole.

The work of Runia and Ankersmit has made a persuasive case that parallel processing occurred in NIOD's production of the Srebrenica report. Despite the voluminous documentation of the events, it still succeeded in historicising a myth of the Dutch nation as decent, tolerant and without prejudice. While there are different processes at work when it comes to the literal documentation of past events and their collective memory, we can suggest that similar outcomes are possible, since the myth has become cemented in the collective understanding, regardless of what doubt has been cast on it by historical scholarship.

What is at issue is not the use of comparison itself, which can be useful, particularly if looking at wider trends in how things are remembered, or to ascertain common trends in zones of conflict. This point was articulated by Sinn Féin's Danny Morrison, who compared the response of the US Army commanders during the Battle of Fallujah in Iraq in 2004 to those of British Army leaders during the Falls Road Curfew in 1970:

> I know that the scale in human death and suffering is not the same and these are different scenarios *but there are some parallels*, not least the hackneyed script the Americans appear to be working from and the claims that their actions are aimed at liberating people. (Morrison, n.d., a, my emphasis)

This observation is all the more interesting since Morrison has previously drawn on the pogrom narrative in the remembrance of the events of 1969 (Morrison, n.d., b).

Finally, the essay has noted that this tendency towards catastrophising, and the importation of external experience in collective memory is not just confined to Irish nationalists and republicans, but also in evidence among some unionist and loyalist communities, although this tendency to internationalise experience may be more recent in the latter case. The ways in which the past is remembered in both communities, therefore, may be more similar than either side might care to admit. It remains to be seen if any recognition of the culture of parallel remembrance of suffering in the past can form the building blocks for mutual understanding in the hoped-for 'united community … that has equality and mutual respect to the fore' in the future (NIO, 2020: 14).

References

Ankersmit, F. R. (2006) '"Presence" and myth', *History and Theory*, 45 (3): 328–36.

An Phoblacht (1999) 'Never again: Bombay Street 30 years on' (19 August). Available at: www.anphoblacht.com/contents/5259 (accessed 5 July 2022).

Arnold, R. (2016) *Russian Nationalism and Ethnic Violence: Symbolic Violence, Lynching, Pogrom and Massacre*. Abingdon: Routledge.

Bloxham, D. (2009) *The Final Solution: A Genocide*. Oxford: Oxford University Press.

Cochrane, F. (2013) *Northern Ireland: The Reluctant Peace*. New Haven, CT: Yale University Press.

Cohen, H. J. (1966) 'The anti-Jewish Farhūd in Baghdad, 1941', *Middle Eastern Studies*, 3 (1): 2–17.

Confino, A. (1997) 'Collective memory and cultural history: problems of method', *American Historical Review*, 102 (5): 1386–403.

CRC (Community Relations Commission) Research Unit (1971) *FLIGHT: A Report on Population Movement in Belfast during August 1971*. Extracts available at: https://cain.ulster.ac.uk/issues/housing/docs/flight.htm (accessed 10 January 2020).

De Waal, T. (2015) *Great Catastrophe: Armenians and Turks in the Shadow of Genocide*. New York, NY: Oxford University Press.

De Zayas, A. (2007) 'The Istanbul Pogrom of 6–7 September 1955 in the light of international law', *Genocide studies and prevention*, 2 (2): 137–54.

Dixon, P. and O'Kane, E. (2014) *Northern Ireland since 1969*. Abingdon: Routledge.

Farrell, M. (1976) *Northern Ireland: The Orange State*. London: Pluto Press.

Fein, H. (1993) *Genocide: A Sociological Perspective*. London: Sage.

Ghassem-Fachandi, H. (2012) *Pogrom in Gujarat: Hindu Nationalism and Anti-Muslim Violence in India*. Princeton, NJ: Princeton University Press.

Glennon, K. (2013) *From Pogrom to Civil War: Tom Glennon and the Belfast IRA*. Cork: Mercier Press.

Government of Northern Ireland (1972) *Violence and Civil Disturbances in Northern Ireland in 1969. Report of Tribunal of Inquiry* [Scarman Report] (Cmd 566, April). Belfast: HMSO. Available at: https://cain.ulster.ac.uk/hmso/scarman.htm (accessed 23 January 2020).

Hagen, W. W. (2005) 'The moral economy of ethnic violence: the pogrom in Lwów', November 1918', *Geschichte und Gesellschaft*, 31 (2): 203–26.

Hart, P. (2003) *The IRA at War, 1916–1923*. New York, NY: Oxford University Press.

Hennessey, T. (2005) *Northern Ireland: The Origins of the Troubles*. Dublin: Gill & Macmillan.

Himka, J. P. (2011) 'The Lviv pogrom of 1941: the Germans, Ukrainian nationalists, and the carnival crowd', *Canadian Slavonic Papers*, 53 (2–4): 209–43.

Irish Republican News (2009) 'Burning of Bombay St remembered' (20 August). Available at: https://republican-news.org/current/news/2009/08/burning_of_bombay_st_remembere.html (accessed 5 July 2022).

Kallis, A. (2007) '"Licence" and genocide in the east: reflections on localised eliminationist violence during the first stages of "Operation Barbarossa" (1941)', *Studies in Ethnicity and Nationalism*, 7 (3): 6–23.

Kenna, G. B. (1922) *Facts and Figures of the Belfast Pogrom, 1920–22*. Dublin: The O'Connell Publishing Co.

Kennedy, L. (2016) *Unhappy the Land: The Most Oppressed People Ever, the Irish?* Sallins: Merrion Press.

Kennedy-Pipe, C. (1997) *The Origins of the Present Troubles in Northern Ireland*. London: Routledge.

Lewis, M. and McDaid, S. (2017) 'Bosnia on the border? Republican violence in Northern Ireland during the 1920s and 1970s', *Terrorism and Political Violence*, 29 (4): 635–55.

Lynch, R. (2008) 'The people's protectors? The Irish Republican Army and the "Belfast Pogrom", 1920–1922', *Journal of British Studies*, 47 (2): 375–91.

McCann, M. (2019) *Burnt Out: How 'The Troubles' Began*. Cork: Mercier Press.

McCleery, M. J. (2015) *Operation Demetrius and its Aftermath: A New History of the Use of Internment Without Trial in Northern Ireland, 1971–75*. Manchester: Manchester University Press.

Morrison, D. (n.d., a) 'From the Falls to Falluja'. Available at: www.dannymorrison.com/wp-content/dannymorrisonarchive/175.htm (accessed 23 January 2020).

Morrison, D. (n.d., b) 'Writing oneself out of history'. Available at: www.dannymorrison.com/wp-content/dannymorrisonarchive/147.htm (accessed 23 January 2020).

Murray, S. (2009) 'The Clonard Pogrom, 1969', *An Phoblacht* (23 July). Available at: www.anphoblacht.com/contents/20389 (accessed 5 July 2022).

Nelson, S. (1984) *Ulster's Uncertain Defenders: Loyalists and the Northern Ireland Conflict*. Belfast: Appletree Press.

Newry and Armagh Sinn Féin (2019) '"Founding of the Orange State is nothing to celebrate" – Murphy' [Facebook post] (7 January). Available at: www.facebook.com/newryarmagh.sinnfein/posts/2040504436017325 (accessed 5 July 2022).

NIO (Northern Ireland Office) (2020) *New Decade, New Approach*. Belfast, HMSO. Available at: https://bit.ly/3ArE6ym (accessed 23 January 2020).

O'Brien, J. (2000) *The Arms Trial*. Dublin: Gill & Macmillan.

Penkower, M. N. (2004) 'The Kishinev pogrom of 1903: a turning point in Jewish history', *Modern Judaism*, 24 (3): 187–225.

Petrovic, D. (1994) 'Ethnic cleansing – an attempt at methodology', *European Journal of International Law*, 5 (3): 342–59.

Prince, S. (2007) *Northern Ireland's '68: Civil Rights, Global Revolt and the Origins of the Troubles*. Dublin: Irish Academic Press.

Prince, S. and Warner, G. (2012) *Belfast and Derry in Revolt: A New History of the Start of the Troubles*. Dublin: Irish Academic Press.

Runia, E. (2004) '"Forget about it": "parallel processing" in the Srebrenica report', *History and Theory*, 43 (3): 295–320.

Runia, E. (2006) 'Presence', *History and Theory*, 45 (1): 1–29.

United Nations (1951) *Convention on the Prevention and Punishment of the Crime of Genocide*. Available at: https://bit.ly/2JC00oo (accessed 5 July 2022).

Visoka, G. (2016) 'Arrested truth: transitional justice and the politics of remembrance in Kosovo', *Journal of Human Rights Practice*, 8 (1): 62–80.

White, H. (2014) *Metahistory: The Historical Imagination in Nineteenth Century Europe*, anniversary edn. Baltimore, MD: Johns Hopkins University Press.

3

'Touching the third rail?' The problems of dealing with the past in Northern Ireland

Eamonn O'Kane

Speaking in 2009 to the House of Commons Northern Ireland Affairs Committee on the publication of the *Report of the Consultative Group on the Past*, one of its co-authors, Denis Bradley, made a telling observation: 'the past is the "third rail", as I think they describe it in American politics. If you touch it, you get burnt!' (NIAC, 2009: EV9). The comments were made as Bradley, and his co-chair of the process, Archbishop Robin Eames, discussed with MPs the findings of their examination into how Northern Ireland should deal with the legacy of the conflict commonly known as the Troubles.

While the reaction to the Eames–Bradley Report (as it became known) may not have left the authors 'burnt', many saw the report as incendiary. The process, which had lasted two years, held 141 private meetings with groups and individuals, saw over 500 people attend public meetings and received 290 written submissions and almost 3,000 standardised letters (CGP, 2009: 23), resulted in a 192-page report. Yet, upon its publication, most of the commentary (and criticism) focused on one proposal: the suggestion that a 'recognition' payment of £12,000 be paid to the nearest relative of anyone who died as a result of the conflict. This was contentious as it made no distinction between those killed by paramilitaries and those paramilitaries who were killed. While this proposal diverted attention from what was actually a thoughtful contribution to the debate on how to deal with the past, both the reaction to the proposal and Bradley's comments on the 'third rail' were indicative of the problems that have bedevilled attempts to deal with the past in Northern Ireland. This chapter seeks to do three things: outline the proposals that have been made to deal with the past; examine the tensions that exist between aspirations to achieve justice and truth to assist reconciliation in relation to the proposal; and suggest that a new approach is needed to break the logjam that exists in Northern Ireland.

Designing an architecture to deal with the past

The issue of how to deal with the past was on the agenda from the time of the negotiations which led to the Belfast/Good Friday Agreement (GFA) in April 1998. In November 1997, the British government tasked former senior Northern Ireland Office (NIO) civil servant Sir Kenneth Bloomfield to lead a commission, 'to examine the feasibility of providing greater recognition for those who have become victims in the last thirty years as a consequence of events in Northern Ireland' (Bloomfield, 1998: 8).

Bloomfield's report highlighted several issues that have continued to shape the debate about how to deal with the past, and indeed that have hindered progress on that question. In the report, Bloomfield raised the vexed question of who constitutes a victim. While acknowledging that, for many people, anyone who was killed or injured while undertaking illegal activity 'is only a victim of his own criminality and deserves no recognition for it', he suggested that a wider focus on the impact of those deaths should be adopted. The report further argued that 'any individual's involvement in unlawful activity does not lessen the grief and loss of close family who mourn him or her, many of whom may well have been unaware of the nature of involvement. We need to remember that our society does not attribute guilt by association. The degree of guilt to be borne by any individual is a matter, in the civil sphere, for courts of law, and in the moral sphere for a higher jurisdiction' (Bloomfield, 1998: 14). The focus of the report was on the impact that the conflict had had on the wider society and did not seek to apportion blame for the events.

Given that over 3,700 people died in the thirty-year conflict and over 40,000 were believed to have been injured, the violence had a wide impact within Northern Ireland and beyond. (For a wider discussion of the impact on the violence in Northern Ireland, see

McKittrick et al., 1999.) It was how to deal with this legacy that Bloomfield was concerned with. His suggestions, although more limited than some of the reports which followed, were primarily focused on how victims could be better supported, but it also noted that it might be useful to consider a truth and reconciliation process in the future, and also the possibility of a 'memorial and reconciliation day' as well as the creation of a 'Northern Ireland memorial'.

Although Bloomfield's was a serious and useful report, its impact was rather limited. This was, perhaps, a result of its timing. It was published in April 1998, just as the GFA negotiations reached their conclusion. As a result, it was somewhat overshadowed by that development. The GFA did mention the need for reconciliation and the issue of assisting victims, albeit briefly. The agreement stated that the signatories 'look forward to the results of the work of the Northern Ireland Victims Commission', and noted the challenges faced by victims and the 'work being done by many organisations to develop reconciliation and mutual understanding and respect between and within communities and traditions' (Secretary of State for Northern Ireland, 1998). It also pledged to 'positively examine the case for enhanced financial assistance for the work of reconciliation'. However, there was no detailed discussion in the GFA of practical steps related to dealing with the past.

At that stage, it was far from clear that the violence was coming to a permanent end in Northern Ireland. It was a difficult task to decide how to deal with the legacy of a conflict and support its victims until it was clear that it had ceased. Indeed, this was something that Bloomfield himself noted in his report:

> While no-one can guarantee that there will be no further victims, it could seem grotesque to contemplate a memorial if, unhappily, full-scale violence was to resume. The question of memorialisation can only appropriately be addressed after the definitive entry into the new and more forward looking era in the life of Northern Ireland. (Bloomfield, 1998: 51–52)

If the Bloomfield report did serve as a marker in terms of the necessity of dealing with the past and the legacy of the conflict, the issue continued to cause friction in Northern Ireland's politics and the functioning of the devolved structures and Executive. The next major examination of the issue was the Eames–Bradley Report. In addition to the contentious recognition payment mentioned above, the report contained more detailed recommendations for how to deal with the past than Bloomfield's had. It proposed the creation of a Legacy Commission, to be headed by an international chair and limited for five years. The Legacy Commission would identify themes that emerged from their work related to the Troubles. There was to be a new unit to replace the work being done by the Police Service of Northern Ireland's Historical Enquiries team (HET) and Police Ombudsman in investigating unsolved murders during the Troubles, which had come in for criticism.

It also proposed an information recovery body under a separate commissioner and unconnected with the policing investigations process to seek to secure information of importance to relatives. It agreed with the conclusions of Bloomfield's commission that it would not be appropriate to have a shared memorial to those who died in the Troubles, given how contentious it would be, and also supported Bloomfield's proposal for a shared day of remembrance each year (CGP, 2009).

As noted earlier, the arguments over the recognition payments somewhat overshadowed the discussion of the Eames–Bradley Report, and the proposals were never implemented. Bradley argues that he did believe that the government would adopt the report but suspects that there was opposition to it from advisers to Secretary of State Shaun Woodward (interview with the author, 25 June 2019). In 2010, the Northern Ireland Office published a summary of responses to the report, which showed that twenty of twenty-eight organisations that had responded opposed the payments, as did 169 of 174 individuals who responded. The then Northern Ireland Secretary of State, Owen Paterson, stated that the report 'should be seen as an important contribution to the debate about the past' (*News Letter*, 2010), but the government did not seek to implement its recommendations.

The issue of the past and how to deal with it did not go away, however. By 2013 it was one of three areas (along with issues related to parades and flying flags) that was undermining the governance of Northern Ireland and causing instability within the Northern Ireland Executive. As a result, the Executive invited former US diplomat Dr Richard Haass and US academic Professor Meghan O'Sullivan to lead an all-party group to consider these matters. The issue of dealing with the past was the one on which most progress was made. However, Haass and O'Sullivan could not get the parties to endorse their proposals. These mirrored elements of the Eames–Bradley Report in that they called for the creation of a new Historical Investigations Unit (HIU) to take over investigations of unsolved conflict-related deaths from the HET and Police Ombudsman.

In addition to the HIU, Hass–O'Sullivan proposed a new Independent Commission on Information Recovery (ICIR), which would be separate to the HIU and be tasked with seeking to provide information from (paramilitary) organisations to the families of those who died, if the families requested such information. The ICIR would also accept information from individuals about killings they were involved in, but would not pass such information on to the victims' families unless the family requested a report.

They also proposed that the ICIR should identify patterns or themes that their work uncovered and the establishment of an Implementation and Reconciliation Group (IRG) to oversee the work of the bodies tasked with dealing with the past. It suggested the creation of a Historical Timeline Group to 'develop a factual chronology of the Troubles' and called for greater support for victims and survivors (Hass and O'Sullivan, 2013).

The divisions over the proposals for flags and parades were more to blame for the inability to get agreement on the Haass–O'Sullivan proposals, but the failure of the initiative did lead to disappointment. Another factor which attracted some criticism was the absence of the British and Irish governments from the process. It was a creation of the Executive, and Secretary of State, Theresa Villiers, while noting the progress that had been made in Parliament, did observe that although the government 'were not formally a participant in the Haass process, we have been fully engaged with it from the start' (Hansard, HC vol. 573, col. 303, 8 January 2014). For some, this lack of direct engagement by London and Dublin was a problem. It had been a marked feature of the peace process since the mid-1990s that progress was largely only made when the government engaged directly in talks. Their failure to do so on this occasion was criticised (see, for example, O'Donnell, 2014).

As 2014 progressed a sense of crisis increased in Northern Ireland; in addition to the problems related to dealing with the past, flags and parades, a new challenge emerged over proposed welfare reform.

The Westminster government was forced to re-engage directly, as it seemed increasingly likely that devolved government might collapse. The First Minister, Peter Robinson of the Democratic Unionist Party (DUP), argued that 'the present arrangements are no longer fit for purpose' (Robinson, 2014). To prevent such a crisis, Theresa Villiers launched an eleven-week talks process between the five power-sharing parties in Northern Ireland, and the two governments, which led to the Stormont House Agreement (SHA), which all parties endorsed on 23 December 2014. In terms of the proposals to deal with the past, the SHA was very similar to the Hass–O'Sullivan ideas.

In many ways, the SHA had succeeded in the aspiration of the Americans' documents to agree to the 'creation of an architecture' to enable people to 'contend with the past' (Haass and O'Sullivan, 2013: 20). This architecture comprised: an HIU to replace the HET; an ICIR; an IRG to oversee information recovery; and an oral history archive (OHA). The IRG would be made up of eleven members. The chair was to be jointly nominated by the First and Deputy First Minister; one member would be nominated by the British government, one by the Irish government and the other eight members by Northern Ireland's political parties in relation to their representation in the Assembly. (The DUP would nominate three members, Sinn Féin two and the Ulster Unionist Party, Social Democratic and Labour Party, and Alliance Party one each).

This architecture was to be the basis which would allow Northern Ireland to come to terms with its past; however, despite the endorsement of the proposals by all the parties in 2014, there has been little progress. The collapse of the Northern Ireland Executive over the (unrelated) Renewable Heat Incentive issue in January 2017 delayed progress (see McBride, 2019). However, the government sought to push the process forward and issued a proposed Stormont House Agreement Bill and an associated consultation process in 2018. The government produced a summary of the seventeen thousand responses it received to the consultation in July 2019 but had not set out what it viewed as the next steps by the end of 2019.

This chapter will now discuss the criticisms that have been levelled at the proposals for dealing with the past in Northern Ireland and examine whether it is likely to be possible to deal with the issues along the lines proposed.

The problems of dealing with the past

As noted, Northern Ireland seems to be in a rather strange position. It is almost universally accepted that the past needs to be dealt with and that the failure to do so is having a detrimental impact on society and politics there. The issue has been the subject of significant work, scrutinised by official commissions; the focus of at least three reports (and many more academic examinations); and detailed proposals were agreed by all the main parties and two governments in 2014. Yet no real progress has been made.

The process is attempting to do several things at the same time. It is seeking to bring justice to the relatives of those whose loved ones were killed, discover the truth about what happened in Northern Ireland and help facilitate reconciliation in the region over events during the conflict. These are undoubtedly laudable aims; however, there are barriers to the achievement of each and tensions between them, which need to be acknowledged to a greater extent than they have been so far.

Justice

The fact that the majority of Troubles-related killings were never solved, and no one jailed for the deaths, can be taken as indicative of the fact that there has been a lack of justice in Northern Ireland. While there were certainly a significant number of prosecutions and incarceration during the conflict (around thirty thousand paramilitary prisoners were jailed during the period), the fact that people have not been held to account for murders of individuals has been extremely difficult for many of those who lost loved ones in the conflict. These cases remain open and responsibility for their pursuit falls to the HIU proposed under the SHA, which was intended to be, as the government's 2018 consultation document explained, 'an independent, investigative institution responsible for completing outstanding investigations into Troubles-related deaths' and have 'full policing powers' (NIO, 2018: 13). As well as examining outstanding cases (those which the predecessor HET had not yet examined), the Director of Public Prosecutions (DPP) can refer a case to the HIU, 'where the DPP has reasonable grounds for believing the HIU is likely to find new evidence that could lead to the identification or prosecution of a person involved in the death'. It was estimated that the proposed HIU would have to investigate around 1,700 Troubles-related deaths spanning the period 1968–98 (NIO, 2018: 26). However, no one really envisaged that these investigations would lead to many prosecutions. The Eames–Bradley Report was explicit on this point, noting that:

> the conduct of investigation needs to take full account of the increasing difficulties facing investigators and the question of where best to allocate scarce resources. With the lapse of time, it may be increasingly difficult to find new evidence or substantiate old evidence. Potential witnesses are more difficult to discover and may be regarded as less reliable. (CGP, 2009: 127)

The record of the HET's work – Peter Shirlow (2018: 422) has pointed out that the HET only managed to secure two convictions and eleven prosecutions from its review of 1,850 cases – would also seem to support this cautionary note.

It is not, however, simply the passing of time and difficulty in uncovering evidence that is relevant to discussions over the issue of conflict and justice in Northern Ireland. This debate also needs to be set in the wider context of decisions taken during, and the purpose of, the peace process. There was arguably a tension inherent between the quest for peace and demands for justice in Northern Ireland throughout the period that became known as the peace process (which can be roughly dated from the early 1990s). The purpose of the peace process was to seek to persuade those who used violence for (political) ends, to cease their armed campaigns and agree to pursue their objectives by non-violent means. The primary focus of this attention was the IRA, as they were the group that had killed more people than any other, and because other notable (loyalist) paramilitary organisations had long claimed that their violence was a response to republican actions. The question was how could the IRA be persuaded to end their campaign? By the early 1990s there was a growing belief within British and Irish government circles that elements of the republican movement might be receptive to a new approach. The peace process resulted in the IRA agreeing to end its campaign (with a ceasefire from 1994 to 1996, and again from 1997 onwards); the political party associated with them, Sinn

Féin, were invited into the political process and given a seat at the talks which led to the GFA of April 1998 and, ultimately, seats in the devolved power-sharing Executive.

This was a remarkable development, but it was one that was, in part, built upon compromises and concessions, some of which were related to issues normally associated with justice. Significantly, the deal allowed for the release of all prisoners within two years if they were linked to groups that had abandoned violence. This meant that all IRA prisoners (as well as those associated with loyalist groups such as the Ulster Volunteer Force (UVF) and Ulster Freedom Fighters (UFF)) were released by 2000. Many of these individuals had served significantly less than their sentences. While the HIU investigations are ongoing, it also means that anyone who might be convicted as part of one of those investigations for a Troubles-period crime will serve comparatively little jail time if they are connected to one of these groups. (Interestingly, the rules do not apply to members of the security forces, so any soldier or former police officer who might be convicted of a Troubles-related killing as a result of an HIU investigation would not be in the same situation.)

A few years after the conclusion of the GFA it became apparent that the British government had given assurances to members of the IRA who were 'on the run' that they would not face prosecution. It was also the case that incidents of criminality and the use of violence were 'overlooked' by the British government in the early period post-GFA, notably related to 'punishment beatings' by paramilitary groups. Despite such activity, the government resisted calls to suspend prisoner releases or declare the IRA's ceasefire over.

Tony Blair noted in the House of Commons in January 1999 that it was an 'imperfect peace' but 'better than no process and no peace at all' (quoted in Dixon, 2019: 175). Such incidents and decisions highlight that pragmatism was a key factor in the establishment of the peace process. Questions related to 'justice' were considered in relation to wider considerations of 'peace' and, at times, peace was prioritised over justice. This prioritising of peace has cast a shadow for some over the resulting process and dealing with the legacy of the past. There is pressure from some quarters to redress what they see as this imbalance at the heart of the peace process.

Shirlow has offered a useful distinction of approaches between what he terms 'apologia' and 'humiliation'. For Shirlow, apologia is a tactic that tends to be used by non-state actors who seek to justify previous violence, without admitting guilt by suggesting it was explicable and justified in the context in which it occurred. Shirlow argues that 'humiliation seeking', linked to 'criminalisation discourses', is employed by 'the British and Irish states and sections of Irish nationalism and aims for non-state actors to show contrition figuratively, emotionally and in practice through an admission of guilt uncoupled from the assertion of extenuating or mitigating circumstances' (Shirlow, 2018: 424). It is this strand of opinion which is pressing the justice arguments and claims that there has been a problem at the heart of the process which needs to be addressed. Some argue that those (non-state) actors who were responsible for the deaths during the Troubles need both to show contrition and 'pay' for their crimes. (For a strong example of this argument, see Matchett, 2016, and some of the contributions in Dudgeon, 2016.)

There is also, however, something of an inversion of this in play as well: some non-state actors, notably within republican circles, feel that their side was targeted by the state throughout the period and many of their 'combatants' were prosecuted and incarcerated for their crimes, but they believe that the same did not happen to members of the security forces who were involved in killings or crimes. Those who hold such positions have views towards the security services that would fit Shirlow's 'humiliation' characterisation.

This issue of who should be the focus of investigations into Troubles-related killings has also caused problems related to justice considerations. Paramilitary groups accounted for 90 per cent of killings during the Troubles while the state actors were responsible for 10 per cent of those who died. Some of these 10 per cent died in contentious circumstances and there have been demands that those responsible be investigated and prosecuted. There have been some high-profile cases, such as the decision to prosecute 'Soldier F' for two murders and five attempted murders during the Bloody Sunday shootings in 1972 (*Guardian*, 2019). Many within the unionist community, and politicians at Westminster, have decried what they see as too much focus being given to 'state killings'.

Speaking in 2016 on the decision to charge a seventy-three-year-old former soldier, Denis Hutching, for the killing of John Pat Cunningham in 1973, the DUP MP Sammy Wilson told the House of Commons that the decision 'is not about opening cases to find out who is guilty or not guilty. It is about political revisionism, rewriting history, and trying to move the blame from the terrorists to those who served their country faithfully' (Hansard, HC vol. 618, col. 295, 13 December 2016). The then prime minister Theresa May expressed similar sentiments to Parliament in 2018 when she argued, 'we have an unfair situation at the moment, in that the only people being investigated for these issues that happened in the past are those in our armed forces or those who served in law enforcement in Northern Ireland. That is patently unfair – terrorists are not being investigated. Terrorists should be investigated and that is what the Government want to see' (Hansard, HC vol. 640, col. 677, 9 May 2018). May's assertion that terrorists were not being investigated was challenged by many, including Northern Ireland's Victims' Commissioner, Judith Thompson. Thompson stated that the comments were 'completely in contravention of the facts' (Walker, 2018). But such sentiments illustrate the divisive nature of attempts to investigate the past and bring about prosecutions.

The belief that former soldiers and police officers were being unfairly targeted by those who wanted to 'rewrite history' to portray the state rather than terrorists as the aggressors, led to consideration of introducing a statute of limitations for prosecutions against security forces' personnel. It was widely expected that this would be in the proposed SHA Bill, but it was allegedly dropped when legal advice suggested that such a statute would have to apply to all those suspected of killings, not just state actors. The DUP and Sinn Féin both opposed such plans but for different reasons (the DUP did not want to see paramilitaries potentially escaping prosecution, and Sinn Féin felt the same about former soldiers and police officers). The dropping of the proposals led to a row in Cabinet between the Secretaries of State for Defence and for Northern Ireland (Osborne, 2018).

However, the view by some in government that security forces personnel should not be investigated appeared to linger. In 2019, the Northern Ireland Secretary of State Karen Bradley was criticised for asserting in Parliament that: 'Over 90 per cent of the killings during the Troubles were at the hands of terrorists, every single one of those was a crime. The fewer than ten per cent that were at the hands of the military and police were not crimes.' She later had to backtrack, and asserted that, 'where there is evidence of wrongdoing it should always be investigated, whoever is responsible' (quoted in Moriarty, 2019).

Given the issues related to passage of time and availability of evidence, the pragmatic favouring of peace over justice that underpinned the peace process and the differences between parties on why the violence occurred and who should be investigated for killings in the period, there are significant questions over whether it will ever be possible to get justice for those who died during the conflict.

Truth

In addition to the fact that the majority of conflict-related deaths in Northern Ireland are unsolved, there is a good deal of debate about many aspects of the Troubles and who was responsible for specific acts of violence that killed and maimed people. The proposals that have been developed during the commissions discussed earlier and the plans for the ICIR and the OHA (discussed below) seem to offer a way to reduce this level of ignorance and help discover the truth about what happened. However, there remain significant obstacles to achieving this goal.

For the ICIR to work, it will require individuals and organisations who were involved in the conflict and responsible for violent acts to engage with the commission and provide the necessary information. There are several reasons why this may not be as straightforward as the SHA appears to suggest. Firstly, there is a battle for control of the narrative around the conflict with organisations seeking to suggest that what their side did was a justifiable and measured response to the provocation they faced, while suggesting that what was done to them or by the 'other side' was unjustified and excessive. (There are overlaps here with the apologia/humiliation distinction discussed earlier.) Organisations might be unwilling to allow former members to offer accounts to the ICIR that challenge their preferred narrative.

Secondly, although it is the case that under the SHA proposals information given to the ICIR is not admissible in court (a step taken to encourage people to disclose information to the ICIR for their reports to the families of those killed), the explanatory notes for the proposed Bill caused some to question how distinct the two processes of the ICIR and the criminal investigations are. The notes stated that 'policing authorities or a coroner' were entitled to carry out investigations as a result of information in an ICIR report. If these investigations 'led to evidence being generated, then that new evidence would not fall under the inadmissibility provisions (despite the report itself being inadmissible)' (Explanatory Notes to the Northern Ireland (Stormont House Agreement) Bill, para. 155; see also McEvoy *et al.*, 2018). This may well act as a disincentive for people to disclose information to the ICIR; the concern being that it might invite further investigation into events they were involved in.

Thirdly, Northern Ireland's DPP, Stephen Herron, raised concerns in 2018 that organisations could seek to implant false information into ICIR reports in order to 'prejudice a potential or actual prosecution' (Archer, 2018).

Fourthly, beyond the fear of subsequent prosecution, individuals may be concerned about criticism of their previous actions if they disclosed information to the ICIR. Tom Roberts, a former UVF prisoner who now works with a group helping loyalist ex-offenders, has noted that, 'they'd be pointing at you walking down Royal Avenue; it's a very small society here ... People draw analogies sometimes with South Africa – South Africa is a vast country (nearly sixty million people), we're less than two million people, to a degree everyone knows who everyone is anyway' (interview with the author, 27 June 2019). As a result, questions remain as to how effective the ICIR's quest to produce reports is likely to be.

The second major strand of the SHA that is related to information recovery and the quest for the truth regarding what happened in Northern Ireland is the proposal for an OHA. The OHA would be located in the Public Records Office Northern Ireland. This proposal has been less contentious and could have historical value for researchers in years to come. There are some points worth noting, however.

The proposal that the OHA will also produce a factual timeline of the Troubles would be helpful but, inevitably, given the number of incidents which occurred in Northern Ireland, there is likely to be some who complain about omitted events. More substantially, however, given that contributions to the OHA would be voluntary, some of the issues related to the willingness of individuals to contribute and the narrative they may offer, similar to those discussed above regarding the interaction with the ICIR, may also be in play. There is a danger that a distorted impression of the conflict and the impact it had on society emerges if groups seek a large input into the process and offer a particular version of events.

There is also the issue of the absent voices, which could skew the impression that the OHA may ultimately give. It is possible that many people may decide not to engage with the project, and as a result there may be important perspectives that are not recorded. McGrattan and Hopkins (2018: 5) have noted that: 'The process of selecting what to "remember" and what to "forget" is itself intensely politicised.' If these absences are not filled and the voices not heard, it may distort what historians draw from the OHA in the future.

The other aspect related to the quest to discover the truth is the proposed role for academics. The IRG is to receive reports from the ICIR, HIU, OHA and Coroners' Service that identify 'patterns and themes' which have become apparent during their investigations. These reports would be produced by the bodies at the end of their five-year terms of operation. The IRG 'must commission academic experts to identify, and then report to the IRG on, patterns and themes' in these reports. The draft bill lists a range of other sources which the academics may draw upon, all of which are in the public domain (see Art. 62 (3) of the Draft Northern Ireland (Stormont House Agreement) Bill (2013)).

The proposals state that the academics must be independent, but there are no real details about how this is to be achieved or what the selection process will be. The explanatory notes simply state that 'the academic experts must act independently and free from political influence' (Explanatory Notes to the Northern Ireland (Stormont House Agreement) Bill, para. 190). The bill itself offers a rather basic definition of an academic expert as 'a person who, in the view of the IRG, is of proven academic standing' (Art 62 (9)). The government's consultation paper of May 2018 gives a little more detail and suggests that the academic report might be commissioned through the Economic and Social Research Council (ESRC) funding council in order to ensure independence and academic rigour (NIO, 2018: 47).

The government's summary of responses to the consultation noted that some respondents had 'argued that the academics commissioned to prepare a report should have access to a wider range of material and reports, than is currently set out in the draft Bill, to assist their work'. There was also a call for a wider role for academics, noted in the consultation summary: 'Other respondents argued that the IRG should establish a formalised role for historians, such as through an advisory research board or commission – either to advise the IRG, and/or other institutions, or to provide context in order to help them with their work' (NIO, 2019: 27–28).

These proposals were similar to the recommendations made by the Conference of Irish Historians in Britain, who held a seminar in Oxford in 2016 (and made a submission to the consultation process). The group has called for a larger amount of material to be made available on the conflict from government archives. They argue that access to such material is necessary to enable the independent academics selected to fulfil their role. While they note the problems related to secrecy, they suggest these could be overcome either by names being redacted from documents by officials before they are released to researchers or by having the reports vetted by officials after they have been written (Conference of Irish Historians in Britain, 2016).

Such an approach would undoubtedly help the researchers fulfil their role and lead to more informed reporting. It is not, though, without its own problems. Groups whose own narratives of the conflict are likely to be challenged by academics' reports will seek to question their veracity on the grounds that the material they draw upon is not open to all for inspection and that, given that that material is from the government's archives, it is problematic. Also, no matter how robust the selection process is for the academics who perform the role, accusations of bias will inevitably be made.

Indeed, Elazar Barkan (2009) has highlighted the problems faced by academics who have been involved in similar exercises elsewhere. Barkan noted that those whose accounts are challenged by the work of academics tend to seek to undermine it and that the 'custodians of the nationalist discourse do not disappear; they are likely to mount a counter offensive' (Barkan, 2009: 909).

None of these problems are insurmountable, and it is the case that robust academic work will certainly be an asset to attempts to develop a fuller picture of what happened during the Troubles in Northern Ireland. But the problems do serve to highlight some of the potential challenges that the proposals pose. The quest for the truth is clearly an important aspect of dealing the past, but as designed, it is unclear whether the proposals in the SHA will be as far reaching or transformative as its architects may have hoped. The historian A. T. Q. Stewart offered a more cautionary message about the impact that historians and, indeed, the 'truth' can have:

> There are many people of good intentions who would persuade us that if only we could discover the truth about our history, some of that harm be neutralised. This is an illusion, for the myth is often more potent than the reality, and perhaps a different type of truth. History is not a branch of social welfare, and the only respectable motive for studying it is to explore the past for its own sake. Academic historians must resign themselves to the fact that they have little real influence on a nation's view of its past. What a nation thinks of its history is shaped rather by colourful narrative and the need for a political myth. The reality which is disinterred by patient scholarship is not so much disputed as simply ignored. (Stewart, 2001: 185)

Obviously, the process suggested in the SHA seeks to overcome this problem, and Stewart's view is perhaps too bleak, but it is worth bearing in mind when considering how we access the truth.

Is there a need for a different approach?

Although the ambition and aspiration of the recommendations in the SHA (which as we have seen has drawn from the work of the reports that preceded it) are impressive, the inability to make progress towards their implementation is telling. The hopes that by taking the steps discussed above, progress could be made in both the areas of justice and the search for truth in Northern Ireland, which would help towards reconciliation in the region and enable it to come to terms with its past, have been unfulfilled.

This failure to make progress over the past has become an impediment to governing the present and is casting a long shadow over community relations in the future. The foundations of the peace process were built upon pragmatic decisions, prioritising peace over justice in certain areas. These were difficult decisions, and for many they were wrong, but without them there would have been no peace process (and more killing and continued instability). It was not that these pragmatic decisions made a just society unjust or a truthful society deceitful. They made a violent society far less so. However, it should not be a surprise that once the violence receded there was increased pressure to deal with the past.

The problem, however, is that although the violent phase of the conflict has largely passed, it is not the case that Northern Ireland society was created anew in April 1998. The parties and groups who were the main players in the conflict have remained the main players in the politics of the post-conflict era. These parties, especially those associated with paramilitary groups, have a vested interest in defending a narrative that justifies past actions and present trajectory. In addition, the structural problems related to the passing of time and lack of available evidence mean that in the vast majority of cases there is little likelihood of criminal trials leading to justice for the families of those killed in the conflict. Finding the truth about what happened to them (even if there will be no prosecutions) is a more realistic aspiration. However, this would involve groups and individuals engaging with a process honestly and openly, a process that would lead to some uncomfortable truths emerging and making stated positions by political parties and authorities more difficult to maintain and defend. There has been little indication so far that they are willing to do so.

While groups make demands for information on what was done to them, they are less forthcoming over what was done by them, or those associated with them. The fact that the IRG, the overseer of the process, is to comprise nominees from the political parties may undermine its chances of success. The political parties are divided over not only the legitimacy of what happened during the past but also what the focus of the bodies that seek to investigate it should be (they are on different sides of the apologia/humiliation divide). As a result, it is rather ambitious to expect politicians or political appointees to oversee such a contentious undertaking.

The American author David Rieff has discussed whether attempts to deal with the past in certain deeply divided societies can undermine them further rather than heal. For Rieff, the problem is particularly acute in post-conflict societies where there 'is no clear winner', as 'both sides may be able to sustain their own incompatible memories' (Rieff, 2016: 12). He challenges the view that remembering injustices is cathartic: 'To the contrary, at numerous times and in numerous places, remembrance has provided the toxic adhesive that was needed to cement old grudges and conflicting martyrologies, as it did in Northern Ireland and the Balkans for generations, if not for centuries.' As a result, he argued that, eventually, 'there comes a time when the need to get to the truth should no longer be assumed to trump all other considerations' (Rieff, 2016: 86–89).

Rieff's suggestions have not been universally accepted. Guy Beiner has questioned the suggestion that memory is malleable to the extent that a society could choose to 'forget': 'Appealing as it may seem, the conviction that memory can be turned off on command (presumably at the whim of politicians, with the help of historians) derives from a simplistically conceived notion of collective memory, which assumes that if memory is constructed and malleable it can be easily annulled' (Beiner, 2018, 25). Beiner has discussed the problems that have emerged in other societies that have sought to control how their past is remembered (or not) and argues persuasively that these have led to further tensions and have largely been unsustainable.

However, the situation in Northern Ireland does not have to be a binary one: that is, either deal fully with the past, discover the truth and come to an agreed narrative over what happened, or forget about the Troubles and move on. It is how the past is dealt with, and by whom, that is in question. Beiner is of course correct in suggesting that the past cannot be 'forgotten', especially at a personal level. But Rieff raises an important question when he ponders whether it is possible to find common ground and 'healing' over the past when there is no clear winner.

Northern Ireland's experience is different to many societies that have embarked on truth and reconciliation processes, due to the nature of the conflict. As Henry Patterson has pointed out:

> there is a major difference between Northern Ireland and the vast majority of international examples of truth recovery processes: whereas in the South African and Latin American examples, which are those most referred to by those making the case for a local truth commission, it was the state and its agents which were responsible for the vast majority of deaths and traumatic events, in Northern Ireland it was paramilitary organisations that killed the vast majority of victims. (Patterson, 2016)

In other states, it may be easier to deal with the past as regimes were overthrown, those that were responsible for most of the violence and killing were ousted and, usually, a more democratic and representative government was installed. This fundamental alteration of the society facilitated (often years later) an examination of the past. This has clearly not happened in Northern Ireland.

There are problems in Northern Ireland over political will, a perceived need to defend past actions and an unwillingness to allow narratives to be undermined, which have largely led to the lack of progress. This is despite apparent agreement over the architecture that would be installed to deal with the past. Given the structural and attitudinal barriers to developing a comprehensive process to deal with the past, it seems unlikely that the SHA will be fully implemented.

As Beiner notes, however, the past does not go away and it will need to be addressed (if it cannot be 'dealt with'). It may be that this will be best served by an ad hoc, piecemeal approach. For instance, as the SHA suggests, academic investigation into the past is an important aspect of dealing with it. As Ignatieff has argued, 'the function of honest historians, is simply to purify the argument, to narrow the range of permissible lies' (Ignatieff, 1996: 113).

The problematic narratives that underpin a good deal of the debate about Northern Ireland's past do need to be challenged and academic work will help to narrow the range of permissible lies. The state can play an important role in this by seeking to put as much of their records into the public domain as possible. Similarly, funding made available through bodies such as the ESRC would help facilitate this research, but it does not need to be 'state sponsored' or be a part of a large 'dealing with the past' project in order to get to 'the truth'. Tony Judt argues: 'if history is to do its proper job, preserving forever the evidence of past crimes and everything else, it is best left alone. When we ransack the past for political profit – selecting the bits that can serve our purposes and recruiting history to teach opportunistic moral lessons – we get bad morality *and* bad history' (Judt, 2008).

The other aspects of the SHA again could be considered, but in isolation from each other. There are OHAs in existence, and these could be expanded and supported (albeit with an awareness of some of the potential problems noted above). The debate over investigations into past crimes by a body such as the HET and the necessity to continue coroner investigations into certain killings are more problematic and differences over these are likely to continue. But without significant attitudinal changes in Northern Ireland, an imminent breakthrough appears unlikely.

It may still be too soon for a comprehensive, structured, wholesale process that will resolve the issues and allow society to 'move on' after a five-year period, as suggested. It may be time to seek to examine the component parts of dealing with the past individually and lower expectations. People individually, and society more widely, will have to find ways of dealing with the past, but the 'third rail' appears to be too dangerous to be touched directly at the moment. A way needs to be found to separate dealing with the past from the political present. The proposals as currently set out in the SHA give the politicians too much influence over the process and too few incentives to risk getting burnt by it.

References

Archer, B. (2018) 'Legacy investigation time "may not be achievable" – PPS chief', *Irish News* (9 October). Available at: www.irishnews.com/news/2018/10/09/news/legacy-investigation-time-may-not-be-achievable—pps-chief-1453280/ (accessed 10 October 2018).

Barkan, E. (2009) 'Introduction: historians and historical reconciliation', *American Historical Review*, 114 (4): 899–913.

Beiner, G. (2018) *Forgetful Remembrance: Social Forgetting and Vernacular Historiography of a Rebellion in Ulster*. Oxford: Oxford University Press.

Bloomfield, K. (1998) *We Will Remember Them*. Report of the Northern Ireland Victims Commissioner. Belfast: The Stationery Office.

CGP (Consultative Group on the Past) (2009) *Report of the Consultative Group on the Past*. Belfast: CGP.

Conference of Irish Historians in Britain (2016) 'Historians and the Stormont House Agreement: report on a workshop held at Hertford College, Oxford, 19 October'. Available at: https://irishhistoriansinbritain.org/?p=321 (accessed 16 May 2018).

Dixon, P. (2019) *Performing the Northern Ireland Peace Process*. Basingstoke: Palgrave Macmillan.

Explanatory Notes to the Northern Ireland (Stormont House Agreement) Bill (2018). London: HMSO.

Guardian (2019) 'Bloody Sunday: "Soldier F" case reaches court' (18 September).
Haass, R. and O'Sullivan, M. (2013) 'Haass report – proposed agreement' (31 December). Belfast: Northern Ireland Executive. Available at: www.northernireland.gov.uk/publications/haass-report-proposed-agreement (accessed 10 May 2018).
Matchett, W. (2016) *Secret Victory*. Belfast: Matchett.
Ignatieff, M. (1996) 'Articles of faith', *Index of Censorship*, 5: 110–22.
Judt, T. (2008) 'The "problem of evil" in postwar Europe', *New York Review of Books*, 14 February.
McBride, S. (2019) *Burned*. Dublin: Merrion Press.
McEvoy, K., Bryson, A., Mallinder, L. and Holder, D. (2018). *Addressing the Legacy of Northern Ireland's Past: Response to the NIO Public Consultation*. Belfast: QUB Human Rights Centre. Available at: http://bit.ly/2N0Gzrr (accessed 20 July 2022).
McGrattan, C. and Hopkins, S. (2017) 'Memory in post-conflict societies: from contention to integration?', *Ethnopolitics*, 16 (5): 488–99.
McKittrick, D., Kelters, S., Feeney, B. and Thornton, C. (1999) *Lost Lives*. Edinburgh: Mainstream Publishing.
Moriarty, G. (2019) 'Killings by British soldiers during Troubles were "not crimes" – Karen Bradley', *Irish Times* (6 March). Available at: www.irishtimes.com/news/politics/killings-by-british-soldiers-during-troubles-were-not-crimes-karen-bradley-1.3816483 (accessed 6 March 2019).
News Letter (2010) 'Ulster rejects Eames Bradley report on Troubles' (19 July).
NIAC (2018) *The Report of the Consultative Group on the Past in Northern Ireland*. London: The Stationery Office.
NIO (Northern Ireland Office) (2018) *Addressing the Legacy of Northern Ireland's Past* (consultation paper, 11 May). Belfast: Legacy Policy Team.
NIO (2019) *Addressing the Legacy of Northern Ireland's Past. Analysis of the consultation responses*. Belfast: Legacy Policy Team.
O'Donnell, L. (2014) 'Our government is taking peace process for granted', *Irish Independent* (9 May). Available at: https://bit.ly/3RPBSze (accessed 10 May 2014).
Osborne, S. (2018) 'Government launches consultation on killings during Northern Ireland's Troubles with no amnesty for British soldiers', *Independent* (11 May). Available at: https://bit.ly/3yX3o5b (accessed 16 May 2018).
Patterson, H. (2016) 'Victims and the peace process', *Belfast News Letter* (21 November). Available at: www.proquest.com/newspapers/victims-peace-process/docview/1842159258/se-2 (accessed 9 August 2022).

Rieff, D. (2016) *In Praise of Forgetting: Historical Memory and Its Ironies*. New Haven, CT: Yale University Press.

Robinson, P. (2014) 'Stormont's inadequate set-up and the welfare row... Northern Ireland's First Minister writes exclusively for the Telegraph', *Belfast Telegraph* (8 September). Available at: https://bit.ly/3OrpHpr (accessed 15 September 2014).

Secretary of State for Northern Ireland (1998) 'The Belfast Agreement: An Agreement Reached at the Multi-Party Talks on Northern Ireland' (Cm 3883, 10 April). Available at: https://bit.ly/3RRKQfd (accessed 20 July 2022).

Shirlow, P. (2018) 'Truth friction in Northern Ireland: caught between apologia and humiliation', *Parliamentary Affairs*, 71: 417–37.

Stewart, A. T. Q. (2001) *The Shape of Irish History*. Belfast: The Blackstaff Press.

Walker, S. (2018) 'Victims' commissioner says PM's facts "incorrect"', *BBC News* (14 May). Available at: www.bbc.co.uk/news/uk-northern-ireland-44088827 (accessed 16 May 2018).

4

Collective memory, ethno-national forgetting and the limits of history in misremembering the past

Aaron Edwards

In *Regarding the Pain of Others*, Susan Sontag observes that the past casts a spell on those who choose to remember it: 'Remembering is an ethical act and has ethical value in and of itself. Memory is, achingly, the only relation we can have with the dead.' She goes on to argue: 'So the belief that remembering is an ethical act is deep in our natures as humans, who know we are going to die, and who mourn those who in the normal course of things die before us – grandparents, parents, teachers, and older friends' (Sontag, 2003: 103).

Sontag's remarks go to the heart of ethnic conflicts where competing groups engage in what might be thought of as a seance between the living and the dead. In Cyprus, the former republic of Yugoslavia and Northern Ireland, we see the consequences of the appropriation of historical memories in ways that reinforce pre-existing divisions over ethnicity, nationality and religion (Kaloudis, 1999; Richmond, 2002). In the words of Eric Hobsbawm,

> 'We' recognize ourselves as 'us' because we are different from 'Them'. If there were no 'They' from whom we are different, we wouldn't have to ask ourselves who 'We' were. Without Outsiders there are no Insiders. In other words, collective identities are based not on what their members have in common – they may have very little in common except not being the 'Others'. (Hobsbawm, 1996: 40)

As Rogers Brubaker (2002: 166) has further argued, it is common for 'ethno-political entrepreneurs' to seek to exploit these differences as a means of fuelling conflict. As he observes, by 'invoking groups, they seek to evoke them, summon them, call them into being'. These self-proclaimed ethnic defenders employ a common-sense trope of 'the group' in a way that is 'designed to stir, summon, justify, mobilise, kindle and energise' (Brubaker, 2002: 166). It is necessary for scholars to treat such ethnic discourse with care, particularly where highly selective readings of the past can be used to perpetuate violent conflict (Edwards, 2015).

This chapter examines the dynamics of the Northern Ireland conflict through the broader conceptual lens of ethno-nationalism. In common with the work of Anthony D. Smith, it acknowledges that ethnic forms of nationalism are 'of varying kinds and degrees, some of them relatively peaceful like the Catalan and Czech movements, others aggressive and exclusive of the kind witnessed in pre-war Germany and Italy or present-day former Yugoslavia' (Smith, 2007: 100–1).

It could be argued that both Ulster loyalists and Irish republicans in Northern Ireland represent more 'aggressive and exclusive' fringes of rival ethno-national communities. Not only have they consistently opted to obfuscate or forget the excesses of their violent pasts, they have also actively misremembered these acts in a way that seeks to legitimise present political decisions and positions. This should not be surprising, for, as I have argued elsewhere, '[c]ollective rituals backed up by a strong sense of community identity and a political cause serve as a powerful adhesive during times of rapid sociopolitical upheaval and change' (Edwards, 2008: 215).

Nonetheless, what is intriguing is not necessarily *why* people in divided societies engage in collective rituals, traditions and culture per se but *how* they have sought to employ them in the service of legitimising their claims of ethnic entitlement in ways that are competitive (Horowitz, 2000). Historical memories of a troubled past are conjured and marshalled in support of the continuation of a centuries-old struggle in a way that threatens to destabilise transition processes. Here, Northern Ireland is no exception (Edwards, 2019; Rieff, 2016a). In closing, the chapter advances a normative perspective that sees professional historians as playing an important role in promoting a more objective understanding of the past in a way that can aid the cause of reconciliation.

Divided history; divided memory?

The predominant view of ethno-national conflict is that it is so enduring because it is contested by organised groups that tend to confront each other (Wolff, 2006: 64). Donald Horowitz argues that 'ethnic identity is established at birth for most members' and is based on a 'myth of common ancestry, which usually carries with it traits believed to be innate' (Horowitz, 2000: 52). In deeply divided societies – where competing groups interpret the world around them in diverging ways – these differences reflect broader political identity concerns.

Ethnic groups tend to place emphasis on symbols of identity, customs and traditions, and, as Horowitz notes, such competition manifests itself outwardly in the attachment of meaning to symbols. 'Symbolic conflicts, however, also accentuate points of difference between the groups', Horowitz suggests, 'and generate counter symbols around which opposition to a symbolic claim can coalesce' (Horowitz, 2000: 217).

The strength of such ethnic solidarity is disputed in the academic literature. Brubaker, for instance, challenges what he calls 'groupism' – that is, 'the tendency to take discrete, sharply differentiated, internally homogeneous and externally bounded groups as basic constituents of social life, chief protagonists of social conflicts, and fundamental units of social analysis' (Brubaker, 2002: 164). He rails against the proclivity to enter into a discourse that too readily reifies groups as being conveniently labelled, for example as Catholics or Protestants, Serbs or Croats, Jews or Arabs, or, indeed, Turks and Kurds, as if they were 'unitary collective actors with common purposes' (Brubaker 2002: 164).

Brubaker's analysis is worth acknowledging. It has clear implications for our understanding of why and how people in divided places utilise the past in the ways that they do. Drawing on Brubaker's work, Cillian McGrattan argues that by focusing on ethnic groups, theorists and politicians effectively 'silence questions concerning the importance of historical choices and responsibilities' as well as other perspectives, which help explain the dynamics of 'political entrenchment' and 'communal polarisation' (McGrattan, 2010: 8).

While it is important to appreciate the nuances of conflict dynamics in divided societies, we must also recognise how divergent understandings of the past serve as the adhesive by which people find attachment to broader ethno-national 'imagined communities' (Anderson, 2006: 6). As Hutchinson and Smith observe, these ethnic communities – what they call 'ethnies' – tend to exhibit the following characteristics: 'a named human population with myths of common ancestry, shared historical memories, one or more elements of common culture, a link with a homeland and a sense of solidarity among at least some of its members' (Hutchinson and Smith, 1996: 6).

It is generally accepted that these distinct features help to provide cohesion for heterogenous communities while, at the same time, fuel tendencies towards othering. Moreover, when these shared historical memories are invoked, they risk hermetically sealing the past and avoiding discussion of the real causes of the conflict. Michael Howard likens such myth-making narratives to what he calls 'nursery history' on account of the sustenance it brings to its adherents (Howard, 1993: 26–30; MacMillan, 2010: 39).

Arguably, myth-making in divided societies can limit the scope for reconciliation between parties in conflict and stave off the promise of social justice and redress for human rights abuses long after the guns fall silent (McGrattan and Hopkins, 2017: 489). It is also worth keeping in mind the political connotations of memory work. As Luisa Passerini reminds us:

> It is the reference to the individual or the group that remembers that allows us to situate historically and make concrete what is remembered and what is not. The issues of forgetting and silence are indeed equally important for understanding the political reverberations of memory. (Passerini, 2010: 460)

Understanding how forgetting can be just as powerful as remembering can illuminate key dynamics in the role of historical memory in perpetuating and accentuating ethno-national conflict.

The famous aphorism coined by Spanish philosopher George Santayana runs: 'those who cannot remember the past are condemned to repeat it' (Santayana, 1906: 284). Santayana's quote is often attributed in isolation without seeking to place it amid his more general meditation on historical progress. Progress for Santayana 'depends on retentiveness', for when 'experience is not retained, as among savages, infancy is perpetual'. Santayana describes a mind that in the earliest stage of life is frivolous and easily distracted, missing progress due mainly to a preoccupation with persistence. In the initial phase, common among who he terms 'children and barbarians', 'instinct has learned nothing from experience' (Santayana, 1906: 284).

In the second stage, human beings are 'docile to events, plastic to new habits and suggestions, yet able to graft them on original instincts'. Eventually, their progress brings them to adulthood and 'true progress'. It is in the last stage, in Santayana's view, where we see retentiveness exhausted and all that has happened is 'at once forgotten; a vain, because unpractical, repetition of the past takes the place of plasticity and fertile readaptation'. As humans grow older, their memories weaken and they become forgetful of the past, becoming 'self-repeating' and degenerating 'into an instinctive reaction, like a bird's chirp' (Santayana, 1906: 285).

In Ireland, it could be argued that memory is more of 'an instinctive reaction, like a bird's chirp'. As Frank Wright observed in his magisterial book on the land question during the Irish Home Rule Crisis of the late nineteenth century:

> It is often said that part of the trouble in Northern Ireland today is that we will not forget our history. For me the real difficulty is that our versions of history are in fact ways of explaining our feelings and especially our fears in everyday life. By contrast, history in societies enjoying normal order does not feel as though it is about relationships that matter today. (Wright, 1996: 5)

If we simply ignore the bird's chirp, rather than acting instinctively, then we might move to something akin to 'normal order' where history is less about relationships today. David Rieff recommends that the best route to achieving great stability is perhaps to avoid remembering altogether. As he argues:

> On such occasions, when collective memory condemns communities to feel the pain of their historical wounds and the bitterness of their historical grievances – and all communities have such wounds, whether at a given point in history they are oppressors or the oppressed – it is not the duty to remember but a duty to forget that should be honored. (Rieff, 2016b: 121)

Although controversial, there is much to agree with here in Rieff's interpretation of historical memory, especially in transitional societies

Collective memory, ethno-national forgetting 83

where there is a real danger of them relapsing back into violent conflict.

Is this possible in places where nationalism 'simultaneously meets emotional, psychological and material or practical needs' of ordinary people? Richard English argues that the people lie at the heart of nationalism's discourse on community and, as such, 'myths of shared national descent intensify attachment in ways which are partly, but only partly, fictionally based' (English, 2006: 13). As George Orwell observed in his essay *Notes on Nationalism*: 'The nationalist not only does not disapprove of atrocities committed by his own side, but he has a remarkable capacity for not even hearing about them.' Orwell went on to argue that every nationalist 'is haunted by the belief that the past can be altered' (Orwell, 1945). The conflict between Ulster loyalists and Irish republicans demonstrates the provenance of Orwell's words, for there is clear evidence of both communities actively choosing to forget the excesses of their past in a way that does injury to history.

The principal weapon for perpetuating and accentuating division comes in the form of 'nursery history' aimed at gaining advantage in a conflict, according to John Nagle, which is 'inextricably bound up with contests over political legitimacy and state sovereignty' (Nagle, 2014: 475). This struggle for recognition by competing groups, Nagle argues, is 'highly resistant to peaceful transformation since both groups' desire for national self-determination cannot be realised' (Nagle, 2014: 475). What makes matters worse, according to Geoffrey Beattie, is the sociopolitical backdrop to this contest between competing actors. In Northern Ireland, where social segregation reinforces differences, the context is 'at least partly responsible for the endurance of violence and tension … because both sides are perpetually trying to avenge the deaths of those that they knew "personally"' (Beattie, 1979: 249–52).

Social forgetting in Northern Ireland

To understand the broader context which gives rise to community mourning, we need look no further than the thousands of annual commemorative parades and rituals organised by Ulster loyalists and Irish republicans. In his empirical-based work on memory and the Northern Ireland Troubles, Kris Brown observes:

> If a shared history of conflict produces a sense of continuity and connection within a national grouping, then memorialisation and commemoration can be seen as playing a vital part in maintaining social cohesion, particularly in times of a lurching peace process. (Brown, 2007: 708)

Brown labels these rituals 'ghostly national imaginings', in many ways echoing Sontag's concept of a seance between the living and the dead. Guy Beiner argues that they tend to obfuscate inconvenient truths, thereby creating a form of 'social forgetting', 'when communities try, or profess to try, to forget discomfiting historical episodes, but actually retain muted recollections'. Beiner continues:

> Social forgetting, by this definition, pivots on tensions between maintaining a facade of public forgetting and the persistence behind the scenes of private remembrance. Ireland, with its rich vernacular traditions of folk memory, which have been mostly veiled from official scrutiny and have seldom been recognised by historians, offers fertile ground for explorations of social forgetting. (Beiner, 2017)

As Brown and Beiner both acknowledge, the past helps to create cohesion while also conferring collective meaning, particularly in marginalised and deprived communities. However, this kind of social forgetting can have negative consequences for people in divided societies. Perhaps the most significant outworking is the tendency for ethno-political entrepreneurs to deny or downplay the violence of loyalist and republican paramilitary groupings.

Underground armies have been a constant feature of Irish history for centuries. Originally emerging as agrarian-based entities that engaged in the ritual of drilling, marching and defending land (Stewart, 1989), they had morphed into sophisticated terrorist organisations by the mid-twentieth century. As Brown argues:

> Northern Ireland's paramilitary groupings function as 'shadow armies', illegal formations organised along quasi-military lines. They are also organisations which have framed their political programmes in terms of sovereignty, defence of communities, and simple patriotism; they have reserved for themselves the right to use force, a right vociferously guarded by the state. In a most basic formulation paramilitary groupings themselves imitate facets of the nation-state, specifically in the latter's

appeal to allegiance and the need to legitimate its monopoly of force. National allegiance and identity, and the historic legitimisation of force, can be grafted together by means of war memorialisation and commemoration. (Brown, 2007: 709)

It is James W. McAuley, the leading expert on loyalist paramilitaries, who reminds us: 'The core philosophy behind much Loyalist paramilitary activity was to engage in some form of "counter-terrorism". Although dressed in a discourse of "taking the war to the republican enemy", in reality, the targets were often ordinary Catholics' (McAuley, 2004: 526). The tendency to demarcate territory and threaten outsiders is a common denominator behind republican paramilitary violence too (Bowyer Bell, 2000: 289–90). As Tommy Gorman, a former member of the Provisional IRA, has put it:

> People around me were in complete denial. We were supposed to be socialist, yet we had all these people who were ultra-nationalist, who were openly right-wing, and even openly sectarian, within the Republican Movement – our movement. And if you look at the pattern of bombing, you never saw Catholic towns getting hit with these massive bombs. You know, the whole thing, when you look back at it, it was just a pure sectarian thing. (Cited in Hall, 2005: 18)

It is worth probing the role of sectarianism further, for it helps explain how a misrepresentation of the past by some ethno-national entrepreneurs can perpetuate and accentuate divisions in Northern Ireland.

For many commentators, the year 1972 has been recognised as the high-water mark in Troubles-related killings. The shooting dead of thirteen unarmed civilians and the wounding of fifteen others by the British Army in Derry on 30 January 'occupies a pivotal position in the unfolding history of the Troubles, not least due to its centrality in Irish nationalist popular memory' (Dawson, 2005: 151). 'Bloody Sunday', as it became known, tends to crowd out other memories of 1972, including the Provisional IRA's bombing of the Abercorn Restaurant in Belfast on 4 March, which killed 2 young women and injured 130 others, and the Official IRA's bombing of a British Army base in Aldershot, England, on 22 February in which one Roman Catholic Chaplain and six civilians were killed.

Many tit-for-tat attacks took place during the year and July 1972, in particular, saw an upsurge in sectarian murders. During a four-week period, the Provisional IRA was responsible for thirty-two murders of Protestants, including the bomb blitz of Belfast on 21 July in which nine people died, subsequently known as 'Bloody Friday', and on 31 July when they bombed the village of Claudy near Derry, killing five Catholics and four Protestants (McKittrick et al., 2001: 240–42). At the same time, Loyalists claimed the lives of twenty Catholics (CAIN, n.d.). Violence continued throughout the remainder of the decade, with one loyalist gang, known as the Shankill Butchers, killing twenty-five people, most of whom were Catholics, in the heavily segregated areas of North and West Belfast (Dillon, 1989; Edwards, 2017).

Sectarian violence continued to ebb and flow in the late 1970s and early 1980s. There were occasional peaks, such as the indiscriminate attack on Protestant worshippers in a church in Darkley, County Armagh, on 20 November 1983. Sixty-five worshippers, including twenty children, were attending a religious service at the Mountain Lodge Pentecostal Church when four gunmen burst in through the doors and opened fire with automatic rifles, killing six men. 'It was like the sound of pebbles tinkling off a windowpane,' recalled one survivor. The gunmen reloaded their weapons and opened fire again, expending some seventy rounds of ammunition in total, with twenty-five rounds being fired as survivors tried to flee the building (Murtagh, 2018).

The massacre was later claimed by the Catholic Reaction Force, generally regarded as a cover name for a local unit of the Irish National Liberation Army (INLA) (McKittrick et al., 2001: 963). The INLA claimed it had carried out the attack in retaliation for sectarian murders of Catholics. However, the reality was that there had been few loyalist murders at this time. On 29 October, the Ulster Volunteer Force (UVF), operating under the cover name of the Protestant Action Force, murdered a member of the Official IRA-aligned Workers Party, David Nocher, in Greencastle in North Belfast (McKittrick et al., 2001: 956–57). A week later the UVF murdered Catholic civilian Adrian Carroll outside his home in Abbey Street, Armagh (McKittrick et al., 2001: 960–61). Despite the INLA's claims, the vast majority of the deaths at this time were in fact attributable to them and to the Provisional IRA. Indeed, the INLA had killed two of its own members and two Catholic civilians in Armagh. It could be argued that Darkley was an attempt to rehabilitate the

Collective memory, ethno-national forgetting 87

INLA's tarnished reputation in the eyes of their supporters for killing members of their own broader ethno-national community. INLA-aligned groups have sought to rehabilitate the rationale for such violent acts since the cessation of major hostilities in the 1990s. We can see this clearly in the commemorative rituals of the INLA and its political associates in the Irish Republican Socialist Party (IRSP). In a parade held in 2012 to mark Easter Sunday, a traditional date in the republican calendar, one spokesman for the IRSP noted:

> So, while today is about remembering the dedication and selfless sacrifice of those who paid the ultimate price for Irish freedom, and pausing to think, how different it would have been if the injustices of military occupation had not been foisted upon us, let us also take the opportunity to celebrate the commitment of an Irish Republican hero and his contribution to the just and noble cause of setting his people free. Let us take the example laid down by Dominic, Mary and others, that only when we begin to look beyond sectional interests and narrow minded sectarianism, can we begin to see the bright horizons of a true Republic, that only when we allow the objectives of the struggle to determine our actions can we create the common purpose needed to complete that struggle. (IRSP, 2012)

The spokesman conveniently eviscerated Dominic McGlinchey's personal complicity in the Darkley attack, as well as the culpability of the INLA in other sectarian atrocities.

The denial of sectarianism is common in other mainstream republican events. In a 'March for Truth' rally held some years earlier in August 2007, Sinn Féin president Gerry Adams told those gathered:

> The objective of this march and rally is to draw attention to collusion and British state violence; a policy which resulted in many thousands of victims who were killed or injured or bereaved; and the administrative and institutional cover-up by the British government and its state agencies. (Sinn Féin, 2007)

There was only fleeting mention of Sinn Féin's associates in the Provisional IRA, with Adams claiming that the armed group had 'apologised to all those non-combatants it killed or injured and their families'. Yet, he conveniently sidestepped sectarian attacks, acknowledging only the '[s]ectarian killings of Catholics', which he complained, 'were routinely described as apparently motiveless murders'. By remaining silent on the 'aggressive and exclusivist' actions undertaken by the IRA (Sinn Féin, 2007), it could be argued that Adams misremembered the past.

Moreover, by attempting to legitimise claims of ethnic entitlement, Adams cast the IRA in the role of defenders. This claim has been challenged, particularly by constitutional nationalists north and south of the Irish border. As the *Irish Times*, the Republic of Ireland's leading national newspaper, pointed out in an editorial amid a crisis in the peace process, 'There is no history or evidence to support the claim that the Provisional IRA has prevented serious loyalist violence against Catholics in Northern Ireland' (*Irish Times*, 2000).

Republican paramilitaries, as noted, were not the only protagonists responsible for sectarian violence during the Troubles. Loyalist paramilitaries were also responsible for over a thousand deaths, many of them sectarian killings. In the period 1990–94, loyalists killed 175 Catholics, 22 of whom were IRA members or former members, and 13 of whom were Sinn Féin activists. From these grim statistics, we can infer that loyalists found it much easier to target Catholic civilians, especially in places where residential segregation was commonplace and where most people were selected for assassination on the basis of perceived community identity (Merari, 2000: 58).

In Belfast the nature of segregation meant such killings happened in clearly demarcated urban spaces, with some human geographers informing us that 'the highest intensities of deaths occurred in highly segregated neighbourhoods in the center of Belfast that were also proximal to physical interfaces' (Mesev *et al.*, 2009: 901). As these scholars make clear, the vast majority of fatalities occurred 'within segregated communities composed of over 90 percent Catholics or Protestants, within areas of high deprivation' (Mesev *et al.*, 2009: 901).

A closer examination of tit-for-tat violence in this period is revealing. On 30 October 1993, a Provisional IRA bomb attack on a fish shop on the Shankill Road killed nine Protestant civilians. This atrocity triggered an upsurge in sectarian murders, with McKittrick *et al.* (1993) describing part of the horror it unleashed as follows:

> At a refuse depot the body of a council worker had been removed, leaving behind a packet of Silk Cut cigarettes and a puddle of his

fresh blood. Strewn all around the yard were dozens of empty bullet cases – Belfast confetti. People now turn on the television news with something approaching dread. Each bulletin seems to bring to the screen another relative of a victim, grieving and in shock and disbelief that death has come to the door.

McKittrick *et al.* quoted the Unionist Party Lord Mayor of Belfast at the time, Reg Empey, asking: 'What has all this proved, other than that we're good at killing each other?' Dr Joe Hendron, the MP for the moderate nationalist Social Democratic and Labour Party in West Belfast, went further: 'Fear is stalking the streets of west and north Belfast and far beyond. It is as bad as I have ever known and I go back to 1969, 70, 71. The situation is as bad now as it was then. There is this palpable fear everywhere you go' (cited in McKittrick *et al.*, 1993).

The Shankill bomb on 23 October 1993, when an IRA squad had allegedly attempted to assassinate the Ulster Defence Association (UDA) leadership, resulting in ten people being killed – one IRA bomber and a UDA member, but the majority being eight Protestant civilians – undoubtedly provided loyalist paramilitaries with the renewed impetus they needed to revisit their coercive strategy of 'terrorising the terrorists'. In practical terms, this strategy enabled loyalist paramilitary commanders to sanction revenge attacks on the republican and nationalist community. Atrocities followed, including a gun attack on a public house in Greysteel, County Derry and the shooting dead of two council workers in Belfast.

Reflecting on these events, loyalist paramilitary leader Johnny Adair explained the actions of those in his grouping, the Ulster Freedom Fighters (UFF), in the following terms:

> And I believe, I don't take credit, it was the men of C Company. They were courageous and dedicated young men. And they were the men who took the war right into the heart of republican West Belfast, an area where loyalists hadn't ventured in almost 30 years of the Troubles. Once we got a safe house in there, we were in there … every single day. The record speaks for itself. Daring raids. Broad daylight … Connolly House. Rocket attacks. Sinn Féin offices and Sinn Féiner's homes. We had them on the run, like. We did. The targets we were going for, they were real good targets, the people who were killing on a daily and regular basis and blowing the place up all the time. (Author interview with Johnny Adair, 17 January 2016)

Juxtaposing Adair's comments alongside those of Tommy Gorman mentioned earlier in this chapter, we can see why sectarianism would be such an inconvenient truth for self-proclaimed ethnic defenders. However, while Gorman acknowledged the role of sectarianism, Adair seeks to obfuscate sectarian killings by loyalists, clinging on to a belief that the UFF was targeting 'the people who were killing [his community] on a daily and regular basis'.

In this respect, it is incorrect to portray all loyalist murder victims in this manner and, therefore, we must counter-balance such claims alongside the objective historical reality. 'Very few people in Northern Ireland today', argued Frank Wright, 'would try to claim that the victims of violence are chosen because of their individual characteristics; they are attacked because they are identified as representing groups of people' (Wright, 1987: 11). This 'representative violence' has had long-term repercussions, as Beattie and Doherty have argued:

> The troubles in Northern Ireland are given meaning through the testimony, the stories, and the folk tales of the community. These accounts are flexibly produced and reproduced by friends, neighbours, and the media and are accentuated, amplified, and changed in the process. (Beattie and Doherty, 1995: 431)

What the misinterpretations of the past above highlight is the tendency to obfuscate those episodes that may impinge upon attempts to reinforce ethnic entitlement in the present (Todorov, 2001: 18).

Condemned to repeat the past?

In his acclaimed study of post-war Europe, Tony Judt pondered the reasons behind individual and collective uses and abuses of the past. 'That history should have weighed so heavily upon European affairs at the start of the twenty-first century was ironic', he observed, 'considering how lightly it lay on the shoulders of contemporary Europeans'. In post-authoritarian Europe, governments 'no longer exercised a monopoly over knowledge and history could not readily be altered for political convenience', argued Judt. Insofar as it posed challenges, he reasoned:

> The threat to history in Europe came not from the deliberate distortion of the past for mendacious ends, but from what might at first have

seemed a natural adjunct to historical knowledge: nostalgia. The final decades of the century had seen an escalating public fascination with the past as a detached artefact, encapsulating not recent memories but lost memories: history not so much as a source of enlightenment about the present but rather as an illustration of how very different things had once been. (Judt, 2005: 768)

Arguably, nostalgia is reflected within and between ethno-national communities in Northern Ireland. With the British state keen to portray itself as an 'honest broker' in the post-Agreement years, London could no longer practise its monopoly over what Graham Dawson calls 'Britain's Official Memory' (Dawson, 2007). Since the election of a Conservative government in 2015 and the Tories' subsequent deal with the Democratic Unionist Party, there are those who dispute whether the government can continue to claim this title (see, for example, former Secretary of State for Northern Ireland Lord Peter Hain in Hansard, HL vol. 799, col. 1338, 9 September 2019). With the collapse of the power-sharing Executive in 2017 and the absence of a robust civil society, not to mention a lack of inter-ethnic consensus, McGrattan and Hopkins argue that even the 'languages and vocabulary of "peace" and "reconciliation" may, in this way, mask continuing antagonism' (McGrattan and Hopkins, 2017: 492).

If, as David Rieff (2016b: 121) suggests, 'it is not the duty to remember but a duty to forget that should be honoured' in deeply divided societies, then how can this be done in a more pragmatic manner? Perhaps we might seek refuge in the moral high ground, which sees violence – especially that of a sectarian nature – as a regressive throwback to a bygone era? Liberal scholar Michael Ignatieff suggests that, 'Ethics matter, not just to constrain the means we use, but to define the identity we are defending and to name the evil we are facing' (Ignatieff, 2005: 167).

If only it were as simple as this. One of the defining features of post-ceasefire Northern Ireland is the prevailing logic of its zero-sum ethno-national dispute. This has manifested itself in a variety of ways, including the linkage of ethnic entitlement to territory, meaning that 'significant symbolic battles remain regarding how the past, present and future understandings of identity and conflict are negotiated' (McDowell et al., 2017). Amid such antagonism, it is difficult to persuade the protagonists to concede ground on their present political beliefs, never mind deeply held historical memories. Perhaps then History (i.e. the professional study of the past) might offer some assistance? The Troubles have exerted a powerful gravitational pull on historians ever since the first stone was thrown in anger in the 1960s. Much of this scholarship looks at the causes and consequences of the violence, placing it in its wider political, economic, social, cultural and security context. Other scholarship has examined the ideological genealogy of unionism or nationalism, loyalism or republicanism. Sometimes, the study of the binary nature of these ethno-national identities has given way to examinations of other forms of identity in Northern Ireland, which, in some ways, helps to refashion our understanding of the past into an interpretation that is more inclusive or appreciative of contingency (see Elliott, 2017; Graff-McRae, 2010, 2017; Prince, 2007; Prince and Warner, 2011).

This work has opened up new avenues for our exploration of identity and place, though it remains insufficient in challenging ethno-national myth-making. Here, it may be possible for historians working on Ireland to learn from other places. For example, in her work on reconciliation in Sino-Japanese relations, international relations scholar Yinan He highlights attempts to agree a form of shared historical memory, established via joint research and dialogue between independent historians not only to 'set straight the historical facts' but also to bridge 'the gap between nationally bounded interpretations of such critical issues as war responsibility' (He, 2007). There is clearly scope for similar work to be undertaken in Northern Ireland in future, especially once legacy issues are resolved by a reconstituted Assembly and Executive. In the meantime, the grassroots work of shared history projects continues to advocate returning to a general public understanding of the past where ethno-national competition no longer defines the islands of Britain and Ireland.

Conclusion

A century on from the tumultuous events which saw the gun first introduced into Irish politics and a generation after the signing of the Belfast/Good Friday Agreement, Irish nationalists and Ulster unionists remain divided, particularly over how they remember the past. The region is governed according to the logic of a peace process that was designed by British, Irish and American governments eager to placate the interests of two major ethno-national blocs. Elements of constitutional engineering were imported into Northern Ireland by academics, policymakers and politicians who believed that the best way to deal with diametrically opposed views was to formalise and entrench them in power-sharing structures, something further consolidated by the St Andrews Agreement of 2006.

Consequently, this deep-freezing of ethno-national competition has forestalled the development of an alternative political culture based on social justice and shared moral values. Social policy expert Robin Wilson maintains that 'ethnic violence is rooted in an internal politics based on manipulating ethnic symbols to generate strong hostile emotions', and that any attempt to forge 'a stable peace requires not just a political settlement but also reconciliation'. For such reconciliation to prosper, argues Wilson, there is a need for parties in conflict to acknowledge responsibility and the 'wounds of others', while attempting to reconstruct such discourses to 'highlight conciliatory strands' and develop 'more co-operative social relationships' (Wilson, 2010: 55). In helping to rebuild a shattered society, while simultaneously fostering cooperation between communities, this chapter has argued that there is a pressing requirement for historians to challenge deeply divisive historical memories as a means of preventing a relapse into violent conflict.

References

Anderson, B. (2006) *Imagined Communities: Reflections on the Origins and Spread of Nationalism*. London: Verso.

Beattie, G. (1979) 'The "Troubles" in Northern Ireland', *Bulletin of the British Psychological Society*, 32: 249–52.

Beattie, G. and Doherty, K. (1995) '"I saw what really happened": the discursive construction of victims and perpetrators in first-hand accounts of paramilitary violence in Northern Ireland', *Journal of Language and Social Psychology*, 14 (4): 408–33.

Beiner, G. (2017) 'Troubles with remembering; or, the seven sins of memory studies', *Dublin Review of Books* (1 November). Available at: www.drb.ie/essays/troubles-with-remembering-or-the-seven-sins-of-memory-studies (accessed 9 October 2020).

Bowyer Bell, J. (2000) *The IRA, 1968–2000: Analysis of a Secret Army*. London: Frank Cass.

Brown, K. (2007) '"Our father organisation": the cult of the Somme and the unionist "golden age" in modern Ulster loyalist commemoration', *Round Table*, 96 (393): 707–23.

Brubaker, R. (2002) 'Ethnicity without groups', *European Journal of Sociology*, 43 (2): 163–89.

CAIN (Conflict Archive on the Internet) (n.d.) 'Sutton Index of Deaths, 1972'. Available at: https://cain.ulster.ac.uk/sutton/chron/1972.html. (accessed 9 October 2020).

Dawson, G. (2005) 'Trauma, place and the politics of memory: Bloody Sunday, Derry, 1972–2004', *History Workshop Journal*, 59 (1): 151–78.

Dawson, G. (2007) *Making Peace with the Past? Memory, Trauma and the Irish Troubles*. Manchester: Manchester University Press.

Dillon, M. (1989) *The Shankill Butchers: A Case Study of Mass Murder*. London: Arrow Books.

Edwards, A. (2008) 'Drawing a line under the past', *Peace Review*, 20 (2): 209–17.

Edwards, A. (2015) 'On the obfuscation of the past', *Peace Review*, 27 (3): 354–62.

Edwards, A. (2017) *UVF: Behind the Mask*. Newbridge: Merrion Press.

Edwards, A. (2019) 'The toxic legacy of the Northern Ireland Troubles', *RUSI Newsbrief*, 39 (5). Available at: https://rusi.org/publication/rusi-newsbrief/toxic-legacy-northern-ireland-troubles (accessed 9 October 2020).

Elliott, M. (2017) *Heartlands: A Memoir of the White City Housing Estate in Belfast*. Belfast: Blackstaff Press.

English, R. (2006) *Irish Freedom: The History of Nationalism in Ireland*. London: Macmillan.

Graff-McRae, R. (2010) *Remembering and Forgetting 1916: Commemoration and Conflict in Post-Peace Process Ireland*. Dublin: Irish Academic Press.

Graff-McRae, R. (2017) 'Ghosts of gender: memory, legacy and spectrality in Northern Ireland's post-conflict commemorative politics', *Ethnopolitics*, 16 (5): 500–18.

Hall, M. (ed.) (2005) *Grassroots Leadership (2) – Father Des Wilson and Tommy Gorman*. Newtownabbey: Island Pamphlets.

He, Y. (2007) 'Remembering and forgetting the war: elite mythmaking, mass reaction, and Sino-Japanese relations, 1950–2006', *History and Memory*, 19 (2): 43–74.

Hobsbawm, E. (1996) 'Identity politics and the left', *New Left Review*, 1 (217): 38–47.

Horowitz, D. (2000) *Ethnic Groups in Conflict*. London: University of California Press.

Howard, M. (1993) 'The use and abuse of military history', *RUSI Journal*, 138 (1): 26–30.
Hutchinson, J. and Smith, A. D. (1996) 'Introduction', in J. Hutchinson and A. D. Smith (eds), *Ethnicity*, pp. 3–16. Oxford: Oxford University Press.
Ignatieff, M. (2005) *The Lesser Evil: Political Ethics in an Age of Terror*. Edinburgh: Edinburgh University Press.
Irish Times (2000) 'IRA claim to role as Catholics' defender unfounded', *Irish Times* (2 February).
IRSP (Irish Republican Socialist Party) (2012) 'Vols. Dominic and Mary McGlinchey commemoration – speech in full', (15 April). Available at: http://newryrepublican.blogspot.com/2012/04/vols-dominic-and-mary-mcglinchey.html (accessed 9 October 2020).
Judt, T. (2005) *Postwar: A History of Europe since 1945*. London: Vintage Books.
Kaloudis, G. (1999) 'Cyprus: the enduring conflict', *International Journal on World Peace*, 16 (1): 3–18.
MacMillan, M. (2010) *The Uses and Abuses of History*. London: Profile Books.
McAuley, J. W. (2004) 'Just fighting to survive': loyalist paramilitary politics and the Progressive Unionist Party', *Terrorism and Political Violence*, 16 (3): 522–43.
McDowell, S., Braniff, M. and Murphy, J. (2017) 'Zero-sum politics in contested spaces: the unintended consequences of legislative peacebuilding in Northern Ireland', *Political Geography*, 61: 193–202.
McGrattan, C. (2010) *Northern Ireland, 1968–2008: The Politics of Entrenchment*. Basingstoke: Palgrave Macmillan.
McGrattan, C. and Hopkins, S. (2017) 'Memory in post-conflict societies: from contention to integration?', *Ethnopolitics*, 16 (5): 488–99.
McKittrick, D., Kelters, S., Feeney B. and Thornton, C. (2001) *Lost Lives: The Stories of the Men, Women and Children who Died as a Result of the Northern Ireland Troubles*. Edinburgh: Mainstream.
McKittrick, D., MacKinnon, I. and McIntyre, D. (1993) 'Crisis in Ulster: assassins are on the rampage: a numbed city awaits fresh horrors after bullets become the confetti of Belfast as gunmen mow down Catholic workers', *Independent* (27 October).
Merari, A. (2000) 'Terrorism as a strategy of struggle: past and future', in M. Taylor and J. Horgan (eds), *The Future of Terrorism*, pp. 52–65. London: Frank Cass.
Mesev, V., Shirlow, P. and Downs, J. (2009) 'The geography of conflict and death in Belfast, Northern Ireland', *Annals of the Association of American Geographers*, 99 (5): 893–903.
Murtagh, P. (2018) 'The shooting sounded "like pebbles tinkling off a window pane"', *Irish Times*, 24 November.

Nagle, J. (2014) 'From the politics of antagonistic recognition to agonistic peace building: an exploration of symbols and rituals in divided societies', *Peace and Change*, 39 (4): 468–94.

Orwell, G. (1945) 'Notes on nationalism'. London: Orwell Foundation. Available at: www.orwellfoundation.com/the-orwell-foundation/orwell/essays-and-other-works/notes-on-nationalism/ (accessed 4 December 2019).

Passerini, L. (2010) 'Afterword', in S. Radstone and B. Schwartz (eds), *Memory: Histories, Theories, Debates*, pp. 459–564. New York: Fordham University Press.

Prince, S. (2007) *Northern Ireland's '68: Civil Rights, Global Revolt and the Origins of the Troubles*. Dublin: Irish Academic Press.

Prince, S. and Warner, G. (2011) *Belfast and Derry in Revolt: A New History of the Start of the Troubles*. Dublin: Irish Academic Press.

Richmond, O. (2002) 'States of sovereignty, sovereign states, and ethnic claims for international status', *Review of International Studies*, 28 (2): 381–402.

Rieff, D. (2016a) 'The cult of memory: when history does more harm than good', *Guardian*, 2 March.

Rieff, D. (2016b) *In Praise of Forgetting: Historical Memory and its Ironies*. New Haven, CT: Yale University Press.

Santayana, G. (1906) *The Life of Reason or the Phases of Human Progress*. New York: Charles Scribner's Sons.

Sinn Féin (2007) 'Speech by Gerry Adams: no turning back for truth campaign' (12 August). Archived in CAIN at: https://cain.ulster.ac.uk/victims/docs/political_parties/sf/adams_120807.pdf (accessed 6 December 2019).

Smith, A. D. (2007) *Nations and Nationalism in a Global Era*. Cambridge: Polity.

Sontag, S. (2003) *Regarding the Pain of Others*. London: Penguin.

Stewart, A. T. Q. (1989) *The Narrow Ground: The Roots of Conflict in Ulster*, new edn. London: Faber.

Todorov, T. (2001) 'The uses and abuses of memory', in H. Marchitello (ed.), *What Happens to History: The Renewal of Ethics in Contemporary Thought*, pp. 11–39. New York: Routledge.

Wilson, R. (2010) *The Northern Ireland Experience of Conflict and Agreement: A Model for Export?* Manchester: Manchester University Press.

Wolff, S. (2006) *Ethnic Conflict: A Global Perspective*. Oxford: Oxford University Press.

Wright, F. (1987) *Northern Ireland: A Comparative Analysis*. Dublin: Gill and Macmillan.

Wright, F. (1996) *Two Lands on One Soil: Ulster Politics Before Home Rule*. Dublin: Gill and Macmillan.

5

Irish republicanisms and radical nostalgia

Stephen Hopkins

This chapter analyses the complex connections between varieties of contemporary Irish republicanism and the notion of 'radical nostalgia', a term adopted from Glazer's (2005) important work on commemoration of the Spanish Civil War. The first section is devoted to examining the relationship between nostalgia and radical (or revolutionary) politics, and some of the characteristic ways in which socialist and/or radical nationalist movements have utilised nostalgia as a means to mobilise support. In the (alleged) context of the 'unfinished revolution' in Ireland, various strands of the republican 'family', including both the 'mainstream' or 'establishment republicanism' of Provisional Sinn Féin as well as many of the myriad so-called 'dissident' groups, have sought to lay claim to the legacies and heritage of the Irish 'struggle' and 'resistance' to British rule in Ireland (see Hoey, 2018: 20).

In particular, there has been an intra-republican effort to mobilise radical nostalgia in the service of divergent contemporary political goals, leading to a mnemonic competition regarding which branch of the movement can most plausibly claim the mantle of authenticity and continuity with the 'heroic' history (both recent and more distant) of Irish republican activism. With that in mind, the second section of the chapter analyses the broad contours of these struggles over 'ownership' of republican memory, with specific reference to the experiences of the 'Troubles' in Northern Ireland from the late 1960s until the late 1990s. The final section is focused upon the 'post-conflict' generation of republicans, which, it will be argued, has often been recruited into 'dissident' organisations, at least in part on the basis of a radical nostalgia, or *exo-nostalgia*, for a past they never knew (Berliner, 2014: 21; Bowd, 2016: 6). The chapter argues that radical nostalgia is closely bound up with the politics of commemoration and memory in contemporary Northern Ireland. The example of the Irish republican family illustrates in a powerful fashion the tensions at the heart of a self-proclaimed revolutionary politics, in which there is both a 'sense of nostalgia as a sentimental search for comfort in the past, and the progressive, activist, unruly connotations of radicalism' (Glazer, 2005: 246). It may be agreed that 'whatever its object, nostalgia serves as a negotiation between continuity and discontinuity' (Atia and Davies, 2010: 184).

However, while nostalgia may usually have been associated in the popular imagination with a wistful, even gentle, backward-looking gaze (Jack, 2017), in the sphere of revolutionary political and ideological movements, nostalgia could more accurately be characterised by its potential to be used as a weapon of struggle (Berdahl, 1999). Certainly, in the context of Irish republican*isms*, a bitter and protracted series of disputes over the historical narrative of the movement have been played out in a competitive struggle for control of its nostalgic memoryscape.

Nostalgia and radical politics

In the historical evolution of socialist and communist political movements, there has almost always been scepticism with regard to nostalgic thinking; in truth, it has often been reviled as the essence of reactionary politics: 'a fatuous form of collective self-indulgence at best and, at worst, a deliberately created cleverly exploited obstacle on the path to reform or revolution ... In Marxian terminology it is a subspecies of false consciousness, moreover, a particularly insidious subspecies in that it ... looks longingly backward to obsolete societal arrangements rather than forward to the better ones destined to emerge' (Davis, 1979: 108–9). Marx himself criticised nationalist movements, specifically, for the 'worldwide necromancy' they peddled, with their backward-looking focus (Bonnett, 2010: 22–26). Glazer acknowledged that 'there is a consensus among many scholars that nostalgia, as a force in culture and society, is reactionary in nature. Its sentimental and uncritical gaze into the past can tend to freeze the present and empower the status quo' (Glazer, 2005: 7).

Identifying the dilemmas of radical nostalgia, Bonnett explored the paradox that 'nostalgia is integral to radicalism; yet, radicalism has been offered as a narrative of anti-nostalgia' (Bonnett, 2010: 7). However, such a dismissive attitude towards nostalgic modes of thought has since been subject to increased scrutiny, particularly as utopian thinking has receded. Atia and Davies argued that, even if 'nostalgia is always suspect' and we should keep a 'sceptical distance from its illusions', nevertheless it may entail a critical potential, that it can involve an 'empowering agency', particularly as a 'potent form of subaltern memory' (Atia and Davies, 2010: 181). Rather than a 'retreat into hidebound certainty', à la Marx, nostalgia may be better understood as an 'interpretative tool', which can on occasion be wielded by progressive forces to imagine alternative futures (Atia and Davies, 2010: 182). Patrick Wright (2009 [1985]: 27) has similarly promoted the idea that nostalgia may have a 'critical and subversive potential'.

In their stimulating book exploring what they term the 'mnemonic imagination', Keightley and Pickering are also anxious to recognise that nostalgia should not simply be 'equated with an uncritical escapism and bland consolation in the past, along with a concomitant loss of faith in the future' (Keightley and Pickering, 2012: 10-11). Their argument is that 'memory' and 'imagination' should not only or always be interpreted as mutually antagonistic, but they can be 'closely akin'. In this reading, the mnemonic imagination can be understood as recognising the 'transformative potential of memory'; the role of remembering the past should not be limited to repetition of it, but instead be seen as 'the creative production of meaning' about the past, present and future (Keightley and Pickering, 2012: 6-7). In other words, while nostalgia can sometimes be 'undesirable and disabling', it can also 'move beyond compensation for mourning over loss and instead represent a more active effort at reclaiming what seems lost'. In terms of the political uses of nostalgia, they argue that 'it can be about keeping certain alternatives open within the public domain and keeping alive certain counter-narratives that rub against the grain of established social orthodoxies and political pieties' (Keightley and Pickering, 2012: 115-16).

A radical nostalgia, therefore, would allow us to move beyond a simple polarity and antagonism between 'progress' and 'nostalgia', in which the latter is dismissively cast as 'trading in a past which is passive and foreclosed' (Keightley and Pickering, 2012: 116). In his discussion of US veterans of the International Brigades in Spain, Glazer noted that many of them became memory activists, indeed 'irrefutable icons of activism', who understood their commemorative zeal in terms of an attempt to re-infuse 'lost histories with credibility, substance and emotional resonance' (Glazer, 2005: 7, 18).

The 'common-sense' definition of nostalgia, as a regretful or wistful memory of a lost past, and a sentimental yearning, may, in this version, not necessarily be accompanied by a paralysing longing, which precludes action in the present. Keightley and Pickering conceptualise nostalgia as a 'composite framing of loss, lack and longing', and it is in their specific synthesis, in any given example, that the precise form of nostalgia comes into being (Keightley and Pickering, 2012: 117). The mnemonic imagination permits 'pasts that have not been experienced to be longed for'; in a deficient present, such as an ideologically transformed age, the 'unregainable past' may still be used to prepare the ground for change in the future. It is this capacity for fusing longing and hope which means that radical nostalgia may not necessarily involve a 'futile attempt to breathe life into a long dead past' (Keightley and Pickering, 2012: 118).

Nationalism and nostalgia

In his work examining Basque nationalism and nostalgia, Diego Muro uses the scholarship of John Armstrong and Anthony D. Smith to analyse the nationalist myth of the 'Golden Age' (Muro, 2005; see also Armstrong, 1982; Smith, 1986). Nostalgia arises from the juxtaposition of the present, often viewed as disastrous, and an idealised, longed-for past. Muro argues that 'nostalgia will emerge as an act of resistance against a specific juncture in time when decay is perceived and loss is likely to occur' (Muro, 2005: 575). Borrowing from Smith, Muro identifies a 'nationalist triad' in the discourse of radical Basque nationalism, based upon three overarching myths: the Golden Age; decline; and regeneration or salvation (Muro, 2005: 581). In terms of nationalist discourse, there was a time (often in the remote past) when the nation 'lived in its pure and authentic form'; the precise content and periodisation of this Golden Age may alter over time, but the nostalgic attitude which it inspires does not change.

In an Irish nationalist context, the historian George Sigerson (in an address to the Irish National Literary Society in 1892) argued that: 'Our [the Irish nation's] deliverance from this thralldom of an enemy's judgement abides in the monuments of the ancient Irish past' (cited in Bonnett, 2010: 89; see also Richards, 1991). If the Irish nation's 'authentic voice' was to be found in its distant past, it was also the case that this knowledge was not simply valuable for its intrinsic worth, but because it prefigured a willingness to challenge colonial power in the present of the late nineteenth century (Bonnett, 2010: 89).

This chapter argues that nostalgia for the Golden Age of the nation as a whole may be replicated in the nostalgia that is internal to the nationalist movement: in the Irish case, there was a time (not in the distant past, but within living memory) when the Irish republican movement (the IRA and Sinn Féin) itself was 'pure' and 'authentic', before it declined into a vehicle for compromise on long-held principles, and a ladder for 'careerists' and 'opportunists', who have bartered away the essence of the struggle. Thus, for contemporary, so-called 'dissident' republicans, the Golden Age may refer not so much to a putative pre-colonial paradise but to a much more recent period, characterised by the unity and purpose of the revolutionary 'resistance' struggle of the Provisional republican movement.

In the second myth, by extension, for 'dissidents the decline is manifest in the sight of a former Provisional IRA leader shaking hands with the British monarch, or Sinn Féin 'Ministers of the Crown' upholding British rule in part of Ireland. 'Dissidents' argued that it was, in fact, Sinn Féin that 'was dissenting from republicanism's ideological roots' (see Hoey, 2018: 21; also Frampton, 2011: 43–89). One example will suffice: Des Dalton, then president of Republican Sinn Féin (which split from Provisional Sinn Féin in 1986 over the latter's decision to take up any seats it won in the 'partitionist' assembly of the south of Ireland), was asked in 2018 for his view on speculation that Sinn Féin might take up its seats at Westminster; he replied that it should be no surprise that this was being mooted:

'They ceased to be Republicans thirty years ago, you know, they're probably not even really Irish nationalists let alone Republican' (cited in McDonagh and Galvin, 2018: 8).

As Muro puts it, 'what is important to point out is that the thread that unites the three constituent myths is violence' (Muro, 2005: 582). Heroism, sacrifice and defeat, to be followed by eventual redemption and vindication constitute the narrative template for this nationalist discourse: 'the heroic dead are essential in maintaining group cohesion' (Muro, 2005: 582). However, we can see that in the case of the Irish republican family, the 'heroic martyrs' of, for example, the 1980–81 hunger strikes are no longer a force for cohesion, but rather a memory field that reflects and magnifies the deep and bitter divisions of the contemporary movement (see Hopkins, 2014: 425–39, 2018: 263–86).

Each element of the fractured republican family is intent on demonstrating its fidelity to the cause enshrined by the martyrs; they attempt to 'sanctify current strategies by association with the memory of dead volunteers' (Patterson, 2011: 81). This question of 'ownership' of the memory of the dead is now part of the strategic and competitive uses of nostalgia that have formed a critical dimension of present-day disputes at the heart of Irish republicanism. It is also significant that the object of nationalist nostalgia does not need to be 'specific autonomous institutions' of the Golden Age, but is more likely to be an 'idealised state', seemingly lost forever (Muro, 2005: 584).

The 'living republic' and the uses of radical nostalgia

The Irish republican movement has always been Janus-faced, on the one hand maintaining a utopian and teleological belief in the 'natural' and organic character of a single sovereign nation-state in Ireland, but also exhibiting a backwards-looking desire to keep alive the purity and sacrifice of the sacred cause, exemplified by the movement's martyrs and heroes. For every generation of republicans (certainly since the United Irish Rising of 1798), the imperative to maintain fidelity, both with 'the Republic' as a (supposedly) living entity and with those who fought and died to uphold it, has produced a cyclical politics.

Both dimensions of this narrative framework can be interpreted as potentially incorporating nostalgia: it can be 'driven by utopian impulses – the desire for re-enchantment – as well as melancholic responses to disenchantment', or as a shifting mixture of both (Keightley and Pickering, 2012: 134). More than two decades after the signing of the Good Friday/Belfast Agreement in 1998, there are many in Northern Ireland who would utterly reject the possibility of nostalgic thinking about the 'Troubles', pointing out the obscenity of such feelings for a conflict in which almost four thousand were killed. But, as Lowenthal observed, 'even horrendous memories can evoke nostalgia' (Lowenthal, 2015: 39). There is a sense, at least for some, that the conflict made this society and territory special, and that is no longer so true.

Turning the legacies of the 'Troubles' into tourist 'attractions' has certainly proven controversial in contemporary Northern Ireland, but the existence of community-based black-taxi tours or museums devoted to paramilitary organisations demonstrate that there is an appetite (in some quarters, at least) for such nostalgia-infused ventures (Patterson, 2019: 156–57). In some respects, the outworking of the UK's (though not Northern Ireland's) majority vote in 2016 to leave the European Union may have reanimated this sense of Northern Ireland as a political laboratory, a polity of interest, both internally and externally. Also in 2016, Irish republicans of all persuasions paid homage at the centenary commemorations of the Easter Rising. Uniting almost the entire spectrum of Irish nationalists, from Fianna Fáil and other establishment parties in the Republic of Ireland, to supporters of Sinn Féin and the diverse 'dissident' groups, was the belief that 'the men of 1916' (with lip-service paid to the small band of women who participated) had paved the way for the creation of 'the Republic'.

However, there was a distinct uneasiness for supporters of Fianna Fáil and Fine Gael, who wished to distance the 'good old IRA' from the Provisional incarnation of the 1970s–1990s (Hanley, 2018). Leading figures in Sinn Féin and some of their sternest anti-republican critics alike rejected this effort to 'quarantine' the mainstream politics in the present-day Republic of Ireland from the Provisional campaign (Hopkins, 2019: 184).

Nostalgic thinking for this foundational moment was rife, with many contemporary republican groups expressing their continuity of purpose with the moral vision of the rebels and executed martyrs, and the ideals enshrined in the Proclamation, even (or especially) if these remained unfulfilled in the contemporary political dispensation. The leaders of the 1916 Rising were, of course, themselves consciously motivated by a nostalgia for the earlier rebels of the Fenian era, as well as the United Irish uprising. Much of Pádraig Pearse's writing and activism prior to 1916 explicitly contained a powerful messianic quality, 'mixing religious testimony with prophecy about an impending Rising by depicting "Ireland's struggle for redemption in terms of Christ's sacrifice at Calvary"' (McCarthy, 2018: 167).

At his trial, Pearse's statement captured a strong flavour of this immensely powerful sense of fidelity to the national past and the national destiny: 'We seem to have lost. We have not lost. To refuse to fight would have been to lose; to fight is to win. We have kept faith with the past, and handed on a tradition to the future' (cited in Foster, 2014: 248). As Foster comments, almost from the immediate aftermath of the executions, 'the language of mystical Catholicism fused with national purism in a new – or ancient – revolutionary rhetoric' (Foster, 2014: 248). Such rhetoric, and specifically its potential use by radical nostalgics in the revolutionary republican movement, proved hugely valuable as a means of recruitment and motivation for successive generations of Irish republicans during the twentieth century and beyond. Many republican intellectuals wrestled with the myths of the Irish revolution in the post-independence era, often combining a nostalgic gaze with a degree of disenchantment (Flanagan, 2015).

Two examples from young recruits to the movement will illustrate the significance of this psychological disposition, which Kearney characterised as the 'mythic resuscitation of some sacred national "tradition"' (Kearney, 2006 [1978]: 34). Mick Ryan joined the IRA in his home city, Dublin, in 1954 as a teenager, and proceeded to play an active role in the 'border campaign' after 1956. In his memoir, he expressed his 'deep sense of regret' at having been born too late to experience the 1916 Rising and subsequent revolutionary era. When he attended the commemoration of the rising held at the General Post Office (GPO) in Dublin on Easter Monday, he 'would feel a tremendous elation at the folk memories that stirred within me, and I longed to have lived at that great time and played my part alongside the heroes' (Ryan, 2018: 31, 49). Despite a recognition that the border campaign was doomed to fail from an early stage, Ryan maintained his commitment until it was ignominiously suspended in 1962: 'we did so more for the sake of the "dead who died for Ireland" than from any belief or hope that we were going to succeed' (Ryan, 2018: 221). The 'mystique that surrounded Ireland's heroic past' inspired in the young man an 'intense pathos and affection' for figures such as Constance Markievicz (Ryan, 2018: 38).

In early 1971, another teenage recruit, Richard O'Rawe, joined the Provisionals in his home district of Ballymurphy, West Belfast. Later, he was imprisoned in the cages of Long Kesh along with many others of the founding generation of Provisionals, and he testified to the romantic nostalgia of this group for the men of 1916, saying:

> I remember thinking how wonderfully uplifting it would have been to be standing beside Pádraig Pearse as he spoke those beautiful words [of the Proclamation]. The fact was that we existed in an idealistic time warp, wallowing in the vision of historical Irish heroes struggling for freedom. There was an almost biblical reverence for the 1916 Proclamation. … We justified all our actions and the entire struggle on the basis of the Proclamation – sometimes elevating the sacrifice of the signatories to a hallowed act. (O'Rawe, 2005: 79–80)

For subsequent generations of Provisional republicans – but also for those recruited by splinter groups – as well as this reverence for the martyrs of Easter, the ten hunger strikers who died in 1981 would occupy a similar place in the republican pantheon (see Morrison, 2006; also Hopkins, 2018).

Alongside this nostalgic fantasising about the actual historical individuals of the rising, it has also been true that the *idea* and (alleged) *substance* of the 'living Republic' has also been immensely powerful as a mobilising force. Pearse himself was a critical exponent of this discourse, both millenarian and saturated with nostalgia for those previous generations who had steadfastly remained true believers in the Irish nation and its destiny. Charles Townshend has referred to 'the Republic of the imagination' (Townshend, 2014), and Colm Tóibín similarly argued of the 1916 rebels that they 'wanted to storm the Bastille of the imagination since they did not have the numbers or the arms to storm the real one' (Tóibín, 2016). 'The

Republic' may therefore be understood as not simply an ideological 'home', inspiring nostalgic yearning, but for many successive republican generations a type of spiritual lodestar.

Townshend cites a contemporaneous but external observer of Sinn Féin during the War of Independence. Roger Chauviré suggests: 'what strikes one most in Sinn Féin thought ... is its extremist character. ... I mean the clear and deliberate determination to ignore what is, and to take account, nay to admit the very existence, only of what ought to be' (cited in Townshend, 2014: 21). The Irish republican movement was primarily motivated, according to Chauviré, by 'illusion', but this belief in the power of ideas to transcend mundane realities helped to encourage an unwillingness to compromise. Townshend concludes his study with the argument that for generations of republicans, 'the Republic was an actually existing entity; it had been created by the action of the Irish volunteers'. Even if it seemed to outsiders to be a 'projection of political imagination, rather than a functioning political structure', this did nothing to invalidate the absolute belief in its existence among 'true' republicans, nor its capacity to invoke emotions of nostalgic yearning (Townshend, 2014: 449).

As noted previously, if the Easter Rising is the example *par excellence* of a radical nostalgic act on behalf of Irish republicanism, for the founding generation of mainly Northern Provisionals, their equivalent was the 1981 hunger strike. As with the rising, the leaders of the hunger strikes saw their actions very deliberately as commemorative, with an explicit connection to previous 'links in the chain' (Graff-McRae, 2010: 163–74). Thus, Bobby Sands, the 'officer commanding' the Provisional prisoners in the H-Blocks, asserted his attachment to the memory of earlier hunger strike martyrs much more than he articulated the 'five demands' (which would constitute political status in the eyes of the prisoners, and the ostensible reason behind the strike): 'I remember, and I shall never forget, how this monster [the UK state] took the life of Tom Ashe, Terence MacSwiney, Michael Gaughan, Frank Stagg and Hugh Coney, and I wonder each night what the monster and his black devils will do to us tomorrow' (cited in O'Donnell, 2015: 199; see also O'Malley, 1990: 50).

It is significant that Sands drew no distinction between the deaths of Ashe and MacSwiney (in 1917 and 1920, respectively), and those of his fellow Provisionals, Gaughan and Stagg (in 1974 and 1976);

they were each martyrs in the same struggle, and the era in which they died was only of secondary import. As O'Donnell put it: Sands 'possessed a keenly historical mind and both embodied and extolled the militant republican ideology of succession, continuity and lasting contribution through martyrdom' (O'Donnell, 2015: 199). It is important for the argument here that Sands's vision was simultaneously utopian and nostalgic, but certainly not prosaic (in terms of concentrating upon conditions in the jail).

Strategic nostalgia and 'the memory of the dead'

In the post-1998 era, it is more important than ever, for both Sinn Féin and its tenacious band of republican critics, to assert their claims to 'ownership' of the 'property of the past' (See Cossu, 2011: 386–400). Sinn Féin is unwilling to vacate the mnemonic ground of the Provisional movement's past, particularly because it has understood the value for its contemporary political project in being seen to maintain its fidelity to the sacrifices of that past. Precisely because Sinn Féin has moved from the periphery to the centre-ground of Irish political life, it has sought to reassure its core supporters that it has not 'sold out' the struggle, and it is not denigrating the memories of those who paid the ultimate cost. The assiduous fashion in which Sinn Féin commemorate the 1981 hunger strikers in an annual ceremony, comprising a history pageant with 're-enactors', *tableaux vivants* and branded merchandise, demonstrates the extent to which it remains determined to control the historical narrative of these years (see Whelan, 2016).

The so-called 'dissidents', however, contest this account vigorously. Critics of Sinn Féin's control of the Bobby Sands Trust, including some members of the Sands family, have accused the party of 'using Bobby's memory as a commercial enterprise' (see Hopkins, 2018). This 'retrotyping' or 'regressive nostalgia' (Keightley and Pickering, 2012: 150–54) for the hunger strikers has proven highly controversial among contemporary republicans; the sensitivities surrounding these mnemonic practices were on display at the 2019 national commemoration in Strabane. Martina Anderson (Sinn Féin MEP) managed to offend unionists with her reiteration of the IRA slogan, *Tiocfaidh ár lá* ('Our day will come'), but also drew criticism from many republicans for dancing in the street, at what was supposed to be a solemn, even sacred, commemoration (Patterson, 2011: 105).

This mnemonic politics is a delicate balancing act for Sinn Féin, because it seeks at one and the same time to appeal to a new audience (especially in the South), which is not steeped in republican discourse and history, but also to maintain its firm grip on the framing and retelling of the Provisional movement's past. The former group is likely to be bemused by, or even hostile to, any Sinn Féin radical nostalgia for the IRA campaign, which it tends to view as the product of a different (worse) time and place, and ultimately not its concern. Yet, Sinn Féin could not afford, and its long-term activists did not wish, to jettison the IRA past completely. Instead, the Gerry Adams and Martin McGuinness leadership engaged in a process of historical revisionism, repurposing the IRA past in an effort both to deny the 'dissidents' ownership of legacies such as the 1981 hunger strike and to claim a continuity of vision – that the contemporary strategy was not a renunciation of the goals of those heroes and martyrs, but rather their fulfilment in a new era (Robinson, 2012: 147).

The response of 'dissidents' to this 'strategic nostalgia' has been to relentlessly highlight alleged Sinn Féin hypocrisy in claiming fidelity to its previous vision, and to engage in their own efforts to mobilise nostalgic modes of thought in order to keep the pure republican flame alight. The paramount significance of 'continuity' and the 'unbroken thread' between different generations of Irish republicanism is emphasised in the oration of ninety-six-year-old John Hunt at the Republican Sinn Féin (RSF) centenary commemoration of the Easter Rising in 2016. Hunt had been interned at the Curragh camp and then sentenced to four years in Mountjoy jail between 1940 and 1945, and his presence at the GPO in 2016 was deployed as a 'living link' with the republican past, designed to confer legitimacy upon RSF and the Continuity IRA (CIRA) (McGlinchey, 2016, 2019: 187). The 'line of succession' stretched back 'to the Fenians, the Young Irelanders, Robert Emmet, Wolfe Tone and the United Irishmen'. Hunt was explicit about the purpose of this radical nostalgia for his republican past: 'as a young man, in the darkness of my prison cell, I understood that the sacrifices of the republicans before me would inspire generations yet unborn' (cited in McGlinchey, 2016). Des Dalton reminded the audience that there were currently CIRA prisoners in Maghaberry jail, so this was no mere theoretical or abstract sense of continuity.

In the Basque context, a similar discourse has been noted, 'creating the impression that "repression" is suffered endlessly by the same people ("us") at the hands of the same enemy ("them")' (Hamilton, 2003: 129). RSF and CIRA statements vehemently reject the label 'dissident', for they understand themselves to be upholding the only legal and legitimate Republic: that declared by Pearse in 1916, and maintained by the Second Dáil in 1919.

'Dissidents' who remain committed to the use of violence have no short-term expectation of succeeding in their 'armed struggle', given that the much stronger and better-armed Provisional IRA ultimately failed to force a British withdrawal. But 'success' in this worldview may mean simply providing an example for future, more propitious times, or undermining the 'normalisation' of current arrangements in 'British-administered' Northern Ireland. It may also be true that the motivation is largely internal to the republican family: 'radical republicans view their highlighting of the "failures" of the Provisional leadership as a form of success in itself' (McGlinchey, 2018: 141; see also White, 2017: 341–56).

Keeping alive memories of sacrifice and heroism will, they hope, plant the seed for future generations, in the hope that better times may transpire. In the meantime, even if many non-republicans view this republican purism as an anachronism, nonetheless the dwindling band of those who 'keep the faith' will not be moved by lack of popularity. Hoey has argued that 'RSF stayed loyal and true to the principles of republicanism upon which it was founded. The age of its activist base had grown older without being significantly replenished by new membership' (Hoey, 2018: 48).

Indeed, such external criticism merely serves to confirm these 'diehards' in a dual politics of complacency (effectively arguing, 'We remain on the moral high ground, incorruptible, awaiting the eventual vindication of history'), as well as a politics of isolation (the critics, and especially the apostate ex-republicans of Sinn Féin, are less authentic, even if 'we' are small in number) (see Hearty, 2016: 269–91). This strategic use of nostalgia has been easily available to 'dissident' groups, in part because it has been a staple element of *all* previous incarnations of Irish republicanism, including the Provisionals.

Both 'dissidents' and Sinn Féin sought to reclaim a language of conservation and protection for radical ends: the slogan 'Defend the Republic!' in the run-up to the centenary commemorations was complemented by the campaign to 'Save Moore Street!', one of the key sites of the Easter Rising, threatened by developers (Moloney, 2016). In the British context, the ambivalence of this nostalgic political mode is mirrored in a critique of the 'leftist austerity nostalgia' inherent in Ken Loach's documentary *Spirit of '45*, which could be titled, 'Defend the NHS!' (Hatherley, 2017: 49–54).

The structural similarities between the competitive mnemonic politics of both Sinn Féin and the 'dissidents' are the reason that non-republican critics have tended to view contemporary republican commemoration and nostalgia as depressing and dangerous, without recognising the diverse strategic purposes underlying such politics. As Andy Pollak argued in response to the sentiments expressed on republican commemoration websites, there is 'an utterly unrepentant glorifying of the young IRA members who died in the squalid internecine violence of the thirty years of the "Troubles", revering them as noble martyrs in the tradition of the rebels of 1916 and the War of Independence' (Pollak, 2018). He further argued that in the event of a small majority for Irish unity in any future 'border poll', there is very likely to be a resumption of large-scale violence as unionists mobilise to resist; in such circumstances, 'a new generation of young republicans, brought up on such a diet of uncritical hero worship, will be only too eager to fight to defend their newly won unity' (Pollak, 2018; see also Mallon with Pollak, 2019: 187–96). Some senior nationalist critics of the republican movement (in all its guises) have warned against, in the words of Maurice Hayes, 'the glorification in song or story of what was mean and nasty and dirty [i.e. the IRA's campaign]' (cited in Pollak, 2018).

Conclusion

The founding generation of the Provisional movement, formed in the crucible of violent conflict in 1969–72, was a 'resistance generation' that experienced the conflict first-hand, killed and died for their vision of 'the Republic', and collectively served thousands of years in jail. This generation, exemplified in the leadership of Gerry

Adams and Martin McGuinness, has deployed counter-memories of the 'Troubles' to contest the UK state's version of events like the hunger strikes.

This mnemonic strategy, however, also represents an attempt to exercise control within the republican and nationalist community. Increasingly, however, there are republican counter-memories – witness Richard O'Rawe's accusation that the hunger strike was prolonged by the movement's leadership for hoped-for political gains (O'Rawe, 2010) – and a 'counter-nostalgia' (Foucault, 1977) utilised by 'dissident' factions in their quest to challenge the Provisionals' master narrative of the post-ceasefire period.

Unsurprisingly, supporters of Sinn Féin have been dismissive of what they disparagingly term the 'micro-groups' which have, in a fragmented and piecemeal fashion, sought to challenge the trajectory of the 'mainstream' movement. Former Sinn Féin publicity director Danny Morrison appealed to 'dissident' groups to 'consider just how wrong and pointless' their campaigns have been: 'because you have an AK47, it doesn't make you a freedom fighter' (Morrison, 2016). He argued that the founding generation of Provisionals did not, in fact, take their mandate to prosecute the IRA's 'war' from the 'theological [republican] position which a lot of the older people were burdened with'; instead, 'our mandate was the sense of oppression, physically, that we lived under' (McGlinchey, 2019: 130).

Some former Provisionals, such as Anthony McIntyre, would concur with the idea that recourse to violence is unjustifiable in the contemporary era, but McIntyre points out that Morrison's logic is flawed: the Provisionals have effectively settled for a share of governmental power in a British-administered Northern Ireland, accepting the 'majority consent' principle for constitutional change and ditching many of the core principles which lay at the heart of the republican tradition (McIntyre, 2018: 219–37). This was an outcome which republicans like Bobby Sands had explicitly rejected in the early and mid-1970s (McIntyre, 2008: 111–14; see also Hopkins, 2018). For McIntyre, those republicans who maintain their allegiance to traditional principles are not criminals, even if their violence has no realistic chance of success and it has been a first instead of a last resort: 'I regard them as people caught up in a legacy, or the product or victims of a legacy' (cited in McGlinchey, 2019: 125).

Some of the leading figures among the 'dissident' organisations were experienced Provisional IRA operators; they are now stalwarts 'beyond the bugle's dying echo'. Yet, others are post-Good Friday Agreement recruits, often too young to have personal memories of the 'Troubles'. For this younger generation, the republican tradition is a 'chosen history', albeit often one with close familial and communal identities and bonds (Glazer, 2005: 219). Maintaining fidelity to this tradition is, in part, motivated by exo-nostalgia, and the attraction of the rituals of commemoration represents 'the effort of one political generation to maintain contact with the felt, dynamic, lived structures of its forebears' (Glazer, 2005: 219).

Bonnett recognised that such exo-nostalgia may be fuelled in part by the attractions of 'the cathartic power of revolutionary violence' (Bonnett, 2010: 98). McAlister has pointed to the complex set of factors which help to explain recruitment of the 'Agreement generation' into 'dissident' groups: these include familial and communal belonging; peer pressure; the 'historical relationship between cultural identity, masculinity and violence'; the potential for 'status, power and money' in districts which are characterised by 'long-term historical underinvestment, gaps in essential services'; but also the critical tendency to 'live the past in the present – surrounded by reminders of the conflict in their communities and families, in divided space, in the daily news and in opposition politics' (McAlister, 2019).

McAlister was writing in the wake of the killing of a twenty-nine-year-old journalist, Lyra McKee, in Derry in April 2019. Shots were fired by a young, possibly teenage, gunman during a riot in the Creggan, when police officers were attempting to carry out searches for weapons, as 'dissident' republicans prepared to commemorate the Easter Rising. The New IRA, an amalgam of Real IRA members and non-aligned Derry republicans formed in 2012, was responsible. The office of its political 'wing', *Saoradh*, was picketed by McKee's friends and family. Ironically, McKee had been forging a reputation for investigative journalism, often exploring the ways in which the stress and trauma of the 'Troubles' had been transmitted, as a kind of post-memory, to the post-ceasefire generation (Hirsch, 1997). McKee's killer occupied the same physical territory *and* the same mnemonic landscape as the resistance generation had; they were both deeply imbricated in the memories and politics of local republicans.

Yet, this episode may be interpreted as a palimpsest or a poor facsimile of riots of the past; another journalist present at the riot described the ritualism of the occasion – there was 'no sense of threat or danger', with local youths 'capturing the flames for Snapchat' (O'Neill, 2019: 4). It was inspired to a significant extent by radical nostalgia; as the film-maker Sinéad O'Shea recorded, for some of these young militants, 'it is not that there may be a return to the Troubles, but that the Troubles have never ended'. She had interviewed an eleven-year-old (the younger brother of a teenager whose mother had taken him to be shot by 'dissidents' for alleged drug-dealing) who told her that he 'wanted the Troubles back: "The madness, the riots, the shootings, the bombings, everything." It's an extraordinary statement, not least because he doesn't remember the Troubles. They were over by the time he was born. They do, however, evoke a time of heroism and purpose for him and his friends' (O'Shea, 2019: 46).

Even before McKee's murder, observant critics had noticed a similar nostalgia at work among some young republicans. The writer Garrett Carr, during a walk he took the length of the border between Northern Ireland and the Republic, came across a 'white line' protest on the bridge between Blacklion in Co. Cavan and Belcoo in Co. Fermanagh. It was organised by the 32 County Sovereignty Movement (a 'dissident' group), and the majority of the sparse participants were young men. Carr wonders whether 'the protest's real energy comes from frustration, frustration at having missed the Troubles. If these lads had been born a decade or two earlier, they could have been fighters, they could have had rank, instead they look awkward. … They consider the border a relic. For others, it is they who are the relics' (Carr, 2017: 183).

These 'generations of nostalgia' are characterised by 'persistent and shifting shapes' (Hirsch, 2003: 82), and there are many republicans, both old and young, who continue to be, in the words of Seán O'Faoláin, 'blinded and dazzled by our icons, caught in the labyrinth of our dearest symbols' (cited in Kearney, 2006 [1978]: 42). The poet Michael Longley argued in 1995 that the Irish 'are good at resurrecting and distorting the past in order to evade the present. In Ireland, we must break the mythic cycles and resist unexamined, ritualistic forms of commemoration' (Longley, 1995: 158). More than a quarter of a century later there is little sign that the Irish republican family is running out of past, or that the power of those 'mythic cycles' is entirely exhausted.

References

Armstrong, J. (1982) *Nations before Nationalism*. Chapel Hill, NC: University of North Carolina Press.

Atia, N. and Davies, J. (2010) 'Nostalgia and the shapes of history', *Memory Studies* 3 (3): 181–86.

Berdahl, D. (1999) '"(N)Ostalgie" for the present: memory, longing, and East German things', *Ethnos*, 64 (2): 192–211.

Berliner, D. (2014) 'Are Anthropologists Nostalgist?', in O. Angé and D. Berliner (eds), *Anthropology and Nostalgia*, pp. 17–34. New York, NY, and Oxford: Berghahn Books.

Bonnett, A. (2010) *Left in the Past: Radicalism and the Politics of Nostalgia*. New York, NY: Continuum.

Bowd, G. (2016) 'Introduction', *Twentieth Century Communism*, 11: 1–11.

Carr, G. (2017) *The Rule of the Land: Walking Ireland's Border*. London: Faber and Faber.

Cossu, A. (2011) 'Commemoration and processes of appropriation: the Italian Communist Party and the resistance (1943–1948)', *Memory Studies*, 4 (4): 386–400.

Davis, F. (1979) *Yearning for Yesterday: A Sociology of Nostalgia*. New York, NY: The Free Press.

Flanagan, F. (2015) *Remembering the Revolution: Dissent, Culture and Nationalism in the Irish Free State*. Oxford: Oxford University Press.

Foster, R. (2014) *Vivid Faces: The Revolutionary Generation in Ireland, 1890–1923*. London: Allen Lane.

Foucault, M. (1977) *Language, Counter-Memory, Practice*. Ithaca, NY: Cornell University Press.

Frampton, M. (2011) *Legion of the Rearguard: Dissident Irish Republicanism*. Dublin: Irish Academic Press.

Glazer, P. (2005) *Radical Nostalgia: Spanish Civil War Commemoration in America*. Rochester, NY: University of Rochester Press.

Graff-McRae, R. (2010) *Remembering and Forgetting 1916: Commemoration and Conflict in Post-Peace Process Ireland*. Dublin: Irish Academic Press.

Hamilton, C. (2003) 'Memories of violence in interviews with Basque nationalist women', in K. Hodgkin and S. Radstone (eds), *Contested Pasts: The Politics of Memory*, pp. 120–35. London: Routledge.

Hanley, B. (2018) *The Impact of the Troubles on the Republic of Ireland, 1968–1979: Boiling Volcano?* Manchester: Manchester University Press.

Hatherley, O. (2017) *The Ministry of Nostalgia*. London: Verso.
Hearty, K. (2016) 'From "former comrades" to "near enemy": the narrative template of "armed struggle" and conflicting discourses on Violent Dissident Irish Republican activity (VDR)', *Critical Studies on Terrorism*, 9 (2): 269–91.
Hirsch, M. (1997) *Family Frames: Photography, Narrative and Postmemory*. Cambridge, MA: Harvard University Press.
Hirsch, M. (2003) '"We would never have come without you": generations of nostalgia', in Hodgkin and Radstone, *Contested Pasts*, pp. 79–95. London, Routledge.
Hoey, P. (2018) *Shinners, Dissos and Dissenters: Irish Republican Media Activism Since the Good Friday Agreement*. Manchester: Manchester University Press.
Hopkins, S. (2014) 'The chronicles of Long Kesh: Provisional Irish Republican memoirs and the contested memory of the hunger strikes', *Memory Studies*, 7 (4): 425–39.
Hopkins, S. (2018) 'Bobby Sands, martyrdom and the politics of Irish republican memory', in Q. Outram and K. Laybourn (eds), *Secular Martyrdom in Britain and Ireland: From Peterloo to the Present*, pp. 263–86. Cham: Palgrave Macmillan.
Hopkins, S. (2019) 'Dublin Provisionals remember the Northern Ireland "Troubles": Irish republican memoir-writing and southern perspectives', in F. Barber, H. Hansson and S. Dybris McQuaid (eds), *Ireland and the North*, pp. 177–99. Oxford: Peter Lang.
Jack, I. (2017) 'A generation hooked on nostalgia is trying to return Britain to the past', *Guardian*, 1 April.
Kearney, R. (2006 [1978]) 'Myth and martyrdom: foundational symbols in Irish republicanism', in *Navigations: Collected Irish Essays, 1976–2006*. Dublin: Lilliput Press.
Keightley, E. and Pickering, M. (2012) *The Mnemonic Imagination: Remembering as Creative Practice*. Basingstoke: Palgrave Macmillan.
Longley, M. (1995) 'Memory and acknowledgement', *Irish Review*, 17/18: 153–59.
Lowenthal, D. (2015) *The Past Is a Foreign Country Revisited*. Cambridge: Cambridge University Press.
McAlister, S. (2019) 'Northern Ireland: how some of the "agreement generation" are drawn into paramilitary groups', *The Conversation*, 26 April. Available at: https://theconversation.com/northern-ireland-how-some-of-the-agreement-generation-are-drawn-into-paramilitary-groups-116033 (accessed 27 July 2022).
McCarthy, M. (2018) 'Making Irish martyrs: the impact and legacy of the execution of the leaders of the Easter Rising, 1916', in Outram and

Laybourn, *Secular Martyrdom in Britain and Ireland*, pp. 165–202. Cham: Springer.

McDonagh, J. and Galvin, M. (2018) 'Without principle and not interested in advancing the goal of a free and independent Ireland', *Saoirse* (August): 8.

McGlinchey, M. (2016) 'Unbroken Continuity', *Village Magazine* (26 August). Available at: http://villagemagazine.ie/unbroken-continuity/ (accessed 27 July 2022).

McGlinchey, M. (2019) *Unfinished Business: The Politics of 'Dissident' Irish Republicanism*. Manchester: Manchester University Press.

McIntyre, A. (2008) 'The price of our memory', in *Good Friday: The Death of Irish Republicanism*. New York, NY: Ausubo.

McIntyre, A. (2018) 'Republican fragmentation in the face of enduring partition', in P. Burgess (ed.), *Contested Identities of Ulster Catholics*, pp. 219–37. Basingstoke: Palgrave Macmillan.

Mallon, S. with A. Pollak (2019) *A Shared Home Place*. Dublin: Lilliput.

Moloney, M. (2016) 'Moore Street victory', *An Phoblacht* (April): 13.

Morrison, D. (ed.) (2006) *Hunger Strike: Reflections on the 1981 Hunger Strike*. Dingle: Brandon.

Morrison, D. (2016) 'Because you have an AK47, it doesn't make you a freedom fighter', *An Phoblacht* (July): 22–23.

Muro, D. (2005) 'Nationalism and nostalgia: the case of radical Basque nationalism', *Nations and Nationalism*, 11 (4): 571–89.

O'Donnell, R. (2015) *Special Category: The IRA in English Prisons*, vol. 2: *1978–1985*. Dublin: Irish Academic Press.

O'Malley, P. (1990) *Biting at the Grave: The Irish Hunger Strikes and the Politics of Despair*. Belfast: Blackstaff.

O'Neill, L. (2019) 'Her friends, realising she'd fallen, began to scream, "she's shot, she's been shot"', *Irish Independent* (20 April): 4–5.

O'Rawe, R. (2005) *Blanketmen: An Untold Story of the H-Block Hunger Strike*. Dublin: New Island.

O'Rawe, R. (2010) *Afterlives: The Hunger Strike and the Secret Offer that Changed Irish History*. Dublin: Lilliput.

O'Shea, S. (2019) 'The tragic killing of Lyra McKee shows how hard it is for wars to end', *Guardian*, 21 April.

Patterson, G. (2019) *Backstop Land*. London: Head of Zeus.

Patterson, H. (2011) 'Beyond the "micro group": the dissident republican challenge', in P. Currie and M. Taylor (eds), *Dissident Irish Republicanism*, pp. 65–95. London: Continuum.

Pollak, A. (2018) 'Demographics might be shifting to a united Ireland – but divides still have to be bridged', *Irish Independent* (10 February): 28.

Richards, S. (1991) 'Polemics on the Irish past: the "return to the source" in Irish literary revivals', *History Workshop Journal*, 31 (1): 120–35.

Robinson, E. (2012) *History, Heritage and Tradition in Contemporary British Politics: Past Politics and Present Histories.* Manchester: Manchester University Press.
Ryan, M., edited by P. Yeates (2018) *My Life in the IRA: The Border Campaign.* Cork: Mercier.
Smith, A. D. (1986) *The Ethnic Origins of Nations.* Oxford: Blackwell.
Tóibín, C. (2016) '"A terrible beauty is born"', *Guardian* (26 March): 4.
Townshend, C. (2014) *The Republic: The Fight for Irish Independence.* London: Penguin.
Whelan, P. (2016) 'Thousands honour Ireland's hunger strikers', *An Phoblacht* (September): 8–9.
White, R. W. (2017) *Out of the Ashes: An Oral History of the Provisional Irish Republican Movement.* Newbridge: Merrion.
Wright, P. (2009 [1985]) *On Living in an Old Country: The National Past in Contemporary Britain.* Oxford: Oxford University Press.

6

Irish republican commemoration and narratives of legitimacy

Kris Brown

This chapter examines Irish republican uses of commemoration, and will show how, in utilising public memory, mainstream republicans associated with Sinn Féin are engaging in a diligent fostering of political legitimacy and continuity. In a post-conflict setting, this has been of particular importance both in deflecting political attacks and maintaining cohesion within their own political ranks.

Through the 'Troubles', Irish republicans espoused revolutionary, separatist goals and were prepared to sanction the use of force in pursuit of their political aims. But as the Northern Ireland peace process revealed, pragmatic adaptation and political compromise eventually led republicanism down a purely political path. History and ideological roots still matter to Irish republicans, and provide their own political capital too, but there was a clear political will by republicanism to weave between old shibboleths and icons, if not to shatter them.

Memory work and remembrance has played an important role in this process of combining sweeping political adaptation on the one hand, with revered symbols and narratives of legitimacy on the other. Republican sites of memory and ritual activity have mushroomed in the last decade, and the sheer number of republican memory sites is formidable. Commemoration is thus a most important public activity for republican activists and elites.

Memory work has attempted to legitimise the mainstream republican project on three fronts of engagement. Firstly, commemoration has served to underwrite the *internal* legitimacy of the Irish republican project as old ideological positions were evacuated in favour of new policies and political language. Mainstream Irish republicanism has also come under fire from *external* political opponents who argue that its past adherence to militancy and political violence continue to put a question mark over present-day democratic 'fitness'; republican commemorative narratives attempt to repulse this in a variety of ways.

Furthermore, on a *hybrid external/internal front*, 'dissident' republican groups, outraged at what they see as a betrayal of ideology and movement history, challenge the legitimacy of Sinn Féin as heir to the republican struggle per se. On this front, mainstream republican memory work seeks not only to legitimise its own political evolution, but to de-legitimise the republican credentials of radical competitors.

The research on which the essay draws is based on extensive observation of republican commemorative activity, studies of their memorial material culture, including museums, and examination of their commemorative publications. The author conducted field observation of approximately sixty republican commemorative events between 2006 and 2019. Publications surveyed included *An Phoblacht/Republican News*, *Iris*, various local newspapers such as the *Andersonstown News* and *Irish News*, together with speeches and reports published on the Sinn Féin website, commemorative DVDs, pamphlets and booklets. Transcripts from field notes of commemorations and speeches are referenced throughout this chapter.

Memory, meta-conflict and legitimacy

Commemoration is important in peace processes as it plays a role in the 'meta-conflict', a battle over the meaning and rationale of the period of hostilities itself, and the legitimacy of key actors' roles, methods and goals within that period of violence. Memory is often invoked and resuscitated in political competition and contemporary contestation even decades after the guns have fallen silent, as a series of 'memory wars' in Europe illustrates (Casanova, 2016; Koposov, 2017; Stone, 2013). This 'war over memory' and 'war using memory' is still sharper in deeply divided societies only recently emerging from extended periods of violence (McDowell and Braniff, 2014). A meta-conflict is a 'conflict over what the conflict is about' (Bell *et al.*, 2004; Horowitz, 1991; McGarry and O'Leary, 1995), which is 'played out in disputes over the causes, nature and consequences of violence' (Mallinder, 2019).

These are not minor or epiphenomenal processes; rather, they are 'integral and consequential parts of the conflict itself' that manifest in 'social struggles'. These struggles comprise powerful definitional claims that seek to 'label, interpret and explain' violence in a particular interpretative frame that has politically constitutive force and thus 'important consequences' for a divided society (Brubaker, 2002: 174). They thus simultaneously invoke and contest fundamental claims of legitimacy, authority and rightful action. As Horowitz warns, this constitutive force joined with the political sensitivity of these meta-conflicts may act as a 'constraint on the imagination and a constraint on innovation' in stabilising projects and processes of peacebuilding and reconciliation (Horowitz, 1991: 2). Yet, meta-conflicts are 'inevitable' and clearly observable in many deeply divided societies such as Bosnia, Cyprus, Iraq, Israel and Palestine, and of course, Northern Ireland (Mallinder, 2019: 6).

Being able to frame one's actions in recent conflict as rightful, just and legitimate brings many claims-making benefits which actors in peace processes cannot ignore. As is common in deeply divided societies, which see a fundamental and infectiously salient division over questions of identity, decision-making and sovereignty, Northern Ireland is an arena in which political legitimacy has frequently been contested. This is because claims for legitimacy have been constructed in a manner different from those societies with a common civic culture. In Northern Ireland, political authority is not derived from a commonly shared, overarching civic culture, which might be the template in 'Western' liberal democracies, rather legitimacy is founded on the basis of the culture of either one or the other community (Hayward and Komarova, 2014). Collective memory forms an important part of that culture (Ross, 2012); political commemoration is a symbolically rich and narrative infused aspect of that collective memory. Moreover, when it deals with the memory of political violence and political mobilisation it plugs directly into the charged circuits of the meta-conflict, and of legitimacy itself.

Commemoration in deeply divided societies may attempt to construct legitimacy in a variety of ways. Legitimacy can be derived from the invocation of those killed, local heroes and martyrs may act as exemplars of rightful action, resistance to injustice, and proper values (Brown, 2011; Di Lellio and Schwandner-Sievers, 2006; Khalili, 2007; Marschall, 2010). Legitimacy is also tied to commemoration of a broader victimhood; a 'battle for "public victimhood" – the contest over the "right" to the status of "victim" – has therefore become an arena in which the meta-conflict is contested' (Lawther, 2014). Public presentation of victimhood, as seen in commemoration, serves to narrate not only harm and suffering, but also injustice and the illegitimacy of a perpetrator's actions.

Commemorations may serve to elevate some victims while ignoring, lowering or questioning the status of others. Victim hierarchies are thus created, challenged or deconstructed – questions of legitimacy, of legitimate status or legitimate actions, are implicit throughout these processes (Borer, 2003; Bouris, 2007; Brown, 2012; Lebel, 2012; Papadakis, 1994). Furthermore, through commemorative practice, specific political groups attempt to create authoritative 'genealogies' linking to previous conflicts, struggles and organisations. This provides their organisations with a contemporary warrant for status and action, together with a constructed ideological continuity with past mobilisations on whom history has conferred a wider legitimacy (Brown, 2011; Lebel, 2012). The contemporary group thus invokes 'family resemblances' of similarities in method, ideology or even name, in a process of legitimacy by association, or imagined lineage.

A snapshot of mainstream Irish republican commemoration

There are a number of important aspects to mainstream republican commemoration. These are numerous and geographically well spread throughout Northern Ireland; a strong commemorative calendar has been created and diligently reproduced year on year. Between 2009 and 2014 there were some 676 mainstream republican commemorations across Belfast and the six counties of Northern Ireland (out of a total of 1,036 commemorations by republicans from all factions) (Brown and Grant, 2016).

This is clearly an activity which is seen as purposeful and sees buy-in at all levels of the political project, from local *cumainn* (party branches) to the Sinn Féin leadership. Numerous memorials dot streets, lanes and townlands throughout republican areas of political support in the province; many, if not all, serve as space for commemorative acts to take place. Notifications of local commemorations are frequently advertised in party organs, local newsletters, on posters and by social media accounts. Local party branches plan and undertake these commemorations assiduously on an annual or at least periodic basis. Easter sees a very attentive commemoration at multiple neighbourhood sites. Many commemorations are thus very locally attuned, and feature personalities, speakers and speech-givers with deep local knowledge and a sharpened personal recall of contentious, violent or traumatic events in the locality. Many localities, whether urban neighbourhoods or counties, produce pamphlets or even coffee-table books outlining the history of the conflict in Northern Ireland from a distinctly local, republican perspective (Beechmount Commemorative Committee, 1998; Magee, 2011; Quinn, 2004).

As well as being frequent and locally attuned, we can also note that republican commemoration is symbolically very rich; a typical commemorative parade will feature banners, flags, painted drums and band uniforms. It will take place at a memorial site which may feature statuary or colourful murals; the immediate area may have been dressed with posters and still more flags. Larger commemorations will also feature participants wearing historic costumes, street theatre, historical artefacts, floats and accompanying temporary exhibitions.

These representations in the commemorations comprise powerful condensation symbols – map images and metonyms of country, depictions of heroes, victims and martyrs, representations of violence or injustice, images of sacrifice and mourning, and portrayals of communal bonding, protest and organised armed resistance. This intense symbolism supplies a powerful, and variable, political palette allowing political actors to advance key narratives and evoke emotion. Commemorations are thus ready-made, almost perfect social practices for the production and transmission of 'myth-symbol' complexes, those short-hand narratives and schema which leaderships use to present arguments and mobilise groups (Kaufman, 2001).

Commemorative adaptivity to the political needs and peace processing of the present (Brown, 2019) might indicate its continued value to organisers; commemorative frequency and local reach also indicate that it may be seen as useful in outpacing the commemorative narratives of others, from within republicanism or without. Another valuable aspect for republican organisers lies in narrative strength and re-enforcement. The 'sacralisation' of speeches and arguments via linkages to history and sacrifice, the invocation of 'lived' memory by speakers and the symbolic richness of commemorative practice itself also allow the creation of robust, affective narratives that have a strength in representational depth and multiplicity.

Establishing internal legitimacy: the internal memory front

The internal memory front sees mainstream republicans seeking to underline their continued commitment to key republican principles sanctioned over time. In terms of claiming legitimacy within the internal memory front mainstream, republicans face a number of challenges. The first we may consider to be historically structural. The search for an ideological template, transmitted down through an uninterrupted line of republican history 'ascribes a continuity to Republicanism which does not in fact exist, or at least is so fractured by periodisation that continuity as a concept is seriously compromised' (McIntyre, 1995: 100–1).

Republicanism has frequently been pragmatic and flexible; indeed, some of its iterations have lacked firm ideological coherence (McGarry, 2003). This at first might be seen to give a large degree of latitude to those who seek to establish connections to the past. Yet although the ideology-in-practice may be less fixed, certain tropes and keynotes of Irish republicanism remain resistant to erasure or radical adjustment. A commitment to separatism and radicalism, and the acknowledgement of the legitimacy of armed resistance are lines marbled through modern phases of republicanism. It is difficult to establish unbroken organisational and ideological links down through republican history, but key ideals are ever present, and maintain a rhetorical and symbolic surety.

Secondly, the compromises of the peace process have induced real strain on mainstream republicans' hold on traditional republican ideals. There have been enormous political changes from the days of the strategy of the 'Armalite and ballot box'. Sinn Féin has signed up to the Mitchell Principles on non-violent political activity, endorsed the Good Friday Agreement (GFA) and participated in a Northern Ireland Executive and Assembly; it has signed up to policing structures and endorses the Police Service of Northern Ireland; it has engaged in periodic unionist 'outreach'. The Provisional IRA, for its part, has called ceasefires, decommissioned its weapons and 'left the stage', or at least drastically reduced its presence and function. It supports the Sinn Féin peace strategy. As these dramatic processes unfurled it became necessary to anchor the republican project in changing currents. It was necessary to bestow legitimacy using the weight of historic ideals, to re-imagine and project continuity with the past, albeit in an updated and recalibrated fashion.

Surveys of publications and field observations of commemorative activity reveal several prominent and recurrent themes in the construction of legitimacy along the internal memory front. There should be no surprise at the primacy of Easter Rising commemorations within the mainstream republican calendar and reflecting this prominence, republicans assert that they remain faithful to the same ideals that motivated the rising. For modern Sinn Féin, the 1916 ideal as guiding light remains a powerful, recurring motif invoked at Easter and often in other periodic commemorations.

The components of this ideal are routinely elaborated in the reading of the Proclamation at Easter commemorations. Radical rejection of British rule, the justness of the cause of national freedom, the necessity of mobilisation and a vision of a new Ireland in the form of the Republic are important and venerated constituents of this ideal. The 1916 ideal is framed as a beacon illuminating the end goal of the republican project, which contemporary republicans must continue to keep sight of.

Emphatic commemoration of this symbolic keystone represents continued adherence to the founding ideals and mission of republican resistance. Commemorations become sites where republicans vocally and publicly re-commit and re-dedicate to these ideas. Commemorations often underline that their *End Goals Remain the Same*; the means and methods may have changed but the destination of the political project is set in stone – independence and unity. What has occurred through the peace process is simply the development of a 'new phase' or 'new type' of struggle. The republican project (and unfolding story) has simply, and appropriately, evolved to a different point which sees no need for political violence and military resistance, and which develops the struggle into new zones – even into institutions which would have once been seen as partitionist and counter-revolutionary.

In some instances, an *Augmented Republican Chronology* has been constructed during commemorative speeches. The 1916 Rising, the 1918 Election, the 'Tan' War, the Civil War are obviously foundational and heroic phases that modern republicans wish to evoke and directly connect to; and for some decades they have appended the 1969 'uprising' and the 1981 hunger strikes (struggles of their own generation) as new phases of exactly the same continuous fight for freedom.

This chronology has been further augmented as the peace process has developed and drawn Sinn Féin further into the institution of state. The 1998 GFA, and even the Hillsborough Agreement of 2010, can be implanted into the timeline of republican struggle and advance. The most modern and reformist of political advances are appended to the most traditional 'magic number' dates of republican chronology. In a similar reformist vein, civil rights mobilisation of the 1960s has also been attached to the timeline of republican resistance.

Republicans do not simply invoke morality, political tradition, fidelity to values and the memory of sacralised heroes in constructing internal legitimacy. They also make more pragmatic, consequentialist arguments in their commemorations, as a means of legitimising their political evolution. Thus, a theme we might call the *Utility of the Recalibrated Struggle* is elaborated. Speeches frequently identify and group together the direct political 'wins' of a republicanism engaged in the peace process: the Orange state has gone and can never return; the loathed security presence has been removed; advances have been made in issues of equality; all-Ireland bodies and institutions have been created and embedded in the new dispensation; new positions have led to electoral dividends for the party; and unionism has been weakened.

Clearly, some re-imagination of both history and the processes that led to the wide-ranging reforms of the GFA is at work. The fact that the Orange state ended in 1972 with the prorogation of Stormont, and that the language of equality and cross-border institutions was birthed and nurtured within constitutional nationalism does not feature in the narrative. Yet, such has been the electoral advance of modern republicanism, and the sincerity of its gradualist turn, that this party capture of reformist vocabulary from within the wider nationalist family has been made more credible. During commemorations, this reformism can now be re-imagined and internalised for the party base as distinctly republican advances.

The symbolism of the 'fallen' is a most powerful legitimising theme. Republican commemorations do not simply stress that ideals are embedded and historically continuous; they also envision the dead as being of the same political stock, calibre and moral standing as the republican dead of previous generations, including the War of Independence and the 1916 Rising. There is no difference in the republican martyrs of the past and present. They are thus all part of the same ideological genealogy, a close-knit family of martyrs who incarnated ever-present republican values running down through time.

The guardianship of the republican project is thus relayed from historically sanctified 'founder icons' such as Pearse, Sweeney or Connolly to the martyrs of the recent conflict that mainstream republicans can best claim – the dead of the Provisional republican movement. Different phases of conflict are noted, but historical boundaries are not to be so hardened as to dissect legitimacy. As Caoimhghín Ó Caoláin noted at an Easter commemoration in 2009: 'We pay tribute to those who died in every phase of the struggle and we make no distinction between the martyrs of 1916 to '23 and those who died in more recent years including the IRA Volunteers and members of Sinn Féin whose names are on the Republican Roll of Honour' (Sinn Féin, 2009a). Similarly, republican exhibitions relating to the hunger strikes of 1981 are continuously tied back to 1916. As Jim McVeigh of the National Hunger Strike Commemoration Committee stated in an interview in *An Phoblacht*:

> Like the volunteers of 1916, the Hunger Strikers were fighting for the Republic, not just political status. As I have already said, the Hunger Strikers were this generation's 1916. Like those who participated in the rising, they inspired a whole new generation to strike out for the Republic. We will be making this point all the time and we will be drawing clear parallels between the two events. (*An Phoblacht*, 2006)

'Family' means more in commemoration than ideological genealogy or the fictive kinship of communal remembrance. Family also provides a very concrete and invested presence. The 'Presence of Families of the Dead' is strongly and routinely noted, and appreciated, at republican commemorations. At an important human level, this represents solidarity with the bereaved and shared sense of loss, but it also contains an important legitimising component. The continued presence of the families of the martyred dead further underlines the authenticity and credibility of the modern republican project.

Those closest to those who sacrificed life in decades past impart a degree of approval for the modernising face of republicanism by their attendance. Mainstream republicans by valuing this family presence accentuate their sense of continuing connection to the radical values of past mobilisation.

'The battle of ideas': the external memory front

As noted above, mainstream Irish republicanism has come under pressure from external political opponents who contend that its former adherence to political violence continues to undermine its present-day democratic 'fitness' and sincere commitment to dealing with still-poisonous legacy issues. A 'war over memory' rattles on in which different players in the Northern Ireland conflict and political process pursue their own interests in terms of constitutional goals, present-day political claims-making, the reproduction of identity and communal solidarity, and, of course, the legitimacy of past positions and actions.

This latter point is a crucial component of the meta-conflict. Mainstream Irish republican commemoration plays a significant part in this meta-conflict. However, given its inward-facing nature, commemoration is seldom for projection to other constituencies; rather, it serves to bolster republicanism's own constituency against external, competitor narratives, which include (but are not limited to) unionists, many victims' groups, the British state and parties from the Republic of Ireland.

This external memory front has been acknowledged as something of a battlefield; as one republican article put it, a new phase of struggle had opened up 'the battle of ideas and the battle for truth about the armed conflict' (*An Phoblacht*, 2005). As Caoimhghín Ó Caoláin noted at a commemoration for Kieran Doherty, the Irish republican prisoner who died on hunger strike in 1981, this battlefront is an attempt to use the past as a brake on republican electoral acceptance and growth:

> The opponents of Sinn Féin are attempting to place the responsibility for 25 years of conflict on the shoulders of Irish republicans. They do so in an effort to thwart the growth of Sinn Féin. (*An Phoblacht*, 2005)

In reinforcing their external memory front, Sinn Féin use commemorations to advance three broad themes – rightfulness of armed response, popular representativeness and support, and equality of victimhood and memory.

The theme of 'rightfulness of armed response' attempts to explain, contextualise and ultimately legitimise the pursuit of armed struggle. One component of this theme comprises a strong contextualisation of the lot of northern nationalists and republicans. A chronology of persistent injustice and state repression is often illuminated in speeches, all evolving from the birth of an illegitimate northern state. As the new Sinn Féin leader Mary Lou McDonald asserted: 'a generation [was] betrayed by a counter revolution and a carnival of reaction. An Orange state was born, repression, discrimination and pogroms were used to consolidate a perpetual unionist majority' (field notes, Mary Lou McDonald speech, Belfast, 21 April 2019).

In intoning republican resistance and political success, commemorative speeches typically spool back through a remembered litany of abuses and government repression ranging from political and military dominance through to assassination, incarceration and censorship, hence:

> The Orange state is gone. One-party rule at Stormont is gone. The RUC and the UDR [Ulster Defence Regiment] and the RIR [Royal Irish Regiment] are gone. British militarisation is almost gone. Good riddance to them all. They failed to break republicans just as internment and shoot-to-kill and paid perjurers and death squads and prisons and censorship failed to break us. (Sinn Féin, 2010a)

Reference to a deeper history of centuries-long British oppression may also be attached to this narrative of twentieth-century subjugation.

The legitimacy of armed struggle as a rightful response is often underlined by commemorative messaging that it was an option of purely last resort as presented here by Declan Kearney:

> Armed struggle is only an option of last resort. In Ireland of the 1980s just as in 1919, no viable political alternatives were available to nationalist and republican people. Armed struggle was the only means available to resist injustice and inequality and to effect political change. (Field notes, Declan Kearney speech, Dungiven, 29 November 2009)

Political violence was not the result of a militaristic ideology but the only means to effect the emancipation of an entire community, as Gerry Adams put it at an Easter commemoration in Belfast: 'I am not a militarist and I never have been but without the IRA the nationalist people of this state would still be on our knees. We would still be second-class citizens' (field notes, Gerry Adams speech, Belfast, 3 April 2010).

The point was reiterated in 2019 by Mary Lou McDonald when she said: 'they fought because there was no other way. The denial of democratic rights and repressive regimes left no other pathway to unity' (field notes, Mary Lou McDonald speech, Belfast, 21 April 2019). Armed struggle, then, 'is not a philosophy or ideology in itself. It must be a decision of last resort in the absence of any other avenue to achieve justice, equality and freedom. It has to be understood and supported by the community seeking its freedom' (field notes, Gerry Kelly speech, Belfast, 5 April 2015). The legitimate resort to political violence is not driven by revolutionary purism but by the compelling exigencies of a political environment and additionally by popular understanding, approval and support. The reach for the gun is also presented as rightful by invoking notions of simple self-defence in the face of immediate threat.

Commemorations in interface areas of Belfast often elaborate the sense of vulnerability of enclaved nationalists, the burning of nationalist streets and property by loyalists, and the inaction or connivance of the police. The layered commemorations of the 'Battle of St Matthew's' fortieth anniversary (enacted in speeches, drama, parades, pamphlets and memorials) strongly projected this vulnerability and provided it with its narrative resolution – the successful armed 'defence' of the area by a newly emergent Provisional IRA (Brown, 2012).

Rightfulness of armed response is also underwritten by republican categorisation of the conflict during commemorations. As Martin McGuinness was to put it at a speech in Derry in 2011, this was a war between legitimate combatants, between armies:

> There have been attempts by the British media and by our opponents, not all of them British, to present the IRA campaign as a terrorist campaign. Nothing could be further from the truth. The war in this city was between the IRA and the British army. (*Derry Journal*, 2011)

The status of the IRA as a legitimate military force is further constructed and reiterated through many commemorations by emphasising a military vocabulary and phrases as descriptors of the paramilitary group and its environment. It is frequently '*the* Army' fighting a 'guerrilla war' against the 'war machine' that is the British Army. Its members are 'volunteers', 'soldiers' and 'combatants' who face incarceration as 'prisoners of war', or who may die on 'active service' and become the 'patriot dead'. Local commemorations of individual republicans typically augment this narrative frame of legitimate war with approving and nostalgic personal recollection of 'war stories' featuring the commemorated volunteers. The themes are of comradeship, service, hardship, bravery and dark humour, all in keeping with the stereotypical war stories of any conflict.

The emotional register struck is clear, that these men and women were soldiers in an army, not criminals. A consequentialist argument is sometimes advanced in commemorations about the rightfulness of armed response: that it worked, or at least partially. Thus, the armed campaign may not have succeeded in bringing about British withdrawal and self-determination, but nevertheless, the IRA 'destroyed the political basis for the Unionist Regime and fought the British Government to a military standstill; creating the political conditions where Republicans then fought the British government at the negotiation table' (Derry Sinn Féin, 2011).

Thus, armed struggle opened up the political space for dialogue and a just peace. The lines of historical development, and cause and effect, are not fully traced in such a blunt assertion. Neither are the roles of other important actors, but the argument is nevertheless pressed. On other occasions the efficacy of armed struggle is more geographically limited, as when Gerry Adams noted the local success of the South Armagh IRA in its conflict with the British security forces: 'all along this canter, this area, in the lanes and in the fields and in the hills of South Armagh, the decades of war saw a resilient army of the people, the Irish Republican Army take on the might of the British Army and defeat it here in South Armagh' (field notes, Gerry Adams speech, Camlough, 14 August 2011). Historians could easily critique Adams's assertion of local victory, but in a commemoration in republican Camlough the rhetorical pitch had some force.

Commemoration does not simply use speeches and narration to legitimise armed struggle. Symbolic representation in commemoration plays its role in underscoring and normalising the rightfulness of armed response too. The banners of Sinn Féin *cumainn* can feature images of armed IRA members or portraiture of fallen volunteers; the bass drums of republican flute bands are similar. Temporary or permanent exhibitions present photographs, ephemera and material culture which depict armed resistance in the modern 'Troubles' heroically. In commemorative parades, actors in tableaux have appeared as masked and armed IRA volunteers, or in uniform mimicking a volley of shots fired in final salute.

It should be noted, however, that the most militant and militaristic aspects of commemoration are fading as the years progress, perhaps the result of internal debate about the use and impact of commemorative 'gunplay' (Kilpatrick, 2012). Yet powerful and resonant representation is still much valued and symbols and imagery continue to round out the narration of legitimacy in an organised, purposeful and heavily encoded republican 'public sphere' (Mulholland, 2007: 414).

The second theme seeks to buttress legitimacy in the external memory front in a much different manner. It resists attempts at de-legitimisation or demonisation by instead narrating the republican project's connection to the populace, and its activists' emergence from normal communities. We might call this theme 'ordinary people and popular support'. Commemorative rhetoric and narration seek to advance two interconnected points: firstly, that the armed struggle's legitimacy flowed from the popular acceptance by, and support of, nationalist communities themselves; secondly, that republican activists and volunteers were ordinary, indeed typical members of those very communities.

Militarists did not parachute into these communities and impose their activities; rather, 'ordinary people in extraordinary times' emerged from them and nurtured popular approval for their armed resistance. As Martin McGuinness put it in a 2008 commemoration:

> When I joined the IRA, it was an army of the people – sustained by the people, supported by the people, and answerable to the people. That is why the IRA became the formidable guerrilla army that it did. The IRA was nothing without the support of the people. It had within its ranks men and women who fought when this community had no other option. (*An Phoblacht*, 2008)

The invocation of popular legitimacy flows from across the border too. As Matt Carthy noted during a south Monaghan commemoration, 'I know there are people here today who could attest to this fact, the resistance of South Armagh would simply not have been possible were it not for the active support of the people of Inniskeen and the refuge, resources and personnel that this parish provided at vital times of struggle' (Sinn Féin, 2016).

That these invocations of popular legitimacy are themselves highly localised does not seem to greatly disturb republicans. For them, wider political units were distinctly lacking in authority. Northern Ireland was a wholly illegitimate, discriminatory and artificial construct while the 'twenty-six counties' was an incomplete partitionist entity whose governing elites opposed true republicans. What matters for republicans is the credible expression of authentic roots and popular support within their own neighbourhoods and townlands; that is where legitimacy was tapped during conflict, and that is where it is re-invoked in commemoration.

Republicans also protect the legitimacy of their project by resisting demonisation or 'othering' of their dead. Republican activists are presented as entirely typical, even laudable, members of their communities. Declan Kearney's description of two IRA volunteers, Henry Hogan and Declan Martin, during their commemoration is entirely typical: 'Henry and Declan were young men. They were sons, brothers, cousins, friends, neighbours of extended networks. Popular local lads at the beginning of adulthood, with options and choices in life' (field notes, Declan Kearney speech, Dungiven, 29 November 2009).

The republican dead are routinely painted not just as patriots, or soldiers, but as friends, comrades, neighbours, and husbands, fathers, wives, mothers, sons and daughters. In other words: 'ordinary people with family and friends who they loved and who loved them' (field notes, Gerry Kelly speech, Belfast, 5 April 2015). What made them different was that they were: 'ordinary men and women who in extraordinary and difficult circumstances found the inner strength, determination and courage to stand against injustice and oppression, and to demand the rights and entitlements of the Irish people' (field notes, Martin McGuinness speech, Carrickmore, 4 April 2010).

This motif of 'ordinary people in extraordinary times' is a recurrent one in republican commemoration of the dead. These were not militants or ideologues, the stereotypical political fanatics, but rather everyday individuals compelled by the force of events (beyond their control) to engage in exceptional forms of political resistance. Republican exhibitions can symbolically enhance this narrative of ordinariness by displaying family photographs, favourite clothing, letters and greetings cards, childhood toys, hobby items and prison crafts, and even the everyday personal affects recovered from the bodies of the dead. Commemoration attempts to underline the common humanity of the dead paramilitaries as a means of resisting demonisation and a de-legitimising, criminalisation of IRA volunteers. This is a most important task for the guardians of republican memory; the IRA engaged in a generation-long conflict in which their group was responsible for almost 1,700 deaths, hundreds of whom were civilians.

Resisting criminalisation and safeguarding memory are important parts of the final external legitimising theme of 'equality of victimhood and memory'. Resistance to the vilification or criminalisation of former volunteers is a periodic theme within commemorations and is often espoused by those in leadership positions. As Gerry Adams expounded:

> The war should never be glamourised or repeated. But neither should the republican involvement in it – the Army's involvement, the involvement our patriot dead be permitted by us to be criminalised or retrospectively delegitimised. This is bigger than me. This is about us as a republican community, especially in this city of Belfast. This is about our integrity and the just nature of our cause. (Sinn Féin, 2010b)

For Martin McGuinness, a broad-based assault on republican memory is underway, which activists must guard against:

> We have a massive responsibility to ensure that the families of our patriot dead are treated with respect and equality that they deserve. We will also resist absolutely ongoing efforts by revisionists in the media and elsewhere to retrospectively criminalise the IRA, its dead volunteers and the proud communities from which it came. And we should be under no illusions that that is what is now underway. Long-time opponents of Irish republicanism are seeking to damage the struggle and sully the memory of our patriot dead through a vile onslaught of negative propaganda. They do this not for monetary gain but also out of hatred for what we have achieved. Unfortunately, a tiny number of former activists who should know better have allowed

themselves to be used in this effort. But just as the revisionists in the past sought to demonise the men and women of 1916 and failed, the Irish people will reject the modern-day revisionists also. (Field notes, Martin McGuinness speech, Carrickmore, 4 April 2010)

Consequently, republicans seek to deconstruct 'hierarchies of victimhood', preferring that there should be 'equality of treatment for all victims and survivors whether it is from state violence and collusion or from any of the other combatant forces' (field notes, Gerry Kelly speech, 5 April 2015). For republicans, political or media led critique of their remembrance of the dead is an attack on the integrity, and thus the underpinning legitimacy, of the republican project, past and present. This very fact alone may explain the frequency of their commemorative calendar, and the undoubted resources poured into it (Brown and Grant, 2016).

Republican commemoration, however, does not stop at the remembrance of dead volunteers in its demands for an equality of victimhood and memory. It can also act to give voice to silenced narratives, particularly those of civilians in areas of republican support. Such a focus is not only standalone but also acts to supplement the contextualising aspect of the rightfulness of armed response theme, and also underlines the responsive and embedded connections to 'the people'.

Republicans have at times presented wider security force wrongdoing very strongly in their commemorations; the 2006 National Hunger Strike commemoration was themed almost entirely around the 'Time for Truth' campaign and featured floats, pageantry and street theatre around issues such as collusion, shoot-to-kill, loyalist attacks, government culpability and cover-ups, and disputed killings of civilians.

The goal of republican commemorative agitation in the equality of victimhood and memory theme is politically challenging but narratively more cautious and limited. They are not seeking to write up republican memory into a grand narrative for wider social acceptance, but instead are attempting to inscribe it as a legitimate strand into a tapestry of other accepted and recognised narratives about the 'Troubles'. This is deemed to be necessary for the expression not simply of memory but fundamentally for identity itself. As Mary Lou McDonald argued at the Easter 2019 commemoration in Belfast:

> There are some who object to us asserting our political identity. They object to us remembering our dead. To them I say no one has the right to censor or deny grief ... A reconciled Ireland must be a place for all with all our experiences and memories. (Field notes, Mary Lou McDonald speech, Belfast, 21 April 2019)

This commemorative approach is not aimed at full social acceptance, but acknowledgement and respect in a pluralised commons of memory; the message is: 'We don't need to accept each other's version of history to acknowledge the rights of everyone to remember their dead' (Sinn Féin, 2018). Conflict in remembrance is acknowledged, the goal is simply finding space for recognition of republican commemoration. As Michelle O'Neill stated at the 2018 Easter commemoration in Belfast: 'Republicans and unionists have conflicting narratives, conflicting histories and conflicting allegiances. That's the reality. Part of the journey to reconciliation is about recognising that to be the case' (field notes, Michelle O'Neill speech, Belfast, 1 April 2018).

A battle is being fought on the external memory front over the legitimacy of the republican movement's founding, rationale and actions. Given that commemoration is inward-facing, it might be construed that the goal is not to project this legitimacy at others but to properly 'school' their own political constituency and reinforce republican argument so as to buttress that argument against rival contestation by the British government, unionists, the media or the Irish government. A similar approach is taken in relation to their approach to another memory rival, that of 'dissident' republicanism, although here the format shifts somewhat and the de-legitimisation of the 'other' is accentuated.

The external/internal front – a hybrid struggle

'Dissident' republican groups view the peace process as a counter-revolutionary betrayal and challenge the legitimacy of Sinn Féin as heir to the republican struggle in their own political, military and commemorative practices (Hearty 2016, 2019; McGlinchey, 2019). On this memory front, mainstream republicanism seeks not only to legitimise its own political evolution, via the internal memory front noted above, but also to de-legitimise the republican credentials of its rejectionist competitors. This is something of a hybridised political front; 'dissident' republican memory is a branch of the same ideological and historical family tree, invoking the same icons and events, but it also represents a sharp rival which competes for republican activists and relentlessly critiques the mainstream's political strategy. It is thus very definitely a potential threat and a distinct 'other' to be repulsed in commemorative narration.

De-legitimisation is the key strategy. Mainstream republicanism has used imagery and pageantry to critique and de-legitimise the activities of British security forces but it avoids the use of imagery and pageantry to de-legitimise the 'dissident' groupings, preferring other strategies. There are no banners or tableaux depicting 'dissident' mass killings, assassinations or kneecapping. Perhaps mainstream republicanism realises the accompanying risks of such blunt depictions, given its own similar history of political violence. Instead, it relies on numerous rhetorical strategies in commemorative speechmaking. Field observation from 2009 to 2019 reveals that these are manifold. A prominent motif is to denounce 'dissidents' as being engaged in a *masquerade*, and to assert that there was only one true IRA (the Provisional one) and that recent groups who use the name are in no way connected to it. 'They are not the IRA, there was only one IRA' is a common refrain in chiding 'imposters'. 'Dissidents' are an alphabet soup of mere 'wannabes'. As Gerry Kelly forcefully proclaimed at an Easter commemoration in 2014:

> These other wannabe groups trying to claim the title of freedom fighters have no strategy to speak of; otherwise they would be presenting it to the world. Whether they call themselves the New IRA, the Old IRA, the Belfast Continuity IRA, the Limerick Continuity IRA, Oglaigh na hEireann, RAAD, CAAD or SAD – a name or title does not give them legitimacy. (Sinn Féin, 2014)

The 'dissidents' are accused of acquiring stolen valour, vampirising the deeds, memory and memorial sites of Provisional republicans. In a direct message to the 'dissidents' at a commemoration for an IRA volunteer, Martin McGuinness angrily stated: 'when you gather at the Cuchulainn monument in the City Cemetery with a handful of supporters just remember that the people commemorated there were not part of your organisation' (*Derry Journal*, 2011). In contrast to the Provisionals' narrated 'popular legitimacy', 'dissidents' are denounced as *unrepresentative*, and a mere flotsam of 'microgroups', and 'small factions' on the 'fringes of nationalism' who hold 'less and less support'.

A further theme speaks of the futility of their actions, which sits in contrast to the sometime narration of the capacity and utility of Provisional use of violence. 'Dissident' violence is so contra 'mainstream' memory (and political strategy) that it is deemed to sit outside the proper unfolding of history itself. It therefore exists in a time warp: the phase of militant history has decisively ended and taken the very notion of armed resistance with it. As Declan Kearney emphasised at a 2009 memorial: 'the IRA fought that war to a conclusion. There is no other IRA today. Nor is there an armed struggle to be finished. Those who choose to masquerade otherwise should disarm and disband' (field notes, Declan Kearney speech, Dungiven, 29 November 2009).

In contrast to the self-narration of mainstream republicans as ideologically and strategically informed, 'dissidents' are presented as irrational, their violence is 'mindless', they are 'militarists' motivated by 'adventurism' and their belief that they are true rivals to Sinn Féin, and can advance to the Republic, shows that they are living in a 'fool's paradise'. Rhetorically, it is now but a short step to criminality. Some 'dissidents' act 'for personal gain; some are involved in drugs. These are the users and abusers of the community who hide behind a façade of political dissent' (Sinn Féin, 2009b). Robberies, extortion and brutal punishment attacks are their day-to-day activity, not the prosecution of armed struggle, they are 'now merely killing people for the sake of killing', and, to date, 'the biggest percentage of any killings carried out by these dissidents have been in internal feuds. This is not a struggle for Irish Freedom! If they are at war it is with each other and the Nationalist community' (Sinn Féin, 2014).

To long-time observers of the 'Troubles', the language and tone of this commemorative messaging of de-legitimisation will seem ironically familiar. But what might the impact of Sinn Féin's narration of both legitimacy and illegitimacy be in the developing political process and attendant issues of legacy?

Conclusion

Irish republican commemoration and the narration of its legitimacy along these three fronts of memory is considerable, and it is worthwhile examining its potential impact across issues of legacy and peace processing. The internal front may be unlikely to impact negatively on peace processing; indeed, it may play a role in pragmatically adapting radical politics to the pragmatics of peace. Its main aim is to reassure constituencies that ideals have not been compromised away, even as it adapts the traditional republican vision of legitimacy and continuity to the exigencies of the peace process (Brown, 2019). The hybrid internal/external front may also have a positive effect on the peace. It is aimed directly at 'dissident' groups, and is designed to bolster peace-process republicanism while rhetorically de-legitimising that of 'dissidents', who can serve a 'spoiler' function in the peace (Stedman, 1997; Trumbore 2018).

Aside from the rhetorical appeals, Sinn Féin's most important function along this memory front may simply be to keep hold of important icons, events and memory sites through frequent commemoration. To do otherwise may allow the symbolic capital and evocative narratives of republican commemoration to be seized and even monopolised by spoiler groups. The impact of the external front is more problematic. It seeks in large part to bolster the integrity of republican armed struggle in the past and to protect the memory of the IRA dead. This strikes at the heart of the meta-conflict in Northern Ireland and may reduce the chances of a future 'meta-bargain' (Mallinder, 2019; Mac Ginty and Du Toit, 2007) on issues of legacy and conflict resolution.

Consider the potential out-workings of the Stormont House Agreement (NIO, 2014): commemorative narration along the external memory front does not sit easily with possible prosecutions of republicans; truth recovery may produce an understanding of the past which complicates or shames; the identified 'themes' emerging from the process may be cherry-picked to support some republican narratives but may collide forcefully with others. The Implementation and Reconciliation Group's academic report, produced by historians and social scientists will have its own narrative difficulties, but should seek to evidence and test positions, not underwrite powerful political myths. The question to be put from those who seek societal reconciliation may be much simpler. Does this prolific commemoration inhibit any broad, shared understanding of the root causes of conflict and the heavy toll of political violence?

References

An Phoblacht (2005) 'Establishment politicians slammed at Cavan commemoration' (1 September).
An Phoblacht (2006) 'The hunger strikes – this generation's 1916' (9 March).
An Phoblacht (2008) 'McGuinness slams micro groups over Derry killing' (3 July).
Beechmount Commemoration Committee (1998) *Green River: In Honour of Our Dead*. Belfast: Beechmount Commemoration Committee.
Bell, C., Campbell, C. and Ní Aoláin, F. (2004) 'Justice discourses in transition', *Social and Legal Studies*, 13 (3): 305–28.
Borer, T. A. (2003) 'A taxonomy of victims and perpetrators: human rights and reconciliation in South Africa', *Human Rights Quarterly*, 25 (4): 1088–116.
Bouris, E. (2007) *Complex Political Victims*. Bloomfield, CT: Kumarian Press.
Brown, K. (2011) 'Bound by oath and duty to remember: loyalism and memory', in J. W. McAuley and G. Spencer (eds), *Ulster Loyalism after the Good Friday Agreement: History, Identity and Change*, pp. 226–43. Basingstoke: Palgrave Macmillan.
Brown, K. (2012) '"What it was like to live through a day": transitional justice and the memory of the everyday in a divided society', *International Journal of Transitional Justice*, 6 (3): 444–66.
Brown, K. (2019) 'Political commemoration and peacebuilding in ethnonational settings: the risk and utility of partisan memory', *Peacebuilding*, 7 (1): 51–70.
Brown, K. and Grant, A. (2016) 'A lens over conflicted memory: surveying "Troubles" commemoration in Northern Ireland', *Irish Political Studies*, 31 (1): 139–62.
Brubaker, R. (2002) 'Ethnicity without groups', *European Journal of Sociology*, 43 (2): 163–89.
Casanova, J. (2016) 'Disremembering Francoism: what is at stake in Spain's memory wars?', in H. Graham (ed.), *Interrogating Francoism: History and Dictatorship in Twentieth-Century Spain*, pp. 203–22. London: Bloomsbury.
Derry Journal (2011) 'McGuinness slams dissident republican "imposters"' (22 August).

Derry Sinn Féin (2011) 'Martrina [sic] Anderson speaking in Derry Easter Sunday 2011' (25 April). www.derrysinnfein.ie/news/2011/04/ (accessed 3 May 2011; dead link – print copy on file with author).

Di Lellio, A. and Schwandner-Sievers, S. (2006) 'Sacred journey to a nation: the construction of a shrine in postwar Kosovo', *Journeys*, 7 (1): 27–49.

Hayward, K. and Komarova, M. (2014) 'The limits of local accommodation: why contentious events remain prone to conflict in Northern Ireland', *Studies in Conflict and Terrorism*, 37 (9): 777–91.

Hearty, K. (2016) 'From "former comrades" to "near enemy": the narrative template of "armed struggle" and conflicting discourses on Violent Dissident Irish Republican activity (VDR)', *Critical Studies on Terrorism*, 9 (2): 269–91.

Hearty, K. (2019) 'Spoiling through performative nonviolence: ritualistic funerary practice as a Violent Dissident Irish Republican (VDR) spoiling tactic', *Studies in Conflict and Terrorism*, 42 (6): 581–99.

Horowitz, D. (1991) *A Democratic South Africa? Constitutional Engineering in a Divided Society*. Berkeley, CA: University of California Press.

Kaufman, S. (2001) *Modern Hatreds: The Symbolic Politics of Ethnic War*. Ithaca, NY: Cornell University Press.

Khalili, L. (2007) *Heroes and Martyrs of Palestine: The Politics of National Commemoration*. Cambridge: Cambridge University Press.

Kilpatrick, C. (2012) 'Ex-IRA chief calls for end to military-style parades', *Belfast Telegraph* (11 September).

Koposov, N. (2017) *Memory Laws, Memory Wars: The Politics of the Past in Europe and Russia*. Cambridge: Cambridge University Press.

Lawther, C. (2014) 'The construction and politicisation of victimhood', in O. Lynch and J. Argomaniz (eds), *Victims of Terrorism: A Comparative and Interdisciplinary Study*, pp. 10–30. London: Routledge.

Lebel, U. (2013) *Politics of Memory: The Israeli Underground's Struggle for Inclusion in the National Pantheon and Military Commemoralization*. Abingdon: Routledge.

Mac Ginty, R. and Du Toit, P. (2007) 'A disparity of esteem: relative group status in Northern Ireland after the Belfast Agreement', *Political Psychology*, 28 (1): 13–31.

Magee, G. (2011) *Tyrone's Struggle: ar son Saoirse nah Eireann*. Omagh: Tyrone Sinn Féin Commemoration Committee.

Mallinder, L. (2019) 'Metaconflict and international human rights law in dealing with Northern Ireland's past', *Cambridge International Law Journal*, 8 (1): 5–38.

Marschall, S. (2006) 'Commemorating "struggle heroes": constructing a genealogy for the new South Africa', *International Journal of Heritage Studies*, 12 (2): 176–93.

McDowell, S. and Braniff, M. (2014) *Commemoration as Conflict: Space, Memory and Identity in Peace Processes*. Basingstoke: Palgrave Macmillan.

McGarry, F. (2003) *Republicanism in Modern Ireland*. Dublin: University College Dublin Press.

McGarry, J. and O'Leary, B. (1995) *Explaining Northern Ireland: Broken Images*. Oxford: Blackwell.

McGlinchey, M. (2019) *Unfinished Business: The Politics of 'Dissident' Irish Republicanism*. Manchester: Manchester University Press.

McIntyre, A. (1995) 'Modern Irish republicanism: the product of British state strategies', *Irish Political Studies*, 10: 97–122.

Mulholland, M. (2007) 'Irish Republican politics and violence before the peace process, 1968–1994', *European Review of History: Revue européenne d'histoire*, 14 (3): 397–421.

NIO (Northern Ireland Office) (2014) *The Stormont House Agreement*. London. HMSO.

Papadakis, Y. (1994) 'The national struggle museums of a divided city', *Ethnic and Racial Studies*, 17 (3): 400–19.

Quinn, R. J. (2004) *The Rising of the Phoenix: The Battle of St. Matthew's and the Events around the Historic Weekend of the 27th June 1970*. Belfast: Belfast Cultural and Local History Group.

Ross, M. H. (2012) *Culture and Belonging in Divided Societies: Contestation and Symbolic Landscapes*. Philadelphia, PA: University of Pennsylvania Press.

Sinn Féin (2009a) 'Make Fianna Fáil pay at the ballot box – Ó Caoláin' (12 April). Available at: https://web.archive.org/web/20200128102329/https://www.sinnfein.ie/contents/15759 (accessed 29 July 2022).

Sinn Féin (2009b) 'Gerry Kelly – address to Lurgan Commemoration, 2009' (13 April). Available at: https://web.archive.org/web/20200128104721/https://www.sinnfein.ie/contents/15761 (accessed 29 July 2022).

Sinn Féin (2010a) 'Caoimhghín Ó Caoláin Easter speech 2010 The Loup, County Derry' (4 April). Available at: https://web.archive.org/web/20200128103009/https://www.sinnfein.ie/contents/18399 (accessed 29 July 2022).

Sinn Féin (2010b) 'Gerry Adams' Easter Speech 2010, Milltown Cemetery, Belfast' (4 April). Available at: https://web.archive.org/web/20200128104444/https://www.sinnfein.ie/contents/18398 (accessed 29 July 2022).

Sinn Féin (2014) 'Loyal orders need to step up to the plate' (20 April). Available at: https://web.archive.org/web/20190525023421/https://www.sinnfein.ie/contents/29677 (accessed 29 July 2022).

Sinn Féin (2016) 'Notions that 1916 leaders would have settled for a 26-county state "ludicrous & laughable" – Matt Carthy' (26 March).

Available at: https://web.archive.org/web/20190524201136/https://www.sinnfein.ie/contents/39139 (accessed 29 July 2022).

Sinn Féin (2018) 'Unionist leaders need to engage in United Ireland debate – Carthy' (2 April). Available at: https://web.archive.org/web/20200128115219/https://www.sinnfein.ie/contents/48863 (accessed 29 July 2022).

Stedman, S. J. (1997) 'Spoiler problems in peace processes', *International Security*, 22 (2): 5–53.

Stone, D. (2013) 'Memory wars in the new Europe', in D. Stone (ed.), *The Holocaust, Fascism and Memory*, pp. 714–31. Basingstoke: Palgrave Macmillan.

Trumbore, P. F. (2018) '"The movement moves against you": coercive spoiler management in the Northern Ireland peace process', *Terrorism and Political Violence*, 30 (3): 524–43.

7

Ulster loyalism, memory and commemoration

James W. McAuley and Neil Ferguson

> [I]t is not the truth which matters in Northern Ireland, but what people believe to be the truth.
>
> (Brian Faulkner, *Irish Times*, 5 January 1972)

The Troubles in Northern Ireland produced huge social turmoil and political division that still structures and provides guidelines for that society. Much of its legacy is encapsulated in, and presented through, expressions and representations of collective memory. The memories projected through various acts of commemoration retain a political intensity and relevance to everyday life that are almost impossible to overstate, and the consequences for contemporary social and political relationships and formations remain with us. Such deposits of memory rest on a series of exclusive community myths and understandings; memories which add to long-standing adversarial readings and understandings of the past, and those narratives which different groupings draw on to reinforce their sense of self-identity and Self.

This chapter considers the construction of loyalist narratives and the use of memory within the political mobilisation of that section of society. In particular, it will consider how collective memories are shared and displayed by those identifying as loyalists, and particularly among loyalist paramilitary groupings and their immediate constituency. Further, it will explore the place of memory in the development of a conflict culture, and the understandings of those who still set their beliefs within the framework of conflict. It places these views within the collective memories utilised within their communities of origin to present a particular worldview and suggests that those who affiliate with paramilitary organisations drew upon a specific view of the past for their motivation.

Understanding collective memory

As this volume indicates, much has been written concerning collective memory, but broadly it can be understood as a narrative from which a group takes meaning and security, through a collective understanding of a constructed past. These views are often transmitted across generations, in ways that directly link past to present, and ensure the prolongation of group beliefs and identity (Olick and Levy, 1997; see also Olick *et al.*, 2011). This process of bonding encompasses those memories passed across generations through oral and cultural events (Vansina, 1985), by narratives and written texts, forms of popular culture, and through other artefacts such as murals, emblems and flags (Epstein, 2001).

There are a multitude of ways of reminding people of particular memories, the interpretation of community histories and where as individuals they should stand on certain events from the past. This constant exposure to a bonded culture, through written material, songs and prose, alongside visible physical manifestations such as commemorative murals and gardens of remembrance, to name a few, creates frames of understanding. In Northern Ireland, even personal jewellery and tattoos, or inscriptions on gravestones, provide ways in which collective memories are made real and living. It is within this framework that contemporary social and political attitudes are formed.

Particular chosen and constructed linkages with the past are made overt and are presented in a highly accessible – if often simplified – way to explain current circumstances and project possible futures. This is based on particular readings of the past, surrounding memories that are far from historically accurate. Rather, these memories mark an interpretation of the past that is subject to contemporary political anxieties and pressures. In response, the political symbolism adopted and that which is recalled is filtered through the needs of contemporary events. It is through the assemblage of ideas and culture that the beliefs a group holds about itself and of others is reaffirmed and identified as loyalism.

Loyalist identity and the remembered past

Loyalism can be thought of as largely the creation of particular socio-economic circumstances, and an identifiable, differentiated understanding of the past. This is perpetuated (and opposed) by various memory actors, ranging from nations, large religious and political groupings, down to local communities (Weedon and Jordan, 2012). Those who identify with loyalism, albeit sometimes in very different ways, highlight a common understanding of chosen historical reference points used in its composition. These collective readings of the past are presented as reasons for the history of unity to group members. References to collective memory carry great weight in the self-identification of loyalism.

In communicating this sense of self-identity from one historical period to another, and from one generation to the next, the use of symbolism and narrative are crucial in transmitting the central values and beliefs of loyalism. At the core of these narratives is the identification of key locations for loyalist collective memory and identity. Through readily available and everyday stories, images and artefacts, children and young people are presented with a coherent narrative, used to explain conflict and history (Cairns and Roe, 2002). This narrative treats time and space in a particular manner, rolling disparate events together across different historical periods and foreshortening experiences.

Connections are made to events as diverse in time as the Enniskillen bombing (1987), the Siege of Derry (1688–89), the Battle of the Boyne (1690), the Battle of the Somme during the First World War (1916), the signings of the Anglo-Irish Agreement (1985) and Good Friday Agreement (1998), the disbanding of the B-Specials (1970), which are foreshortened to be regarded as central to loyalist memory and identity. These, and many other events, are directly linked within loyalist explanations of the past, and in so doing any historical gaps between these events are abridged, suggesting a permanency of action and thought across loyalism.

While membership of political groups may fluctuate and their interpretations of events may differ, loyalism draws on an overarching collective memory and a broadly agreed collective understanding of the past. This comprehensive exhibition of loyalism's history is constructed and passed on through a coherent presentation of a narrative, which not only 'explains' the past but also presents contemporary values and aspirations within loyalism.

Simultaneously, the construction of a loyalist narrative clearly identifies those who do not hold this interpretation of the past, who are deemed to be outside of the self-categorisation of loyalism and clearly presented as the 'Other'. Collective memory plays a central role in consolidating group cohesion by further strengthening ethnic myths and symbols while clearly distinguishing between the group and the Other (Schwartz, 1982). Part of this involves evoking anxieties about the aims and goals of the Other. Fears concerning the likelihood of having to undergo a repeat of past attacks and traumas is never far below the surface.

Hence, current political events affecting the loyalist community are often interpretated and presented within the broad historical context and collective memory surrounding the fate of Protestants in Ireland. This is seen as part of a long-standing story that depicts the Protestant community as constantly under attack for the last four hundred years (as discussed, for example, in the August 2008 issue of the Grand Orange Lodge of Ireland's newspaper, the *Orange Standard*). Many loyalist interpretations suggest that contemporary circumstances are best seen simply as the latest phase in a struggle to preserve Northern Ireland's position within the United Kingdom, and their broad sense of their identity. This is seen as constantly threatened by other cultures and identities – of which Irish republicanism is always to the fore – hence the need to highlight eternal vigilance in an ancient struggle, the current phase of which remains very much alive. In response, loyalism draws on a pre-structured narrative, presenting the past and the present as amalgamated and fused, and a very restricted set of political responses. It is possible to identify constantly recurring themes within this loyalist construction of the past, of which three – defence, sacrifice and the trauma caused by the Other – are recurring.

One grouping offering particular readings of the broader loyalist narrative are found within the constituency of paramilitarism. The origins of loyalist paramilitary groupings rest in the early 1970s. At the time, many unionists were expressing an open sense of dismay that the state was under attack, alongside broader grievances at the loss of political power. Part of the fragmented response to the situation then gave rise to the formation of paramilitary groupings.

Two main organisations came to dominate: one was the Ulster Defence Association (UDA)/Ulster Young Militants grouping, the other the Ulster Volunteer Force (UVF)/Red Hand Commando grouping. The UDA, founded in 1971, grew out of the wide network of vigilante groups that had appeared in loyalist districts. Alongside this, the UVF, which had surfaced and organised in 1966, began to organise and recruit heavily. While not downplaying the viciousness of their campaign, it is important in the context of this chapter to point to how these groups have sought to reference the past and how they have sought to establish distinctiveness within loyalism, while engaging in the broad process outlined above.

Memory and cultures of violence

Not everyone who lived through the Troubles joined or supported paramilitaries (far from it), or even directly encountered violence. But it was not necessary to have been directly involved in political violence to have been affected by it. Once a conflict has been in progress for some time, as John Darby and Roger Mac Ginty point out, 'violence and its effects' are woven 'into the very fabric of society and become part of normal life', and people 'become accustomed to the routine use of violence to determine political and social outcomes' (Darby and Mac Ginty, 2000: 260).

The Troubles comprised a long-term, if low-intensity, conflict. Daniel Bar-Tal (2002) has suggested that in response to prolonged physical violence, a culture of violence may develop and become engrained in society. Such long-term conflicts influence cultural formation and the maintenance and dissemination of four key sets of societal beliefs (Bar-Tal, 2000). These concern, firstly, societal beliefs about the nature of the conflict itself; secondly, beliefs about the (de-)legitimacy of the opponent; thirdly, beliefs concerning the victimisation of one's own group; and finally, societal beliefs concerning what Bar-Tal terms 'patriotism' (which most often manifests in commemoration). We will discuss each of these in the context of how loyalists use collective memory to enforce their sense of social identity and to legitimise to their response:

Societal beliefs about the conflict

Loyalist interpretations of the conflict are mostly built up though reflections of their own experiences and understandings. These include the causes for the outbreak of the conflict and those major events that shaped it, as well as the move towards violence in the late 1960s. In particular, those malign actions by the Provisional IRA are placed in direct opposition to the perceived sacrifices made by loyalist paramilitaries during the Troubles. The resultant competing readings of the conflict offer different explanations as to who was responsible for the emergence of the Troubles and who was to 'blame' for the subsequent patterns of conflict that developed. The collective memories of the conflict are, of course, highly selective (as are republican constructs of the past). The loyalist narrative seeks to capture and hold the moral high ground in many of the explanations it offers.

Beliefs that de-legitimise the opponent

As Northern Ireland descended into organised and assiduous communal violence, the number of killings and the loss of civilian lives rose. Societal beliefs surrounding legitimisation and de-legitimisation of political violence and those involved in it came to the fore, and those engaged often drew on interpretations of the past for their motivation. All of the groups engaged in political violence in Northern Ireland were constantly involved in a struggle for acceptance as the state as well as loyalist and republican groups were all constantly at pains to justify the legitimacy of their own and illegitimacy of the other's campaign. De-legitimising beliefs fulfil several important functions.

Attaching or associating certain names or handles to particular groups, such as 'terrorists', or 'murderers', or 'freedom fighters', or 'defenders', fits directly into differing collective interpretations. Drawing on collective memories offers reasons as to why the adversary's acts are inhuman and immoral, as opposed to those actions undertaken by the in-group. At the same time, the arguments forwarded to rationalise violence are expanded beyond combatant groups, to possibly include members of the civilian population. Hence, such beliefs are used to justify the in-group's acts of violence, either through sectarian ideology or simple revenge, categories still meaningful for some.

Daniel Bar-Tal suggests that as widespread conflict becomes more prolonged and severe, the negative categorisation of the Other leads to them in essence as being seen as evil and inhuman (Bar-Tal, 2013). Moreover, John Cash has identified what he terms as the splitting of 'the political and social order into good and evil' (Cash, 1998: 230). It is clear that in Northern Ireland, as the perceived level of threat intensified during the Troubles, the categories of 'friends' and 'enemies' became clearly differentiated and the actions of the Other were increasingly seen as unjust and without any moral underpinning.

Societal beliefs about the group's own victimisation

Involvement in political violence and experiences of victimhood all form crucial ingredients in the collective memory of both unionists and nationalists, republicanism and loyalism, influenced directly by how each conceive their own identity and that of the Other (Schwartz, 1982). These views were in turn reinvigorated, underpinned and reinforced by community myths and narratives of collective memory, blame and injured party (White, 1991).

As the number of deaths throughout the conflict grew, beliefs and explanations about being victimised by the opponent also developed. For loyalism, such understandings concentrated on the violence and atrocities committed by the evil adversaries of the republican movement and responsibility for the conflict was laid squarely at their feet. This self-perception frames loyalists as both martyrs and victims. Within republicanism there is an equivalent narrative which projects a risen people and martyrdom. Both opposing communities engage in a process that selectively highlights and focuses on the political violence undertaken by the other side. They collectively remember particularly vicious and brutal acts perpetrated by the opponent (Hunter *et al.*, 1991).

It was, in part, such views that allowed for the continuation of the devastating cycle of reprisal violence which was a feature of much of the Troubles. Such encounters were reinforced by beliefs about the evil nature the Other (Ferguson and Cairns, 1996) and the use of negative stereotypes to de-legitimise the perceived enemy (McAuley, 2010). In the case of loyalism, this is well represented by the following:

> The IRA wants to present themselves as victims. And sadly, the Government has pandered to this narrative. ... They demand countless inquiries, and countless prosecutions of elderly veterans. Their objective isn't justice, but rather building a narrative that justifies their actions. The state were murderers and the IRA were defenders of a poor oppressed people, or so they would have you believe. ... They live in a self-created and self-perpetuating myth whereby they were somehow the innocent ones, whereby the IRA terrorists that called themselves an army all of a sudden became victims when someone returned fire. (*Unionist Voice*, n.d.: 12)

Memorialisation of conflict

Loyalist explanations of the conflict are sheathed in distinctive forms of recall and collective memory. It is important to recognise, as Jeffrey Prager (1998) points out, that remembering is a dynamic and interpretive process, not a passive one. The memory of those most deeply engaged in the 'loyalist cause', and particularly those who fought and lost their lives, is deemed most worthy of memorialisation. This generates the production of memorials, monuments, murals and other physical forms dedicated to upholding and defending chosen collective memories. These are increasing reproduced at the local level. Such sites are important, not only because they locate a defined place but also because they give physical expression to the collective memory of loyalism.

Functions of loyalist collective memory

Collective memory fulfils several important functions within loyalism, not least of which is providing lasting and candid reminders about their identity and sense of belonging. These also often highlight the losses that loyalists are seen to have suffered as a group and the need for continual awareness of malevolent and untrustworthy enemies, in particular Irish republicanism. A key role is the function of seeking to inspire others to continue the loyalist struggle. Memorials and commemoration are a way in which loyalist collective memory and collective identity are codified and reproduced.

This also manifests in the enacting of commemorative events, highlighting those people and actions deemed to be of greatest significance to the group. This was clearly seen, for example, in the widespread commemoration and historical enactments on the centenary of the formation of the UVF. Other events are highly ceremonial and formulaic (often mirroring British Army ceremonies), while some involve speeches, music, decorations and displays. These symbolic, codified ceremonies are now commonplace in loyalist communities. Many relate back to the Troubles, commemorating particular events such as the formation of the state, or recall those within loyalism that were killed during the conflict.

Memorialisation and commemoration are elongated to include both recent and historical heroes, making direct links between them. These seek to communicate the dominant values and meanings that loyalists attached to the conflict, symbolically expressing core beliefs and attitudes, and often glorifying perceived victories of the past. One example of this can be seen in the mural depicting Sir Edward Carson and volunteers of the original UVF (Figure 7.1).

For some, Edward Carson best epitomises the intransigent unionist leader whose uncompromising actions took Ireland to the brink of civil war. Within loyalist collective memory, Carson is seen very differently. Alongside James Craig, Carson is a central figure in the foundation myth of Ulster loyalism. It was he who organised unionist opposition to the Irish Home Rule bills and coordinated resistance to breaking the link with Britain (McAuley, 2010: 29–35). At one level the mural is simply a reference to a particular point in history, surrounding unionist opposition to Home Rule, the formation of the UVF and the subsequent enlistment of many UVF members in the 36th Ulster Division. More broadly, however, the mural is used to highlight and reinforce core senses of unionist identity and expressions of Britishness within the loyalist community. There is also another subtext, suggesting that those expressing that identity must remain ever vigilant and be prepared to organise to ensure this.

Since the mid-1990s, loyalist areas across Northern Ireland have witnessed a vast growth in populist memorials surrounding the First World War. In particular, there are many murals commemorating

Figure 7.1 Carson's Volunteers Mural – East Belfast, May 2018

events around the Battle of the Somme, where members of the 36th Ulster Division were killed in large numbers. As such, its commemoration has become directly associated with the unionist and loyalist community (Switzer, 2007). This marks a good example of selection in the construction of collective memory, with others – for example, those who fought for Britain but not from a Protestant, unionist background – being written out of this phase of history (Grayson, 2010). In loyalist circles, the Somme is almost exclusively promoted as a means to laud the exploits of the 36th Ulster Division and the sacrifice of Ulster's manhood (McGaughey, 2012). There is another underlying purpose behind these commemorations. For some, the narrative is extended and used to validate the need for contemporary loyalist paramilitary organisations and to claim a continuation of Britain's role in ensuring the current constitutional position as a form of moral payback for past commitment and sacrifice for the state.

Memory formation around the Somme has assumed ever greater significance within loyalist culture (see Graham and Shirlow, 2002; McAuley, 2016, Officer, 2001; Officer and Walker, 2003; Switzer, 2013) to the point where the memories are part of a foundation myth of Ulster loyalist identity. As Evershed puts it, the Somme 'is a vital part of a memorial cartography that maps the Ulster Protestant experience across time' (Evershed, 2018: 12). The battle was marked in 2016 by both official and unofficial centenary commemorations. Such commemorations were complicated by the paramilitary group that formed around the mid-1960s under the UVF name claiming direct lineage to the UVF assembled in 1913, who subsequently fought with the 36th Ulster Division.

This formulation of collective memory constructs a history running together events and people, separated by the best part of a century, into a coherent narrative. An illustration of this can be seen in a Belfast mural that shows a stylised representation of the 36th Ulster Division going over the top at the Somme (Figure 7.2). To the left of the mural, however, are four smaller posters, each dedicated to modern UVF members killed during the Troubles. The display makes connections across time and political history, which should be obvious. Through the name of the UVF, collective memory is invoked to highlight the fallen, the implication being those who died at the Somme and during the Troubles should be seen as martyrs in the same struggle.

The themes revealed by the mural are apparent at several levels of the loyalist narrative. A further example can be found in the following speech at a commemoration in Belfast in 2018, reproduced in the *Purple Standard*, a newsletter linked with the UVF:

> From the horrors of France and Flanders, and the many campaigns throughout World War One, World War Two, Aden, Korea, the Falklands, Afghanistan and Iraq; when this country called, without hesitation, Ulstermen and women answered.
>
> But as history dictates, war was never far away from our shores, and as the 1960s drew to a close, another enemy reared its head, as

Figure 7.2 Somme/Ulster Volunteer Force Mural – East Belfast, May 2018

the Irish Republican Movement contrived to instigate a vicious murder campaign against the Protestants of Ulster. In response, the ordinary folk of this community forged together, and reconstituted the Ulster Volunteer Force. (*Purple Standard*, n.d.)

The UDA have also drawn on the past to construct a somewhat different narrative, but they have struggled to find as direct and obvious link with the past as the UVF (Viggiani, 2014: 53). In response, the UDA have adopted their own foundation myth, claiming their origins and historical bond lie with the Ulster Defence Union, formed in response to the first two Home Rule bills in 1886 and 1893 (Reed, 2015). These readings of the past, however, tend not to have the same prominence or representation in loyalist popular culture as those associated with the UVF.

Loyalism, commemoration and culture

At the outbreak of the Troubles, loyalist identity tended to be expressed at the macro level, emphasising a distinct sense of Britishness (and increasingly an antagonism to those giving expression to Irishness). The Troubles era brought about stronger articulations of identity at the micro level. This was often through deepening expressions of communal belonging, expressing heightened senses of the circumscribed community of loyalism.

This was based on an identifiable construction of collective memory involving processes of both remembering and forgetting, which shaped 'experience, thought and imagination in terms of past, present and future' (Brockmeier, 2002: 18). Outcomes of this process can also involve the silencing of competing narratives of memory (De Cillia *et al.*, 1999). For Connerton, it remains difficult to disentangle the past from the present, not just because present circumstances 'tend to influence – some might want to say distort – our recollections of the past', but also because 'past factors tend to influence, or distort, our experience of the present' (Connerton, 1989: 2).

The resulting loyalist narrative brings to the fore crucial strands of collective memory, identity and its representations, which are held together by an accepted knowledge and chronology of events (both real and assumed). These subjective histories are told, re-told, transmitted and re-transmitted across generations. Commemoration and memorialisation play a central role in the construction of this imagined community of loyalism. Importantly, these memories are reproduced such that they have everyday meaning in the ways people attach relevance to particular events in their past in understanding the present (Hirsch, 1995).

Loyalism as an identity is built not only on a remembered past but also on a distinct sense of unfinished objectives emerging from that past. To have significance, loyalist collective memory and the meanings within it must be made living and communicated at an everyday level. Loyalist memory 'retains from the past only what still lives or is capable of living in the consciousness of the groups keeping the memory alive' (Connerton, 1989: 97). Both experienced and learned memories play important roles in motivating loyalists, who are mobilised by a broad process of persuasion and through collective memories with which individuals identify (Klandennans, 1998).

Across loyalism there is increasing evidence of collective memory being used to develop cohesiveness within and lionise the in-group, while at the same time dehumanising members of the Other group and solidifying boundaries between them and the in-group (Lambert et al., 2009). Through this engagement with active memory (Schwartz, 1982) loyalists seek to express answers to core questions surrounding community identity, the identity of Self and their social and political relationships with others (Olick, 2008). The past is continually reinterpreted and re-evaluated, and often this remembering occurs directly in relation to factors related to the present.

Patterns of socialisation and the use of collective memory to authenticate and revalidate both Self and group identity (Assmann and Shortt, 2012) are crucial processes in the reproduction of community norms and values. Following Connerton, it is possible to argue that collective memory is maintained 'through a community of interests and thoughts' (Connerton, 1989: 47). In this sense, loyalism draws on specific narratives of past experience, constituted by specific groups to empower particular forms of identity. The institutions that support collective memories, in turn, help to create, sustain and reproduce the imagined community of loyalism by identifying individual experiences as part of a collective experience determined by continuity of history, place and social belonging.

Loyalist narrative performs several roles, not least of which is to provide a point of stability for those individuals and groups struggling to make sense of a socially and politically uncertain world. In this context, identity narratives offer recognisable images and reassurances, which act in reinforcing existing worldviews. Primarily, this works by bringing together events of the past with contemporary concerns and projecting them into the future. The narrative is one that foreshortens history and the distance between political events. This is clearly seen in the following speech made during a loyalist memorial parade held in September 2018:

> For generations, the UVF ... has served with fortitude, gallantry and unmatched steely determination, in the age old Cause of Crown and country. As the conflict raged, time and again our Volunteers stepped forth, engaging and repelling the enemy, and by all means at their disposal, taking the war straight back to the doorsteps of those who would plot our demise, and see the end of British Protestantism on these shores.
>
> Spanning ten decades of conflict and beyond, right up to the present day, our Organisation has never once failed its founding principles.

From the blood soaked, killing fields of France and Flanders, to more recent times, and the terror ridden streets of Ulster, our Volunteers have fought passionately, and relentlessly, against many foes. (*Purple Standard*, 2018)

Memory and the culture wars

While the levels of structured and organised violence may have receded in the period since the signing of the Belfast (Good Friday) Agreement, the intensity of social and cultural difference and conflict between the two communities has, if anything, intensified. The legacy of a culture of violence crystallises at many different levels. The dramatic rise in locally organised memorials, commemorations, walking tours, tours of murals and taxi tours, re-enactments and tributes (both to individuals and events) on both 'sides' in Northern Ireland is noteworthy.

Another trend has seen the increase in localised paramilitary 'museums', which seek to explain the history conflict from a paramilitary perspective. Most of the sites are reasonably small and contain artefacts such as weapons and uniforms. Good examples are found in the Andy Tyrie Interpretative Centre (the main UDA-inspired collection, named after one of its former leaders), or the one organised by the former UVF prisoners' association, the Ex-Prisoners Interpretative Centre (EPIC). Among its stated goals are a commitment to 'to reconciliation and conflict transformation both with and between communities … through social justice, community engagement, restorative justice and the reintegration of former prisoners and their families' (CommunityNI, 2020). In this context, one paramilitary member outlines an interesting reason for what he sees as the purpose of memorialisation:

> Our war of thirty years isn't going to be like the Vietnam War. It's not going to be people sweeping it under the carpet and saying it never happened or it shouldn't have happened. Now, the war in this country happened, and the people that fought it didn't fly in from a different country. They were born and bred here. They fought and defended what they thought was their cause, whether it be republican or loyalist, and it's not something that's going to be swept under the carpet. (Cited in Smithey, 2011: 152)

These localised presentations of memory offer a more detailed and unselfconsciously biased narrative of those who experienced the Troubles first-hand. There is often little pretence of the neutrality or balance that is found in 'official' museums. Central to constructing the core narratives of both loyalist and republican collective memory is the identification within both communities of some central historical reference points and physical sites used in the composition of identity.

These community-level narratives, laid bare by the presentation of these local sites of history and museums (often run and/or organised by former combatants), project reasons for the origins of the conflict and its history. Community discourses, and narratives that often differ radically to official versions of the past, provide members of the group with a coherent narrative, which are integral to the group's self-portrayal. Interpretations of the past, albeit sometimes through skewed accounts, provide trappings to remember and to produce specific understandings of the group.

They also provide one mechanism for such interpretations to be passed on to the next generation. There is continual competition for the ownership of the past, between groupings associated with the UDA and UVF, and in particular their version of history and roles played by particular organisations in defining it. This struggle to impose narratives and understandings of 'history' is, of course, also writ large between unionist/loyalist and nationalist/republican sections of Northern Irish society. Hence, for loyalists, collective memory remains an important instrument in constructing political meaning and directions and how such stories fit into much grander overarching narratives.

Loyalism's use of memory narratives

Loyalism constantly reproduces its own history through formal and informal social contact, everyday conversations, other forms of interaction such as meetings, correspondence, songs, community newsletters, prose, set-piece speeches, forms of popular cultures and so on. While not monocausal or uniform constructs, the broad senses of belonging, common political desires and the emotional attachment to this self-identification are clear. This is bonded by a narrative endorsing and bolstering what is seen as the distinctive cultural and political history of loyalism.

The loyalist narrative emphasises, and in turn is reinforced by, notions of 'us' and 'them', arrived at by interpreting events through a closed narrative which offers only a selective and extremely limited interpretation of the past. It presents the Others as the prime movers of the conflict and the major causes of its protraction. As such, this is typical of other conflict narratives found elsewhere in constructing the idea of a different and menacing Other (Bell, 2003; Edkins, 2003). The greater the perceived or real threat from the Other, the starker the contrast is. In the case of loyalists in Northern Ireland, all republicans, nationalists (and therefore most Catholics) were rapidly seen as part of the dangerous Other.

Within the history of the Northern Ireland state, collective memories were invoked to categorise certain groups as disloyal and untrustworthy. As a result, they were excluded from the dominant political culture and social structure of the state (Kearney, 1997; White, 1991). Alongside this went a host of negative stereotypes applied across all societal levels to describe the Catholic/nationalist/ republican community. These were used to reinforce senses of inclusion and exclusion, applied to all those seen to be outside the social and moral boundaries of the unionist community.

These patterns of difference and construction of the Other were intensified during the Troubles and the cultures of conflict that emerged. More often than not, this manifested as sectarian difference, amplified through intense social division, segregation and protracted exposure to violence, whether directly or indirectly experienced. For some, the resulting negative characterisation of the Other intensified to the point they were seen as undeserving of any level of political empathy or human sympathy. With a minority of individuals, the feeling of hostility aroused towards the Other is so intense as to legitimise a structured violent riposte through paramilitary groups.

Part of the dynamic behind the growth of loyalist paramilitary membership during the Troubles rested on the ability to tap into existing collective memory, especially those narratives involving a community under siege and the need for it to be defended. As shown elsewhere (Ferguson and McAuley, 2016), it should also be remembered that it was the strength and prominence of existing collective memories which, in part at least, provided the motivation for many young Protestants to join armed groups.

Beyond the initial period, decisions to become involved in loyalist paramilitary activity continued to be driven by the loyalist interpretation and use of collective memory. This saw a continued emphasis on the Other as capable of, and sometimes engaged in, appalling acts of violence, while confirming the in-group's status as victims. In such circumstances, the life of a member of the in-group is often seen as being of higher worth than that of a member of the Other. The position was buttressed the reproduction of self-generated myths within each community, which set personal experiences within a collective identity drawing on the strength of collective memory (Misztal, 2003; Olick, 2007).

In Northern Ireland, the identities and cultures of the Protestant/unionist/loyalist and Catholic/nationalist/republican blocs are positioned in direct opposition (Nic Craith, 2002). Both communities rely heavily on identifiable narratives and the intensity of collective memory to strengthen solidarity and assist incorporation within the in-group. These embedded narratives have altered very little with the political settlement; rather, they have been adapted to fit changing historical circumstances. Loyalist interpretations of the past are deeply located within these communal perceptions. They continue to be reproduced on a daily basis, both formally and informally, through narratives, commemorations and other interactions. Take the following:

> we must not be deterred from our task in hand, and in the immortal memory of those who gave their lives for the future of this land, we must forge ahead, never forgetting those who were lost, those who passed whilst incarcerated, and those who fell in more recent years. ...
>
> Never forget, our Cause is just, and as long as one of us remains, it will be maintained. ... On this day, we salute those who gave their all in the Service of Ulster, and to the families who day and daily, mourn their loss. (*Purple Standard*, n.d.)

The loyalist narrative developed in ways that claim legitimacy from the past to explain everyday life. Experiences are placed into the larger discursive frames outlined above to provide the context for explaining and understanding such events (Brockmeier, 2002; Bruner, 1990). Here, the previously mentioned themes of defence, sacrifice and anguish are used as organisational features across the loyalist narratives to explain and account for day-to-day encounters. These bond loyalists together, rallying support for political positions and events. It is the loyalist interpretations and understandings of these past events and circumstances that give direction to political movements and organisation in the present. The ability to highlight continuities with what has gone makes direct appeals to contemporary loyalists. Moreover, the centrality of shared mutual cultural understanding is core in maintaining the imagined community of loyalism. Collective memories provide the cultural means through which members not only view their past but also identify the social and political dynamics of today, and steer the group towards an understood collective future. This involves the entire range of social processes of remembering (and forgetting) that inform loyalist viewpoints.

Conclusions

Collective memory retains a place as a central component in constructing senses of loyalist identity and belonging. Loyalists remember their past in particular ways. Included in this are the formation of specific symbolism and cultural products, rituals, artefacts, commemorations, memorials and murals referred to in this chapter. Participation in the making of collective memory is part of the everyday for loyalists. It reinforces beliefs and attitudes and those senses of belonging, which are at the core of the divisions in Northern Irish society.

There are further considerations as to how collective memory is used to construct and designate those who self-identify as loyalists. Particularly important is how they understand the past from the perspective of the present and how the present guides understandings of the past. Collective memory is drawn upon directly to help individuals conceptualise and contextualise the past. Importantly, memory is used to mobilise politics in the present.

Loyalist collective memory is socially negotiated to determine what can be said about the past and who can legitimately be seen to say it. Further, only certain groups are determined to have an authentic role in reproducing the past. Moreover, this often determines what may qualify as truth in ongoing negotiations between competing societal versions of the past. For many loyalists, a conflict culture continues, and while experiences related to violence have entered the collective memory, these are perpetuated by a cultural memory war over the ownership of the past.

References

Assmann, A. and Shortt, L. (2012) 'Memory and political change: introduction', in A. Assmann and L. Shortt (eds), *Memory and Political Change*, pp. 1–16. Basingstoke: Palgrave Macmillan.
Bar-Tal, D. (2000) 'From intractable conflict through conflict resolution to reconciliation: psychological analysis', *Political Psychology*, 21 (2): 351–65.
Bar-Tal, D. (2002) 'Collective memory of physical violence: its contribution to the culture of violence', in E. Cairns and M. D. Roe (eds), *The Role of Memory in Ethnic Conflict*, pp. 77–93. Basingstoke: Palgrave Macmillan.
Bar-Tal, D. (2013) *Intractable Conflicts: Socio-psychological Foundations and Dynamics*. Cambridge: Cambridge University Press.
Bell, D. S. (2003) 'Mythscapes: memory, mythology, and national identity', *British Journal of Sociology*, 54 (1): 63–81.
Brockmeier, J. (2002) 'Remembering and forgetting: narrative as cultural memory', *Culture and Psychology*, 8 (1), 15–43.
Bruner, J. (1990) *Acts of Meaning*. Cambridge, MA: Harvard University Press.
Cairns, E. and Roe, M. D. (2002) *The Role of Memory in Ethnic Conflict*. Basingstoke: Palgrave Macmillan.
Cash, J. D. (1998) 'The dilemmas of political transformation in Northern Ireland', *Pacifica Review: Peace, Security and Global Change*, 10 (3): 227–34.
Connerton, P. (1989) *How Societies Remember*. Cambridge: Cambridge University Press.
Darby, J. and Mac Ginty, R. (eds) (2000) *The Management of Peace Processes*. London: Macmillan.
De Cillia, R., Reisigl, M. and Wodak, R. (1999) 'The discursive construction of national identities', *Discourse and Society*, 10 (2): 149–73.
Edkins, J. (2003) *Trauma and the Memory of Politics*. Cambridge: Cambridge University Press.
CommunityNI (2020) 'Ex-Prisoners Interpretive Centre'. Available at: www.communityni.org/organisation/ex-prisoners-interpretative-centre-0 (accessed 27 July 2022).
Epstein, J. (2001) 'Remember to forget: the problem of traumatic cultural memory', in J. Epstein and L. H. Lefkovitz (eds), *Shaping Losses: Cultural*

Memory and the Holocaust, pp. 186–204. Chicago, IL: University of Illinois.

Evershed, J. (2018) *Ghosts of the Somme: Commemoration and Culture War in Northern Ireland*. Notre Dame, IN: University of Notre Dame Press.

Ferguson, N. and Cairns, E. (1996) 'Political violence and moral maturity in Northern Ireland', *Political Psychology*, 17 (4): 713–25.

Ferguson, N. and McAuley, J. W. (2016) '"Us" and "them": Ulster loyalist perspectives on the IRA and Irish republicanism', *Terrorism and Political Violence*, 28 (3): 561–75.

Graham, B. and Shirlow, P. (2002) 'The Battle of the Somme in Ulster memory and identity', *Political Geography*, 21 (7): 881–904.

Grayson, R. S. (2010) *Belfast Boys: How Unionists and Nationalists Fought and Died Together in the First World War*. London: Bloomsbury Publishing.

Hirsch, H. (1995) *Genocide and the Politics of Memory: Studying Death to Preserve Life*. Chapel Hill, NC: University of North Carolina Press.

Hunter, J. A., Stringer, M. and Watson, R. P. (1991) 'Intergroup violence and intergroup attributions', *British Journal of Social Psychology*, 30 (3): 261–66.

Kearney, R. (1997) *Postnationalist Ireland*. London: Routledge.

Klandennans, B. (1998) 'The formation and mobilisation of consensus', in B. Klandennans, H. Kriesi and S. Tarrow (eds) *From Structure to Action: Comparing Social Movement Research across Cultures*, pp. 173–96. Greenwich: JAI Press.

Lambert, A. J., Scherer, L. N., Rogers, C. and Jacoby, L. (2009) 'How does collective memory create a sense of the collective?', in P. Boyer and J. V. Wertsch (eds) *Memory in Mind and Culture*, pp. 194–222. Cambridge: Cambridge University Press.

McAuley, J. W. (2010) *Ulster's Last Stand? Reconstructing Unionism after the Peace Process*. Dublin: Irish Academic Press.

McAuley, J. W. (2016) *Very British Rebels? The Culture and Politics of Ulster Loyalism*. London: Bloomsbury.

McGaughey, J. G. V. (2012) *Ulster's Men: Protestant Unionist Masculinities and Militarization in the North of Ireland, 1912–1923*. Montreal: McGill-Queen's University Press.

Misztal, B. (2003) *Theories of Social Remembering*. Maidenhead: Open University Press.

Nic Craith, M. (2002) *Plural Identities – Singular Narratives: The Case of Northern Ireland*. New York, NY, and Oxford: Berghahn Books.

Officer, D. (2001) '"For God and for Ulster": the Ulsterman on the Somme', in I. McBride (ed.) *History and Memory in Modern Ireland*, pp. 160–83. Cambridge: Cambridge University Press.

Officer, D. and Walker, G. (2003) 'Protestant Ulster: ethno-history, memory and contemporary prospects', *National Identities*, 2 (3): 293–307.

Olick, J. K. (2007) *The Politics of Regret: On Collective Memory and Historical Responsibility*. London: Routledge.

Olick, J. K. (2008) '"Collective memory": a memoir and prospect', *Memory Studies*, 1: 23–29.

Olick, J. K. and Levy, D. (1997) 'Collective memory and cultural constraint: Holocaust myth and rationality in German politics', *American Sociological Review*, 62 (6): 921–36.

Olick, J. K., Vinitzky-Seroussi, V. and Levy, D. (2011) *The Collective Memory Reader*. Oxford: Oxford University Press.

Prager, J. (1998) *Presenting the Past: Sociology and the Psychoanalysis of Misremembering*. Cambridge MA: Harvard University Press.

Purple Standard (2018) 'Oration delivered at 2nd Battalion Memorial Parade', Issue 80 (8 September).

Purple Standard (n.d. [*c*.2018]) 'Oration delivered at Mount Vernon, 11 November 2018', Issue 81.

Reed, R. (2015) *Paramilitary Loyalism: Identity and Change*. Manchester: Manchester University Press.

Schwartz, B. (1982) 'The social context of commemoration: a study in collective memory', *Social Forces*, 61: 375–402.

Smithey, L. A. (2011) *Unionists, Loyalists, and Conflict Transformation in Northern Ireland*. Oxford: Oxford University Press.

Switzer, C. (2007) *Unionists and Great War Commemoration in the North of Ireland 1914–1939*. Dublin: Irish Academic Press.

Switzer, C. (2013) *Ulster, Ireland and the Somme: War Memorials and Battlefield Pilgrimages*. Dublin: The History Press Ireland.

Unionist Voice (n.d.) 'Victims mural oration – delivered on Remembrance Sunday', 3: 1–20.

Vansina, J. M. (1985) *Oral Tradition as History*. Madison, WI: University of Wisconsin Press.

Viggiani, E. (2014) *Talking Stones: The Politics of Memorialization in Post-Conflict Northern Ireland*. New York, NY, and Oxford: Berghahn Books.

Weedon, C. and Jordan, G. (2012) 'Collective memory: theory and politics', *Social Semiotics*, 22 (2): 143–53.

White, R. (1991) 'Social and role identities and political violence: identity as a window on violence in Northern Ireland', in R. D. Ashmore, L. Jussim and D. Wilder (eds), *Social Identity, Intergroup Conflict, and Conflict Resolution*, pp. 159–83. Oxford: Oxford University Press.

8

'Remember the women': memory-making within loyalism

Lisa Faulkner-Byrne, John Bell and Philip McCready

Since the Good Friday Agreement, community development and peacebuilding efforts have focused on the men in our area. The fact is that women were never really part of the problem here, so they are not seen as part of the solution.

(Contributor to focus group)

In the post-Good Friday Agreement landscape of Northern Ireland, the marginalisation of women has not gone undocumented. Although women have made some gains in representation in formal politics, they are largely excluded from community development and their contribution to building relations within and between communities is often overlooked and undervalued (Pierson, 2019; Pierson and Radford, 2016). Gender parity at a regional political level has been difficult to achieve in Northern Ireland; likewise, gender parity has also been elusive in memory work.

Over twenty years of the peace process and building peace in Northern Ireland has not translated into gender equality in terms of which stories are told, which voices are heard and how the past is understood. Taking on board the approach of memory studies – that our pasts shape us, but we also shape the ways in which our past contributes to our present and future – exploring the participation of women within memory politics becomes even more salient.

Focusing on the experiences of a small cohort of women from loyalist communities across Northern Ireland, many of which were disproportionately affected by the 'Troubles', this chapter will explore the role of these women in memory work linked to tourism and heritage in their local neighbourhoods, and their opportunities to shape, inform and influence the dominant narratives emerging from, and about, the communities in which they live and 'belong' to. Although they are actively involved in many aspects of community life, it is apparent that the contemporary application of remembering is something which these women feel they are largely excluded from. Based on emergent findings from a series of fifteen facilitated workshops, as well as ten focus groups, thirty women from four loyalist communities in Northern Ireland identify the barriers and challenges pertaining to their participation in memory work, as well as conflict transformation and peacebuilding more broadly. Within each geographical location, peace walls, paramilitarism, legacy issues and multiple levels of deprivation prevail. While we do not suggest that the exclusion of women is endemic across loyalism, our opening quote does, however, demonstrate that within some constituencies, women's displacement throughout the 'Troubles' has persisted post-1998 with impacts on representation, narrative and power dynamics at the grassroots level.

Finally, this chapter will reflect on what we can draw from this gender dynamic when approaching the area of loyalism in memory politics and practice, as well as the implications for women's participation in tourism and heritage, and the peacebuilding space more broadly in those communities where they are underrepresented.

(Wo)men within Ulster loyalism

Prior to documenting the experiences of women participants within some loyalist communities across Northern Ireland, it is imperative to explore the context in which this analysis takes place. Ulster loyalism as an ideology itself has often been portrayed in a simplistic and reductionist manner as a pro-state, reactionary and conservative 'settler nationalism' with almost pathologically sectarian traits (Coogan, 2002 [1995]; Sluka, 2000).

The demonisation of Ulster loyalism, both within academic and media portrayals (Parkinson, 1998), has often been framed around the archetype of the aggressive, sectarian and male paramilitary 'gangster' figure (such as the Ulster Defence Association's (UDA) Jonny 'Mad Dog' Adair or the Ulster Volunteer Force (UVF)/Loyalist Volunteer Force's Billy 'King Rat' Wright), which overlooks the complexity and diversity within Ulster unionism and loyalism (including the voices of men *or* women as paramilitaries, peacemakers or simply just as 'ordinary civilians'; see Coulter, 1994). This has left the appellation of 'loyalist' as one which is often used pejoratively to denigrate a Protestant 'underclass' as paramilitary sympathisers (Greer, 2015) or uneducated 'fleggers' mocked for their working-class accents (Nolan *et al.*, 2014), who suffer from a 'false consciousness' which has been foisted upon them by a now disinterested British state (McAuley, 2016).

Indeed, although Ulster loyalism is often simplistically framed as a manifestation of the desire among many working-class Northern Ireland Protestants to maintain Northern Ireland's place within the United Kingdom (by using political violence if necessary), as Jennifer Todd (1987) suggests, the loyalty of Ulster Protestants to the rest of the UK has often been conditional. There is an element within Ulster loyalism which prioritises the 'imagined community' of the six counties of Northern Ireland ('Ulster') over and above allegiance to the UK (Todd, 1987). Yet, Ulster loyalism must be considered to consist of a multitude of identities delineated by class, locality, religious affiliation and socio-economic status, which sit within this rather broad constitutional commitment to defend either Northern Ireland as an ontological entity or the continuing political link with the rest of the UK (McCready, 2016).

Fortunately, more recent work on Ulster unionism and loyalism has begun to tease out some of these complexities (see McAuley, 2010, 2016; McAuley and Spencer, 2011; Reed, 2015; Shirlow, 2012; Spencer, 2008, 2012; Tonge *et al.*, 2014). Yet, what remains striking about most (re)presentations of Ulster loyalism is the absence of the voices of women. Most studies tend to focus upon the experience and recollections of predominantly male members of loyalist paramilitaries (Bruce, 1992; Crawford, 2003; Edwards, 2017; Mulvenna, 2016; Taylor, 2000; Wood, 2006) and little attention has been paid to the role of loyalist women either during the conflict or within the peace process (although there are a small number of notable exceptions; see McEvoy, 2009; Ward, 2006).

The marginalisation of the voices of loyalist women in textual documentations of the conflict is striking. This to some extent reflects the marginalisation of women within Ulster loyalist politics and paramilitarism during the conflict (perhaps best highlighted by the Latin motto of the youth wing of the UDA, the Ulster Young Militants, of *terrae filius*, which roughly translates as 'Son of the Land'). While Irish republicanism tended to extol the virtues of its female members and activists (generally for the purposes of international propaganda; see English, 2003), a socially (and religiously) conservative and male-dominated Ulster unionist parental culture has generally sought to present Protestant women's experience of the conflict as largely one of victimhood (McDowell, 2008).

Unionist and loyalist women are all too often regarded as *only* the sisters, wives, mothers and daughters of male victims or perpetrators of violence, and are rarely seen as actively participating in politics, community activism, paramilitarism or peacebuilding themselves (Brown, 2014). As McEvoy (2009) notes, this ignores the role of some loyalist women as active members of paramilitary groups such as the UDA and the UVF (albeit they were very few in number and often operating in supporting and auxiliary roles for male members). It also fails to acknowledge the much more substantial role played by women within the community and voluntary sector in grassroots loyalist communities (Ward, 2006), some of whom successfully made the transition into the political arena (such as Dawn Purvis, the former leader of the Progressive Unionist Party).

But if the active role of loyalist women in politics or paramilitarism tends to have thus far been underexplored, the more passive figure of the *mater dolorosa* has a relatively long lineage within symbolic representations of 'Ulster' and 'her' political conflict with Irish republicanism. Some of the most well-known Ulster loyalist propaganda symbols from the early twentieth century relied upon the socially constructed and gendered division of labour between male 'just warriors' who were there to defend their 'beautiful [female] souls' (Elshtain, 1982). The nation ('Ulster' or 'Britannia') itself was often represented in postcard and mural format as a 'vulnerable' and 'defenceless' woman who required 'her' men to protect her from Irish republican aggression (see Wood, 2003: 21, 27).

Yet, symbolic representations of womanhood within Ulster loyalism tend to have been ignored. Rolston's (2018) work on the content of murals is instructive in this regard. He found that in terms of both Irish republican and Ulster loyalist political murals, women were significantly underrepresented, appearing in only 325 out of 2,398 documented political murals across Northern Ireland (13.5 per cent). Yet, in 'republican murals, there were 272 which represented women out of a total of 1,320, that is, 21 per cent. As for loyalist murals, a mere 53 had representations of women out of a total of 1,078, that is, 0.5 per cent' (Rolston, 2018: 371). Most of these representations of women were related to the British royal family, Ulster-Scots culture or famous Ulster Protestant women. Rolston notes that of two hundred murals focusing upon Ulster loyalist politics or paramilitarism, only one contained a female figure. He concludes that, 'in relation to loyalist murals, that absence comes close to being tantamount to silence' (Rolston, 2018: 387).

The visual absence of women in Ulster loyalist commemorative murals is reflected in the absence of women in the expression of conflict memory in loyalist community contexts. Although the peace process was supposed to end an era of male-dominated violence and open up a space for other voices to emerge (including those of women), in reality the burgeoning field of community development remains overwhelmingly male – with former male members of loyalist paramilitaries continuing to play prominent roles in the contemporary period, albeit in a new, peaceful and often positive form (mainly via their work in ex-prisoner support organisations). But given the continuing numeric dominance of men in the field, this research has attempted to provide a voice to those women who feel that more could be done to include their stories and experiences within memory work in some loyalist communities across Northern Ireland.

Pierre Bourdieu, power and the *habitus*

The theoretical underpinning for this chapter is based upon the work of French sociologist Pierre Bourdieu. Although he was not the first to develop the concept of the *habitus*, Bourdieu's work is perhaps the best known in terms of attempts to overcome the challenges inherent in objectivism and subjectivism. Bourdieu described the *habitus* as the relationship between the individual and society in which *habitus* is a 'system of durable, transposable dispositions, structured structures predisposed to function as structuring structures' (Bourdieu, 1990: 53). That is to say that, rather as the subjectivists would have it, whereby society is a series of interactions between individuals, the social elements of our world direct, constrain and enable us in what we do and how we act.

However, the concept of *habitus* also suggests that while our individual choices are bounded by power relations and social structures, this is not to the extent that we lose our capacity to have an impact on our social environment. While we are influenced and at times constrained by our social environment, we also have scope to influence it as active agents (Bourdieu, 1984; Collet, 2009).

The significance of Bourdieu's work is in explaining how structural inequalities in relationships persist in society, particularly between members of different groups (or classes), wherein the dominated internalise the 'taken-for-granted' values or attitudes (*doxa*) promoted by the dominating classes (Bourdieu, 1984). In their study of the reproduction of class privilege through educational structures, Bourdieu and Passeron (2000 [1977]) argued that while the education system in France presented itself as 'neutral' and the system was meant to be equally 'open to all', in reality those students from more privileged social and economic backgrounds, who possessed superior levels of linguistic and cultural capital, were not only more likely to attend college in the first place but were also more likely to gain higher levels of qualifications in 'elite' subjects, which in turn meant that they were rewarded with the best jobs. Yet the facade of 'disinterest' and 'merit' was maintained by the education authorities, which led to students from working-class backgrounds internalising these objective outcomes and structures through their subjective actions, such as choosing not to go to college or choosing more vocational courses as college or science were 'not for the likes of us'.

In the context of the research underpinning this chapter, *habitus* is a useful concept for exploration as structural inequalities in Northern Ireland have relegated the experiences of (loyalist) women to the margins; but many loyalist women have also internalised these experiences, which have become the 'norm', and they therefore have avoided certain spaces (such as the politics of memory and commemoration) because they feel that these spaces remain male-dominated and thus their voices will remain unheard: 'they are not for the likes of us.'

Bourdieu uses a sporting analogy to describe social actors having a 'sense of the game', which refers to a sense of one's relations with other individuals and what those individuals will regard as tolerable, given certain broadly shared out but not definitive understandings

(King, 2000: 420). *Habitus* is therefore a useful tool in examining how agents respond to change, and individuals with the same background might respond differently to the same event; in addition, 'depending on their habitus, some agents promote transformation of the social structure, while others oppose it' (Collet, 2009: 430).

Gender and memory in Northern Ireland

In exploring memory work in Northern Ireland, it is vital to consider how gendered and conservative discourse has shaped the conflict. According to Galligan and Knight (2011), the ethnically divided society in Northern Ireland has been injected with gender constructions of Catholic/nationalism and Protestant/unionism. For unionism and loyalism, conservatism within Protestantism shaped the construction of gender roles within the family, community and public life. Men have traditionally dominated the political sphere and have been very much the voice of unionist and loyalist communities throughout the 'Troubles' and extending into the post-1998 period (Braniff and Whiting, 2016).

Approaches to understanding women's experiences of conflict and peace have made a significant contribution internationally, and locally. Feminist perspectives have helped to challenge the predominant patriarchal approach to memory studies. As this book details, memory work in Northern Ireland relates closely to the politics and policies about the past. But engaging with the past is inherently gendered. Legacy, paramilitarism and processes around demobilisation and reintegration have all been focused on the male experience.

The challenge for memory work within loyalist, working-class and urban communities is that the first- and second-wave feminist approaches have yet to be realised. Women have not been added to the narrative. Gender is individual identity, but it can also be understood as having an impact on shaping meaning, concept and political practice. The nature of power remains a key focus of analysis.

Critical feminist perspectives speak directly to the potential for inclusivity and pluralism rather than selectivity and silencing in memory work in societies emerging from conflict. Within this literature, the urgency to foreground rather than incorporate the experiences of women into narratives and existing structures is paramount. In challenging the liberal peace feminist perspective – add women and stir – a more critical approach prompts for more than weaving women into the patriarchal status quo. Within loyalist narratives about the past, critical feminist approaches have certainly proven a step too far, as this chapter goes on to elucidate.

Ashe's (2012) seminal study exploring radical constructivism with regard to gender, femininity and ethno-nationalism reveals that the intersectional ways in which women participate in ethno-nationalist politics in Northern Ireland can impact on power, position and identities within communities. What Ashe does is centre attention on the aspects of women's lives that shape their participation in politics, memory work and culture: the family, the sense of belonging and agency within a community.

This is vital, as it nuances the dominant discussions within conflict, peace and memory studies from the head-counting it is so often focused upon (number of women signing agreements, number of women elected). Engaging with the past, remembrance and commemoration is a highly gendered process (McDowell, 2008). The way in which the past is represented, explored and symbolised on the muralled walls, remembrance gardens and in commemorative events is dominated by masculine expressions of conflict. Unsurprisingly, within loyalism, where women's voice and role were relegated throughout the 'Troubles,' few spaces to participate in memory processes emerged after the ceasefires.

Curation and commemoration

Communities construct and commemorate history through the ways in which they remember the past (Jovchelovitch, 2012). The narrative that develops from this constructed history, as displayed through the community space, is critical to an individual's and a community's sense of self and identity. The role of non-traditional museum spaces is significant within this context. As Jovchelovitch (2012: 444) notes: 'There is a struggle of sorts between formal and lay histories, which far from being a negative conflict is a necessary reminder of the faulty line that entangles the historical record to narrative, memory and social representations.'

Smithey (2011: 169–75) highlighted five functions of Protestant, unionist, loyalist heritage spaces: celebration, remembrance, education, unity and community relations (see also Bigand, 2018: 71). As Bigand (2018: 71) discusses, it is critical that in commemorating historic events, undue weight is not given to any of the specific functions outlined by Smithey (2011). With regard to community-based conflict commemorations, it is contended that murals, artefacts and conflict commemorations have an important role to play in balancing the social, cultural and educative functions with the more astringent visuals on display.

It is striking how the representation of conflict within loyalist communities denotes a conscious attempt to reflect and remember historic events while also serving to unconsciously reflect contemporary challenges facing loyalism. The expression of culture continues to be a highly contentious macro- and micro-level issue in Northern Ireland. Community-based commemorations aim to reflect loyalist culture from 1969 to 1998 as an adjunct to presenting a narrative on the political developments during that period. The authors were struck that the artefacts displayed in community-based museum spaces, ranging from examples (replicas) of decommissioned weapons to wallets and belts made by incarcerated loyalist prisoners, not only relativise the narrative presented by the museum but also humanise the conflict and challenges faced, not only by prisoners but the wider loyalist community as well. As Doss (2010: 71) noted in relation to memorials, physical objects are important, as they 'evoke memories, sustain thoughts, constitute political conditions and conjure states of being'.

But there is a jarring juxtaposition in the compilation and presentation of artefacts within community-based museum spaces. Given the brutal nature of the images depicted and the narrative of conflict that resonates throughout community museums, it can be confrontational to see weapons and other militaristic objects on display. One museum curator was both bullish and honest in stating in conversation with the authors: 'We are here to tell our truth and the reality was that these items were brought to the streets.'

The underlying argument here is that this particular community-based museum is driven by an objective to tell the narrative of the conflict from the loyalist (UDA) perspective, and the use of militaristic artefacts creates a visceral and emotional tourism experience. As

Bigand (see also Brown, 2008) noted, messages in community-based museums are often

> didactic or moralistic narrative that left little room for debate or alternative interpretation; of a central message articulated around ideas of victimhood, defensiveness or historical misrepresentation; of linear and ordered narratives which left aside difficult questions and highlighted the continuity between past and present; and of a lack of reflective criticism. (Bigand, 2018: 69)

It can also be challenging for visitors to encounter personal items such as wallets and music boxes produced by prisoners, as well as propaganda items such as posters and stickers that are often intended to be humorous but contrast with images of conflict around them. The day-to-day artefacts offer an important insight and social context to the conflict narrative. They also illustrate the role played by women during the conflict as many of the items on display were produced by, or for, wives and female family members of loyalist prisoners. Such artefacts are critical in a museum space that is seeking to evolve into a more gender-balanced narrative of the conflict, given that the prevailing view of the conflict memory within communities could be said to be androcentric with the continued domination of conflict commemorative displays by male figures.

While museum spaces can afford loyalists the opportunity and space to reflect a narrative, it is argued that memory in standalone community-based museum settings can become nostalgia rather than narrative memory. As Smithey (2011: 169) contends: 'Without narratives that provide historical perspective and tie together religious beliefs, political ideologies, and cultural practices, many Protestants can feel alienated and even intimidated, especially as issues of culture and identity have become central in the outworking of the political peace process.' What space then for women within these community processes of memory-making within loyalism?

Memory-making within loyalism – the role of women

Peace walls, paramilitarism and multiple levels of deprivation have characterised the environment and lived experiences of loyalist women both before and after the political peace process. During our focus group sessions, women explained that it was their activities, organising and actions which 'held the family and community together during the darkest days of the Troubles'. It was and remains women who must overcome challenges, at times collaborating with other women irrespective of their religious affiliation, to deal with issues which affect them, their families and community. These issues range from initiating campaigns for better housing or facilities, to ensuring that their sons, in particular, do not engage with paramilitaries or 'fall prey' to them.

Women in these loyalist communities also spoke about times when they were 'in the thick of it', taking part in protests or 'heated' exchanges with the police, or 'turning a blind eye' to the actions of 'the men' within the community. Some also revealed that they had a more active role in the conflict, such as through their service in the armed forces, while others discussed their long-standing engagement with local unionist political parties. Motivated by a desire to improve their lives and the lives of those around them, women have, and indeed remain, active participants in community life.

In spite of this, however, they are cynical as to how their past will contribute to the present and future in Northern Ireland, given that the lack of opportunity for them to participate in loyalist memory work has left a distinct void in Northern Ireland's memory-space. Such sentiments are best captured in the following statements, from focus group participants:

> When it comes to heritage and culture, you would think that women didn't exist. We were there during the Ulster Workers Strike, we have seen many riots, and we have experienced the pain of conflict, but it would seem that our part in history is not as valid as the men's.

> I was in the armed forces, along with other women in my area. We faced the danger; our work shaped every aspect of our lives, and it's not captured anywhere. Rather, I look at the faces of masked men on the gable wall, the non-state actors, who we are forced to remember, whether we like it or not.

> I have been to a number of discussions focused on our conflict and the transformation since 1998, and I've often heard international students and visitors asking, where are the women, what is their story? I'm not saying that women don't get to speak, but there is a greater demand for stories about the actors of conflict and there are definitely more opportunities for men to tell their stories.

Our focus groups revealed several important factors identified by women that link to their lack of empowerment and continued exclusion. While some attributed this to what were defined as the 'distinct factors in women's lives' such as caring responsibilities, others felt that there was a lack of confidence and capacity, and more importantly, a lack of safe space for them to engage in memory-making and conflict transformation processes. In fact, there was a consensus among the women that certain aspects of loyalism were perceived or stereotyped as being aggressive, male-dominated and 'sectarian', which leaves women 'unsure as to where they fit into the narrative'.

With that in mind, women expressed their concerns that their participation may be viewed as merely the supporting act to the narratives of men who tend to take centre stage in the post-conflict arena:

> Over the years, I have found myself saying, 'I'm a loyalist, but I'm not sectarian'. I really feel that there has been a campaign to discredit my community in any way; whereas the republican narrative has been presented as something more valid, it has been romanticised, whereas we are demonised. That makes me a bit wary of leaving myself open to insult and ridicule, women who speak out in loyalist communities are often seen as radical.

> I have numerous examples where women have worked at the peace line to diffuse tensions and stop young people rioting. This to me is conflict transformation at its best. But you will rarely hear about this. I also know of women who have rioted and protested themselves, but the women's groups and community groups wouldn't focus on these things, they would rather get women socialising, particularly across the communities [Protestant/Catholic].

> Even the title of this discussion, 'societies shaped by conflict', makes me think that the focus will be on those who took part in the Troubles [non-state actors]. Funders, visitors, whoever it may be, are only concerned with talking to men about their journeys and influence on politics here. And when us women are asked to take part in discussions, we are often an afterthought or it's merely tokenistic.

Although it was agreed that men (including those with a direct link to the 'conflict of the past' and those with political influence), have played a positive role in community development, many assumed that they would continue to occupy the space and 'write the script' for loyalist memory work. To that end, women felt that funders, academics and/or government departments who are concerned with building peace in Northern Ireland by discerning which stories are told and how the past is understood, are more likely to engage with those males with whom they have already established relationships.

As a consequence of their general exclusion from loyalist memory work to date, some women also felt that while they have a story to tell, they neither have the confidence or capacity to do so, particularly if this involved cross-community engagement:

> I've taken part in cross-community programmes over the years. They are always the same. Republican women use this type of engagement to point the finger of blame at loyalists. They [republicans] have positioned themselves as victims, and we [loyalists] as the perpetrators. The women [republican] are always very confident and articulate about Irish history, whereas our women [loyalists] are not. I think there needs to be a lot of capacity-building within loyalism first, especially as this has been directed at men for so long.

Which stories are told and how the past is understood was viewed by many as a key factor towards improving community relations. Nonetheless, some were less convinced as to how their engagement in community processes of memory-making would achieve real, tangible benefits for them and their communities. Some, therefore, acknowledged that communities such as theirs have not reaped the dividends of peace, particularly in relation to what was described as 'the influx of tourists in recent times'. While some were keen to embrace the opportunity for local community-led tourist initiatives to attract visitors to their area, and ultimately generate much-needed investment and employment opportunities, others were more reluctant to expose their community to outsiders as though they were in 'a real-life museum'. In other words, there was an assumption that their lives would become 'entertainment' for those with no real desire to affect change in what were described as 'under-funded' and 'neglected' communities.

On that basis, these women felt that the current and future prospects of their community would be best served by focusing on the social ills that continue to blight their areas, many of which were disproportionately affected by the 'Troubles'. The following comments were typical:

> I can't see how bringing tourists up to my area would work. What would they be visiting? What do tourists want from a visit to Northern Ireland? And we need to ask ourselves, what would we get out of it? I think I would rather focus on real issues like drugs, poverty and education. I really don't see the benefit of looking back.

> I would hate for our area to become like those parts of Belfast where black taxis are parked along the street and hordes of tourists are gaping in your window at you. They don't seem to hang about and spend money, as far as I have seen, they get out, look around, take a few photos and hop back into the taxi. That's ticked their box for 'experiencing local life'.

While women in these working-class, loyalist communities feel that there are barriers to their participation in community-led tourism, such as power dynamics, many were also keen to note that there has been no overwhelming desire from significant numbers of women themselves to be front and centre. For some, this was due to the fact that the 'past is still very much the present', whereas others felt that heritage and memory work can evoke negative connotations, which may cause hurt and distress for others with diametrically opposing narratives. Such sentiments are succinctly captured in the following statements:

> I think memory and heritage work is still very raw here. I would be mindful of how an event in our community or something I would celebrate could be hurtful to others. That's why I would be happy to take part in work which captures women's lives in the past, the factories, holding the family together or even the wee stories about the craic [fun] and humour which makes this place unique. But when it comes to anything overly political, I wouldn't want to take part.

> Our memories aren't the most pleasant in this part of the world. I don't know what I would like to remember or what would be interesting to outsiders.

The first of these comments opens up the potential of using tourism and heritage projects to explore commonalities of experience across the community divide which do not focus solely upon violence and loss. Aside from the potential benefits to cross-community relations generally, such an approach has the potential to include the voices of those women who up until now tend to have been marginalised by the focus on commemorating and curating male-dominated experiences of conflict.

Conclusion

This chapter has drawn out some of the tensions and ambiguities felt by inner-city loyalist women in relation to conflict transformation more generally and memory work in particular. In some senses the female participants of this study have experienced a form of 'double marginalisation' during the peace process – firstly, as loyalists who feel that their community has been denigrated and portrayed internationally as the aggressor in the conflict in Northern Ireland; and secondly, as loyalist women whose voices tend to have been marginalised while men's conflict-related experiences have been prioritised. Yet, while there are structural factors and power relations between men and women which help to explain the domination of the male experience in memory work with regard to conflict-related tourism and heritage, there are also more subtle dynamics at play which have thus far unfortunately relegated the experiences of many of our participants to the margins.

What came across within the research was that there was a lack of confidence and capacity among participants to 'tell their story', whether this be within their own loyalist community (as women) or in a wider engagement process with Irish nationalists (as loyalists). This suggests that capacity-building remains important in equipping participants with the requisite confidence and skills to fully engage in commemorative, cross-community and memory work. But it also suggests, as does Pierre Bourdieu (1984), that structural inequalities can be internalised by underrepresented groups to the extent that they then begin to exclude themselves from opportunities and processes which are 'not for the likes of us'. This is certainly true of many of the women we spoke with, whether they were reluctant to engage in loyalist tourism and heritage initiatives as women given the dominance of the male experience, or whether they were hesitant to engage in cross-community projects given their perception that Catholic and nationalist women would also dominate the conversation.

As Rolston's (2018) work on commemorative murals in Northern Ireland indicates, if local women from loyalist communities cannot see themselves visually represented for the variety of roles that they have played in their community, then it is not surprising that some women within these communities hold back from engaging in processes which they feel will fail to include them on an equal basis (rather than as tokenistic 'add-ons').

While there has been much useful work conducted by progressive elements within loyalism to date within the area of conflict transformation, it is clear that further efforts are required in the field of memory work linked to tourism and heritage to encourage women, such as those who took part in this research, to feel that such thematic areas are, and should be, 'for the likes of us'. Such work is only made weaker by their absence and would be greatly strengthened by their increasing presence.

References

Ashe, F. (2012) 'Gendering war and peace: militarised masculinities in Northern Ireland', *Men and Masculinities*, 15 (3): 230–48.

Bigand, L. (2018) 'Representing loyalist paramilitary heritage in non-museum exhibitions – aims, practices and challenges', in E. Crooke and T. Maguire (eds), *Heritage after Conflict: Northern Ireland*, pp. 66–83. London: Routledge.

Bourdieu, P. (1984) *Homo Academicus*. Stanford, CA: Stanford University Press.

Bourdieu, P. (1990) *The Logic of Practice*. Stanford, CA: Stanford University Press.

Bourdieu, P. and Passeron, J. C. (2000 [1977]) *Reproduction in Education, Society and Culture*, trans. Richard Nice. London: Sage.

Braniff, M. and Whiting, S. (2016) '"There's just no point having a token woman": gender and representation in the Democratic Unionist Party in post-agreement Northern Ireland', *Parliamentary Affairs*, 69 (1): 93–114.

Brown, K. (2008) 'Living with history: conflict, commemoration and exhibitions in Northern Ireland: the case of sectional displays', *Social History in Museums*, 32: 31–37.

Brown, K. (2014) 'Manicured nails but shackled hands? The representation of women in Northern Ireland's post-conflict memory', in S. Buckley-Zistel and S. Schäfer (eds), *Memorials in Times of Transition*, pp. 149–70. Cambridge: Intersentia.

Bruce, S. (1992) *The Red Hand: Protestant Paramilitaries in Northern Ireland*. Oxford: Oxford University Press.

Collet, F. (2009) 'Does habitus matter? A comparative review of Bourdieu's habitus and Simon's bounded rationality with some implications for economic sociology', *Sociological Theory*, 27 (4): 419–34.

Coogan, T. P. (2002 [1995]) *The Troubles: Ireland's Ordeal 1966–1996 and the Search for Peace*. Basingstoke: Palgrave Macmillan.

Coulter, C. (1994) 'The character of unionism', *Irish Political Studies*, 9 (1): 1–24.

Crawford, C. (2003) *Inside the UDA: Volunteers and Violence*. London: Pluto Press.

Doss, E. (2010) *Memorial Mania: Public Feeling in America*. London: University of Chicago Press.

Edwards, A. (2017) *UVF: Behind the Mask*. Newbridge: Merrion Press.

Elshtain, J. B. (1982) 'On beautiful souls, just warriors and feminist consciousness', *Women's Studies International Forum*, 5 (3–4): 341–48.

English, R. (2003) *Armed Struggle: The History of the IRA*. London: MacMillan.

Galligan, Y. and Knight, K. (2011) 'Attitudes towards women in politics: gender, generation and party identification in Ireland', *Parliamentary Affairs*, 64 (4): 585–611.

Greer, J. (2015) 'Typical unionists? The politicians and their people, past and present', in T. P. Burgess and G. Mulvenna (eds), *The Contested Identities of Ulster Protestants*, pp. 39–54. London: Palgrave Macmillan.

Jovchelovitch, S. (2012) 'Narrative, memory and social representations: a conversation between history and social psychology', *Integrative Psychological and Behavioral Science*, 46: 440–56.

King, A. (2000) 'Thinking with Bourdieu against Bourdieu: a "practical" critique of the habitus', *Sociological Theory*, 18 (3): 417–33.

McAuley, J. W. (2010) *Ulster's Last Stand? Reconstructing Unionism after the Peace Process*. Dublin: Irish Academic Press.

McAuley, J. W. (2016) *Very British Rebels? The Culture and Politics of Ulster Loyalism*. London: Bloomsbury.

McAuley, J. W. and Spencer, G. (eds) (2011) *Ulster Loyalism after the Good Friday Agreement: History, Identity and Change*. Basingstoke: Palgrave Macmillan.

McCready, P. (2016) 'Can Restorative Practices Work in a Loyalist Area? A Case Study on Restorative Responses to Community Conflict of a Loyalist Area in South Belfast' (unpublished PhD thesis, Ulster University).

McDowell, S. (2008) 'Commemorating dead "men": gendering the past and present in post-conflict Northern Ireland', *Gender, Place and Culture*, 15 (4): 335–54.

McEvoy, S. (2009) 'Loyalist women paramilitaries in Northern Ireland: beginning a feminist conversation about conflict resolution', *Security Studies*, 18: 262–86.

Mulvenna, G. (2016) *Tartan Gangs and Paramilitaries: The Loyalist Backlash*. Liverpool: Liverpool University Press.

Nolan, P., Bryan, D., Dwyer, C., Hayward, K., Radford, K. and Shirlow, P. (2014) *The Flag Dispute: Anatomy of a Protest*. Belfast: Queens University Belfast.

Parkinson, A. (1998) *Ulster Loyalism and the British Media*. Dublin: Four Courts Press.

Pierson, C. (2019) 'Gendering peace in Northern Ireland: the role of United Nations Security Council Resolution 1325 on women, peace and security', *Capital and Class*, 43 (1): 57–71.

Pierson, C. and Radford, K. (2016) *Peacebuilding and the Women's Sector in Northern Ireland*. Belfast: Institute for Conflict Research.

Reed, R. (2015) *Paramilitary Loyalism: Identity and Change*. Manchester: Manchester University Press.

Rolston, B. (2018) 'Women on the walls: representations of women in political murals in Northern Ireland', *Crime, Media, Culture*, 14 (3): 365–89.

Shirlow, P. (2012) *The End of Ulster Loyalism?* Manchester: Manchester University Press.

Sluka, J. (2000) '"For God and Ulster": the culture of terror and loyalist death squads in Northern Ireland', in J. Sluka (ed.), *Death Squad: The Anthropology of State Terror*. Philadelphia, PA: University of Pennsylvania Press.

Smithey, L. A. (2011) *Unionists, Loyalists, and Conflict Transformation in Northern Ireland*. Oxford: Oxford University Press.

Spencer, G. (2008) *The State of Loyalism in Northern Ireland*. Basingstoke: Palgrave Macmillan.

Spencer, G. (2012) *Protestant Identity and Peace in Northern Ireland*. Basingstoke: Palgrave Macmillan.

Taylor, P. (2000) *Loyalists*. London: Bloomsbury.

Todd, J. (1987) 'Two traditions in unionist political culture', *Irish Political Studies*, 2 (1): 1–26.

Tonge, J., Braniff, M., Hennesey, T., McAuley, J. W. and Whiting, A. S. (2014) *The Democratic Unionist Party: From Protest to Power*. Oxford: Oxford University Press.

Ward, R. (2006) *Women, Unionism and Loyalism in Northern Ireland: From 'Tea-Maker' to Political Actors*. Dublin: Irish Academic Press.

Wood, I. S. (2003) *God, Guns and Ulster: A History of Loyalist Paramilitaries*. London: Caxton.

Wood, I. S. (2006) *Crimes of Loyalty: A History of the UDA*. Edinburgh: Edinburgh University Press.

9

Visual memory at sites of troubles past: participatory and collective memories in Croatia and Argentina

Máire Braniff

On 25 March 1977 the Argentinian journalist Rudolfo Walsh posted the now infamous '*Carta abierta de un escritor a la junta militar*' ('A writer's open letter to the military junta'), soon after which he was shot, killed and disappeared by the dictatorship (Walsh, 1977). Walsh was one of the estimated thirty thousand people disappeared by the dictatorship (1976–83). Twenty years later, judicial investigations into the crimes of the dictatorship commenced and collective memory-making became commonplace. Walsh's friend Jorge González Perrin, an artist, marked the commencement of trials with a collective approach to the memorialisation of Walsh's life. Disappearance has permanency in Argentina; memorialisation is, therefore, naturally linked to materialisation, to a focus on the imagery of those lives taken.

As part of a group, Art Memoria Colectivo, Perrin worked with families and friends of those who had disappeared, including Walsh, to reproduce photographs using a square grid, paint and tiles. Each tile is a mosaic piece of the picture and, once together, they form the photograph, on a large scale (Figure 9.1). This creative process helps people to collectively remember, in a material way, those disappeared individuals. Working against forgetting and towards materialisation and appearance in a visual way, the tiles technique evolved into participatory action. Participation in memory work informs collective understanding about the past, but it is also subject to sociopolitical dynamics (Chandra, 2006). The collective nature of memory-making is widened beyond family and friends. Each year during the Day of Remembrance for Truth and Justice, the Art Memoria Colectivo has participants paint a tile, leading to another

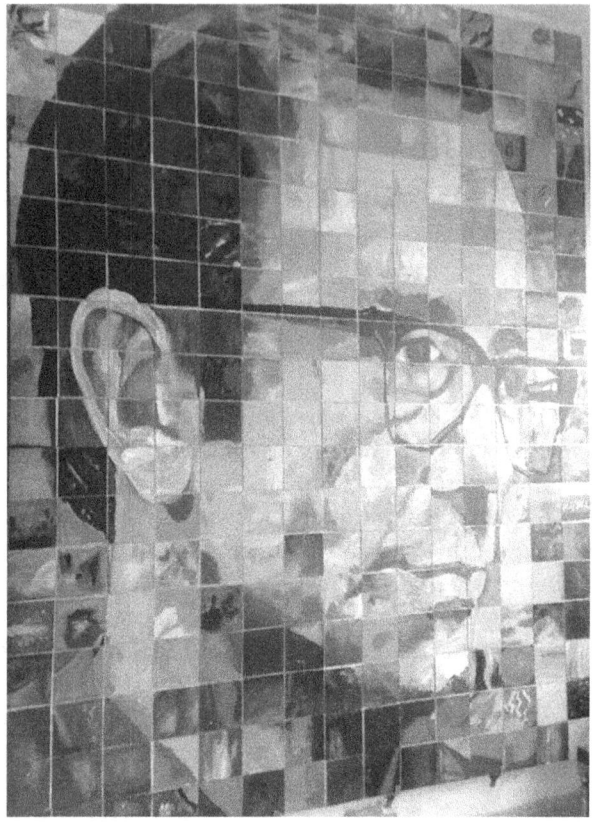

Figure 9.1 Walsh memorial at Perrin's studio, 2015

collective visual representation of a disappeared life. Perrin's approach is multifunctional in making memory: it is disruptive, purposeful, communal and materialising.

Situated within this exploration of memory in Northern Ireland, this chapter is concerned with these aspects of collective memory-making in societies emerging from violent conflict. It considers the ways in which the personal methodologies of creating public acts of memory intersect across different contested spaces and societies emerging from conflict and where appropriate draws comparative points for reflection. In his formative study, Halbwachs (1992) proposed that memory is socially constructed around the concept

Visual memory at sites of troubles past 185

of space and that spatial memory allows us to explore the past in the present. As he shows, a rich and productive field for interdisciplinary research has emerged around public and collective memory after violent conflict.

The chapter centres upon what Pierre Nora (1996) has described as the *lieu de mémoire* (the site of memory) and, specifically, upon the ways in which visual collective memory is utilised at sites and public places impacted by war. In such places, and not unlike Northern Ireland, the past is interconnected with contemporary sociopolitical dynamics. For instance, the failure to engage with the heritage and history of and at the site of Maze Long Kesh prison is a notable point of contrast, for here the decommissioned space communicates its own messages. This chapter shows that in other contested societies, memory practice impacts on how events from the past are understood in the present. This urges questions of agency and power: how is the past engaged with, understood and represented through visual forms?

As discussed elsewhere in this book, the face of the victim is often to the fore, whether at commemorations or in murals in the Northern Ireland context. Zelizer (1998: 2) contends that photographs are the 'building blocks to remembering'. In both Croatia and Argentina, photographs are particularly prescient where bodies remain disappeared; as Sontag (2002 [1979]: 15) famously remarked, 'all photographs are memento mori'. This chapter engages with the intersectionality of memory, exploring intergenerational and gender dynamics to elucidate the contestations within collective memory processes in societies with troubled pasts. Exploring comparative and illustrative examples from physical sites (such as detention centres, killing sites or memorials) of conflict in Argentina and Croatia, it explores visual forms of memory and what this reveals about memory-making in societies living with violent pasts.

Public space and place in memory-making

The societies explored in this chapter offer insights into the often-dichotomous effects that the passage of time and shifting political dynamics have on sites of conflict. Situated within the approach from Jelin (2003) wherein memory is narrative-making and justice-seeking, both examples here demonstrate that memory is disruptive, it is personal and it is political. Families and friends of victims and survivors, communities and political movements demarcate public space through visual methods, adorning streetscapes with plaques, murals and painting. For example, in Buenos Aires, commemorative stone tiles (made of broken crockery and coloured glass and inscribed with personal details) are set into the pavements, marking the spots from which people were disappeared. Space becomes personal and political, providing vivid symbolism of death and injury. What then of the buildings and streetscapes that are intrinsically linked to state and/or non-state violence in the recent past?

In his exposition of memory of war in Lebanon, Haugbolle (2010) connects national identity to cultural spatial memory-making, whereby history is replaced with 'culture'. Personal memory narratives emerge as individual remembrance but can evolve into narratives that are formed as part of the national and public consciousness about the past. In Northern Ireland memory-making has been more partisan, rather than part of a shared and collective understanding of the past. At public sites, the role of memory is therefore critical to how the site is engaged with, represented and understood.

Key questions emerge and tie directly into issues faced in Northern Ireland: how do societies (government, communities, victims and survivors) engage with sites of conflict? Are sites of memory expunged or reconceived? And what role does visual memory play at these sites of memory? As Edkins (2003) advised, memory is not straightforward: it is complex and contested. Memory of violent pasts can also be challenged with subjectivities: memory is active, social and constructed (Ashplant, 2013; Jansen, 2002). Memories are created and fluid; they are what is recalled and brought forward into view about recent violent pasts. Therefore, the visual representation of past injustices and abuses at the sites of conflict serves as an important mechanism not only for remembrance but also for the claims and pursuits of justice, truth and accountability (Burk, 2003).

Here, we explore the collective memory while recognising that this is also selective (McDowell and Braniff, 2014). As Halbwachs (1992) notes, collective memory is a current continuous thought that selectively preserves from the past only what is important to the group. Efforts at commemoration and memorialisation, therefore, are inevitably politicised, and dramatise conflicts that are unresolved from competing histories and identities (McDowell and Braniff, 2014). Visual memory in these societies emerging from conflict raises complex tensions, which speak directly to pressures in terms of ownership of memory; accountability and justice; and representation of victimhood in the public space.

This is particularly the case at sites that were places of death, incarceration, terror or violent acts against the individual(s). The former Escuela Superior de Mechanical de la Armada (ESMA, the Higher School of Mechanics of the Navy, used at one time as a clandestine detention centre) in Argentina (Otálvaro-Hormillosa, 2013) and several memorial buildings in Vukovar, Croatia (Baillie, 2013) are sites of contestation and have presented problems for societies in terms of how to utilise, represent and engage with the past of the site in the present. Crucially, they also intersect with visual memory-making: in the case of the former ESMA, the site is curated with visual markers of loss and disappearance. Similarly, in Vukovar, at the hospital site as well as at the site of mass graves and other key memorials, memory is narrated through visual exhibitions of victimhood, suffering and blame.

Disappearance is shared by both case studies explored in this chapter, and disappearance is a key aspect to the ways in which memory work is represented and presented. Materiality and visual methods have been adopted by families, friends, survivors and communities in aspects of their memory work (Feld, 2012). For, as Barthes (2000) recalls, 'in photography I can never deny that the thing has been there. There is a superimposition here: of reality and of past'. Imagery and photographs become part of the process of interrogating and understanding the past as well as being intrinsically related to memory work (Hirsch, 2001). Reflecting upon these sites calls to mind another where there has been impasse rather than activity in dealing with its recent history, namely Maze Long Kesh prison, Northern Ireland (Neill, 2017).

In reflecting upon the spaces of memory that have been impacted by death, disappearance and trauma during war and conflict, this chapter is concerned with Buenos Aires, Argentina, and Vukovar, Croatia. While the cultural dimensions differ, living with the atrocities and violence of the recent past are important parallels in the two cases. Disappearance and mass killing and the politics of trial, justice and accountability dominate both cases and impact on memory-making processes. Additionally, in each case, victimhood is debated and articulated through commemorative practices, as is blame and culpability.

Furthermore, we have a clear sense that, in both contexts, the types of 'truths' that prevail facilitate the validation of some narratives while others are silenced (McDowell and Braniff, 2014). Drawing upon Jenkins's (2006: 5–7, 19–20) approach of participatory memory work, we are concerned here with the social connectiveness of memory work as well as exploring why memory work is perceived to contribute. In Buenos Aries, spurred by a system of impunity and increasingly against a backdrop of trial and prosecution of the dictatorship, memorialisation became a key methodology of bringing materiality into the public realm – in the absence of grave sites, for example (Clarkson, 2014). Likewise, in remembrance and memorialisation of those who were disappeared in Croatia, Vukovar represents a key public space of memorialisation. At the Ovčara Memorial Centre, the materiality of those who were disappeared is captured in photographs, whereas at the Memorial Museum at the Vukovar hospital, mannequins are used to represent the staff and patients executed.

Memory work is motivated and driven from a range of sources (state, community, cultural or academic, or a mix) and is often intrinsically linked to nation-building or nation-contestation processes (Connerton, 1992). It is both top-down and bottom-up; at times, it is participatory (Gready, 2011). The processes of justice and accountability in both Croatia and Argentina may give an impression of dealing with the past effectively, yet memory work continues to demand and seek truth, justice and remembrance.

What does it mean to remember through materiality, or, specifically, through spaces associated with political violence? In the physical traces, ruins and remains of violent pasts at the sites of conflict, the complex relationship between memory and space is important. Of course, sites of conflict can be preserved, obliterated, reconceived or repurposed (Stoler, 2008). Taking this perspective into account, where sites of conflict provide materiality to the sociopolitical construction of memory, how then can visual forms of memory, such as Perrin's tiled art work, intersect with the sites of memory?

Visual memories of conflict: from the personal to the political

During the Argentinian dictatorship (1976–83), an estimated thirty thousand people were forcibly disappeared, and these lives are at the centre of collective memory-making across public space and place. Since 2010, the initiation of judicial trial and prosecution of the dictatorship has led to further exploration of memory and the past in the public sphere, collectivising memories of disappearance in a visual and material way. The search for justice, truth and acknowledgement of disappearance has been driven by friends and family. Adorning the ceiling of a hallway in a building at the former ESMA are many photographs of those who disappeared.

Sune Haugbolle (2010) reminds us that collective memory is a mixture of both public and private. Therefore, the personal, private photographs donated to this space serve as a highly visible form of establishing narratives about the harm created by the dictatorship. This is emblematic of Graeme Gilloch's point about the 'unknown, unremembered dead who must be redeemed by the historical materialist', particularly in the public space (Gilloch, 2002). In Haugbolle's (2010) approach to memory-making, these types of visual methods do translate the personal memory to the public setting. These family photographs provide an intimacy and a connection, weaving the personal to the public to the political (Hirsch, 1997). This is echoed in Jan Assman's (2008) point that the personal memory often produces and sustains public engagements and understanding about the past.

Writing in 2001, Paolo Jedlowski critiques memory studies for neglecting the role that the personal plays in the construction of narratives and collective memory. Increasingly, and against the backdrop of trial and prosecution, materiality of the personal came to the fore of memory processes in Argentina. As well as the photographs and stories about the disappeared adorning both the inside and outside of buildings of the former ESMA, artists have recreated images using murals on the walls (Figure 9.2), reclaiming space and telling the story of disappearance both within and outside the dictatorship's clandestine site of torture, detention, disappearance and assassination. The visual art forms are demanding of attention, of

Figure 9.2 Mural of Julio López, disappeared, at the former ESMA, 2015

recognition of the life taken. In its materiality, art serves as a mechanism to press against impunity and denial.

Like the Northern Ireland context, most notably Maze Long Kesh, how to engage with spaces and heritage of contested and polarising pasts is rarely uncomplicated. In the years following the end of the regime, deciding on what to do with the ex-ESMA site, located in a residential area of Buenos Aires, was challenging. For instance, in 1998 the government decided to demolish the site and create a park themed on reconciliation. This attempt to destroy the site was emblematic of silencing and elision of history in government approaches to the past. For example, in the 1990s President Menem pardoned military officers who were serving sentences for human rights abuses during the dictatorship. Under the successive Kirchner presidencies since 2003, trials against perpetrators of human rights abuses during the dictatorship were promoted (Levitsky and Murillo, 2008). This extended into the impeachment of Supreme Court judges who were linked to corruption, signalling an end to impunity.

In seeking transformation from impunity to accountability and acknowledgement, the families and friends of the disappeared developed a range of methods to engage, educate and inform about their loss and bereavement. Cognisant of the work of Butler (2009), the range of human rights activists born out of disappearance demonstrates how bereavement and loss act as a spur for political action (Otálvaro-Hormillosa, 2013). Grassroots reaction – not only to reflect on the judicial processes but also to amplify justice and truth-seeking measures through visual methods – was spurred on by this new era in human rights accountability. The Mothers and Grandmothers of the Plaza de Mayo, the HIJOS (sons and daughters of the disappeared) and the Art Memoria Colectivo are some of the organisations active in driving forward public and collective memory-making.

Menem's attempted demolition of the former ESMA in 1998 failed, and by 2004 it became a site of memory to account for and acknowledge what happened during the dictatorship. It also acts as a space for education, to promote human rights and for use by local residents and community organisations. As mentioned previously, at the site of the former ESMA, memory includes photographic exhibitions in which images of the disappeared are in vivid and constant focus. Likewise, the names of those individuals are omnipresent, adorning the windows of the former military swimming pool (Figure 9.3).

Materialising names and faces are central to the practice of visual memory-making at the former ESMA. It is a reminder that these people existed. It is a reminder of the disappeared. Juxtaposing the faces, names and stories of the disappeared at the former ESMA occurs through signage, permanent displays and visiting photographic exhibitions. The relationship between the visual memorialisation at this site of incarceration, torture and disappearance is central to storytelling and engagement with the past, but also to securing a voice for victims and survivors in a landscape that was previously dominated by impunity. These collective memory practices, set against a political landscape dominated by trials of the dictatorship, were

Figure 9.3 Former ESMA swimming pool windows adorned with faces and names of the disappeared, 2015

central in amplifying the impact of the dictatorship on citizens in the past and present.

Collective memory-making in Croatia shares similarities with the processes explored in the examples from Buenos Aries: articulating and representing victimhood set within a sociopolitical context dominated by trials, accountability and searching for those who have disappeared, as well as being linked to nation-building. Vukovar is a city in the north-east of Croatia with a strong connection to the conflict in the 1990s as well as less recent political ethnocentric violence. In 1991, during the Homeland War of Independence, Vukovar was destroyed, with swathes of people killed or displaced. Remembrance of the 938 people killed, as well as those still missing, can be found across the town in places such as the Ovčara Memorial Centre and Memorial Ovčara Mass Grave, the Vukovar hospital, the water tower and public gardens with monuments and plaques.

Not unlike the memory-making in Buenos Aries, the social construction of visual memory has taken place with criminal trials dominating the political and judicial landscape. The International Criminal Tribunal for the former Yugoslavia (ICTY) focused on the events and experiences in Vukovar – specifically, the significant trials of 'the Vukovar three' (Serb military leaders Šljivančanin, Mrkšić and Radić) and the self-proclaimed President of the Republic of Serbian Krajina, Hadžić, as well as the acquittals of Generals Gotovina and Markač (Banjeglav, 2012).

In memorial spaces in Vukovar, similar processes of using visual art to help focus attention on the lives lost represent a primary method of memory-making. Memorialisation has not diminished; thirty years after the start of the war, new memorials and ways of utilising the visual and personal into the political and public still continued to appear. In September 2020 the Vukovar Father and Son monument was unveiled. Petar and Igor Kačic are depicted in this public memorial, of which Igor's mother said: 'It is a monument to all fathers and sons who gave their lives in the Homeland War' (Rowlands, 2020).

The Mothers of Vukovar association has been a key driver in seeking truth and progressing searches for the disappeared, as well as maintaining memorialisation practices. Elsewhere, the digital photographic archive 'Because War Belongs in a Museum' forms part of the familial, personal and collective memorialisation processes regarding the war in Vukovar (Image of War Photography Museum, n.d.). These efforts to personalise and humanise are a bottom-up approach to memory-making in the environment of top-down processes of investigation and prosecution. The ICTY (n.d.) described its role as being responsible for 'combatting denial and preventing attempts at revisionism and provided the basis for future transitional justice initiatives in the region'. Yet, the scale and quantity of memory work in Vukovar and across the region suggests a disconnect between what the ICTY understood as its impact and the motivation of communities to utilise memory work to interpret, narrate and represent their past. These examples also point to the almost cyclical nature of commemoration and its relationship with time. The language at the Ovčara memorial at the mass grave site is clear in the definition of perpetrator and victimhood: 'In memory of the 200 injured Croatian soldiers and civilians from the Vukovar hospital who were executed during the Serbian aggression against Croatia' (MCHW Vukovar, n.d.).

Garrett Sullivan (1998) maintains that Vukovar is at the heart of Croatian nation-building: 'it is the landscape of sovereignty'. What, then, for Serbs who have returned to Vukovar, by the early 2020s making up over one-third of the local population? At a commemoration in November 2020, the Serbian presidential special envoy Matic stated, on laying a wreath at the Ovčara memorial, 'it is important for us to show respect for the victims and solidarity with the families', adding that 'joint commemorations can only help' (Trkanjec, 2020).

Photographs have been utilised in Vukovar's memorialisation as a way of both strengthening and disrupting collective memory. *Faces for Peace* was a 2020 memorial held in Vukovar's town hall to recollect resistance to violence during both the Second World War and the conflicts of the 1990s. Here, photography sat alongside storytelling to uncover and bring to light neglected narratives (Vladisavljevic, 2020). The museum at the Vukovar hospital, meanwhile, comprises mannequins, artefacts and extracts from diaries detailing the experience of the hospital, its patients, and staff throughout the siege between August and November 1991.

The communicating of the history and stories of the early 1990s at Vukovar using visual methods is community-led but also engages public and governmental agencies. For example, the conservation of the water tower and its repurposing as a memorial (opened in October 2020) was mainly achieved through fundraising and community initiatives, yet the memorial is intrinsically linked to nationhood, as evidenced by the national flag that flies above it. Furthermore, retaining as part of the memorial the holes left by the 640 shells that struck the tower, fired by the Yugoslav National Army and Serbs in the 1990s, is a key marker of resistance and culpability.

These examples demonstrate the closely linked relationship between Croatian nation-building and judicial processes from the ICTY, and participatory memory work. Collective memory, therefore, interacts with public space, with implications for how the past is understood and engaged with, and, of course, for how it impacts upon contemporary ethno-national relationships.

Gendered wars, gendered memory

The Homeland War in Croatia and the Argentine dictatorship were situations in which men were much more likely to perpetrate killings and to be killed. Masculinity and nationalism were key drivers of violence and conflict (Bracewell, 2000; Dumančić and Krolo, 2017; Irvin and Lilly, 2007; Milicevic, 2006). Where, then, is there scope for women to participate, and for suffering to be reflected in the memorialisation in both contexts? In the hyper-masculinised wars and subsequent political processes that followed, women were largely absent from both the making of memory and the visual representation of suffering and loss. Women experienced these wars, dictatorships and conflicts in different ways. What is the role of gender at these public sites of memory? The work presented briefly here only seeks to open up comparative engagements with gendered experiences of memorialisation and remembrance.

There is an emerging literature on gender and collective memory that has started to explore the barriers and also methodologies in which women's experiences are represented in the structures of memorialisation (Bosco, 2004; Jacobs, 2008; Mostov, 1995). Intersectionality remains key: women have diverse experiences of war and conflict, and play many roles therein. Confronting a significant issue – sexual violence in war – a visual exhibition by Eliza Hoxha about women victimised during the 1998–99 war in Kosovo confronted memory, space and agency. Hoxha's photographic exhibition comprised women who were victims of sexual violence during the war, and was displayed in the basement of Priština's Grand Hotel, the site where this brutality took place (Begisholli, 2019). While the literature on memory and gender links explicitly to agency and power, the exhibition, titled *Be My Face*, also explored the relationship between memorialisation, gender and public space.

Likewise, in Argentina, important and transformative engagements with the past have reflected upon the gendered aspects of the dictatorship and its victims. Lucila Quieto, at the time a master's student, utilised her university classroom to profoundly shift the ways in which people understood disappearance, loss, violence, bereavement and the impact of the dictatorship. As part of her master's project, Quieto used her university projector and worked with classmates to project a picture of her father, disappeared three months before she was born. No picture existed of her with her father and so she sought to create one by asking a classmate to photograph her in front of the projection. In this way, she maintains ownership of her father's memory, while bringing to the fore the impact of disappearance and bereavement for the children of the disappeared. Quieto went on to photograph, in a similar way, other children of the disappeared, creating an exhibition, *Archaeology of Absence*, which challenges dominant narratives and practices of remembrance (Gaunt, 2011). This work calls to mind tensions around ownership of the past, of those killed or disappeared, and the right to remember in public ways and in public spaces.

Part of the memorialisation through visual methods has raised questions: who owns memory and space? What impact does this have on societal engagement with the crimes of the past? How does this contribute to collective memory-making? Quieto's work reflects a trend in Argentina – for archives, memories and historical work to be encompassing of genders, ages and classes, and to be participatory in origin. Quieto also adds to a more inclusive approach to memorialisation: the grief of a daughter who never met her father; the familial connection; and intergenerational dynamics (Gaunt, 2011).

Internationally, existing literature has lamented the absence of women-centric imagery and participation in the public space, and demanded more diverse approaches to collective memory. Enhanced plurality is further assured by fostering agency within the process of making visual memory at contested sites, though this in itself is impeded by power structures prevailing from a violent, hypermasculinised and militarised society (Ashe, 2012; Braniff and Whiting, 2017). Graff-McRae (2010) emphasises this point when pointing to the gap in gendered analyses of memory – so, even when there is space for women to share experiences, inherent gendered dynamics of war continue to impact on engagement with history and memory.

Visual memory plays an important role to engage the audience, interpret the past and provide a vehicle for remembrance. It interrupts, disrupts and shapes how people reflect upon the violent past. For example, Hrvoje Polan's photographic exhibition *Beyond the Seven*

Camps: From Crimes of Culture to Culture of Crime centred space and memorialisation as two intrinsic and interlinked aspects of memory in Croatia (Vladisavljevic, 2019a). This exhibition dealt with the spaces that were previously cultural centres but that became, during the wars of the 1990s, sites of detention, torture and death. The issue is how to engage with these spaces and memorialise at and about them. At the launch of Polan's exhibition, Zovoko, president of the Croatian Journalists' Association, reflected that the exhibition challenged the accepted narratives and adopted histories of the 1990s: 'It is much easier for many to pretend that there were no war crimes, that there were no camps, that there were no prisons, than to accept the fact that our citizens, as well as [citizens] in other countries, were tortured and killed in the worst possible way' (Vladisavljevic, 2019b).

Beyond the Seven Camps disrupts the ways in which societies engage with the difficult pasts embodied in buildings and public places. This example marks the ability of the acutely felt positionality of imagery to disrupt the silences around place and politics that are too often embedded within the sociopolitical culture that emerges. Polan's exhibition, like Quieto's, serves to interrupt the ways in which people reflect on what happened, where it happened and what this means for contemporary relations. In both Polan's and Hoxha's exhibitions, rather than cleansing the space from its recent past, the focus is centred on what happened, to whom and where.

Since 2005, the trials in Argentina have provided women with the opportunity to utilise visual methods to document, interpret and represent the testimonies and examinations in the court rooms. The exhibition *Dibijos Urgentes* by Eugenia Bekeris and Paula Doberti displayed annotated drawings of the court processes encompassing justice, law and human rights; the images are largely in pencil, but are amplified by red ink (Braniff *et al.*, 2015). What is also striking in the work of Bekeris and Doberti is that these trials are urgent, too: their drawings show the old age of those on trial, a question of timeliness of justice and accountability in this context.

In both contexts, the visual memories created in public spaces by women, either through their family photographs or art work, have had an impact on society. Likewise, the visual memories that complicate, disrupt and nuance the collective narrative due to the featuring or participation of women is striking. Navigating a male-dominated political and judicial space that often saturates memory-making due to its inherent link to nation-building is problematic for ensuring a space and participation for women in these two contexts.

Conclusion

Elsewhere in this book, engaging with or eliding history, the social construction of memory and the role of violence and victimhood in space and place resonate with the discussions in this chapter. In both Croatia and Argentina, place and history have been actively used to foster the narratives of ethnic division and difference, of perpetrator and victim, of guilt and innocence. Like the experiences of memory-making in Northern Ireland, commemoration and memorialisation mark and demarcate territory, bound to ethnicity and community identity. This is often expressed in the partisan and selective practices of memory-making in the form of commemorative plaques and windows, remembrance statues and gardens, as well as murals.

Ethnicised versions of history are resilient, and clearly the predominant focus on blame and accountability is reflective of a judicial and political process that has failed to deliver truth recovery or acknowledgement. This chapter has emphasised the role of visual memory at contested and conflict sites as a method of acknowledgement of loss and injury. It has also pointed to clear examples of how victims and survivors utilise visual methods to seek justice and truth as well as represent pain and bereavement. It has also shown how this visual method intersects with the management of memory at key sites of conflict.

The practices and processes of memory work in the cases considered above draw interesting parallels with memory about the Troubles. What is shared is the omnipotence of memory as part of the present and imagined future: memory is linked to progress. For communities, political movements and parties, as well as the state, memory moves beyond the personal and private to the public and political. What is also shared is the absence of justice and acknowledgement, which helps contribute towards the constant framing of contemporary policy and political debates in the legacies of the past. Despite the saturation of memory in the present, many silences and obfuscations of history prevail.

Marginalisation of voices and experiences of violence is not limited to Argentina and Croatia, as this book has shown. Yet, Northern Ireland does stand out in its failure to deal with a key site of incarceration, Maze Long Kesh. Unlike the key sites at Vukovar and Buenos Aires, Maze Long Kesh remains caught in a political impasse, the prison itself whitewashed and partially demolished. Sidestepping and silencing aspects of history demonstrate the impact of the political context on how the past is utilised and engaged with.

The issues discussed in this chapter reflect, in part, the problem posed by Atwood (1985): 'who can remember the pain once it's over? All that remains of it is a shadow, not in the mind even, in the flesh. Pain marks you but too deep to see.' The urban environment emerging from violent war and conflict can both simultaneously disguise and plainly portray the harms and hurts of the past. This chapter has explored the ways in which the spaces of conflict are conceived after violence. In the places discussed in this chapter, the past is a key part of the fabric of the building – in terms of its memory, representation and how people (locals and visitors alike) engage with it. These spaces also expose the intimate connections to those incarcerated, tortured, assassinated or disappeared at these sites through the visual representation of personal images, photographs, diaries and reflections from victims' families and friends.

Finally, these sites speak to wider political and judicial processes in both contexts where demands for truth and information recovery, justice and accountability remain paramount. They are dominant over other priorities in transitional justice and peacebuilding contexts such as reconciliation and healing. Visual methods of memory work are shaped by and simultaneously inform political and cultural discussions about perpetrator-victimhood, nationhood and inter-ethnic relationships. Public places in both Vukovar and areas of Buenos Aries are demarcated by violence. These memoryscapes are sites for mourning and remembrance, but they move beyond private grief into the political and the public, fostering collective identities.

References

Ashe, F. (2012) 'Gendering war and peace: militarised masculinities in Northern Ireland', *Men and Masculinities*, 15 (3): 230–48.

Ashplant, D., Dawson, G. and Roper, T. (2013) *The Politics of War Memory and Commemoration*. London: Routledge.
Assmann, A. (2008) 'Transformations between history and memory', *Social Research: An International Quarterly*, 75 (1): 49–72.
Atwood, M. (1985) *The Handmaid's Tale*. New York, NY: O. W. Toad.
Baillie, B. (2013) 'Memorialising the "martyred city": negotiating Vukovar's wartime past', in W. Pullan and B. Baillie (eds), *Locating Urban Conflicts: Ethnicity, Nationalism and the Everyday*, pp. 115–31. Basingstoke: Palgrave Macmillan.
Banjeglav, T. (2012) 'Conflicting memories, competing narratives and contested histories in Croatia's post-war commemorative practices', *Politička misao*, 49 (5): 7–31.
Barthes, R. (2000) *Camera Lucida: Reflections on Photography*. London: Vintage.
Begisholli, B. (2019) 'Kosovo exhibition commemorates women raped in Pristina hotel', *Balkan Insight* (11 June). Available at: https://balkaninsight.com/2019/06/11/kosovo-exhibition-commemorates-women-raped-in-pristina-hotel/ (accessed 3 September 2020).
Bosco, F. (2004) 'Human rights politics and scaled performances of memory: conflicts among the Madres de Plaza de Mayo in Argentina', *Social and Cultural Geography*, 5 (3): 381–402.
Bracewell, W. (2000) 'Rape in Kosovo: masculinity and Serbian nationalism', *Nations and Nationalism*, 6: 563–90.
Braniff, M., Norridge, Z. and Vaisman, N. (2015) 'Eugenia Bekeris and Maria Paula Doberti, *Dibujos Urgentes* exhibition', *Children of Political Violence* (4 May). Available at: https://childrenofpoliticalviolence.wordpress.com/2015/05/04/dibujos-urgentes-exhibition-eugenia-bekeris-and-maria-paula-doberti-3/ (accessed 2 September 2020).
Braniff, M. and Whiting, S. (2017) 'Gender, international relations theory and Northern Ireland', in T. J. White (ed.), *Theories of International Relations and Northern Ireland*, pp. 116–30. Manchester: Manchester University Press.
Burk, A. L. (2003) 'Private griefs, public places', *Political Geography*, 22: 317–33.
Butler, J. (2009) *Frames of War: When Is Life Grievable?* London: Verso Books.
Chandra, K. (2006) 'What is ethnic identity and does it matter?', *Annual Review of Political Science*, 9: 397–424.
Clarkson, C. (2014) *Toward an Aesthetics of Transitional Justice*. New York, NY: Fordham University Press.
Connerton, P. (1992) *How Societies Remember*. Cambridge: Cambridge University Press.

Dumančić, M. and Krolo, K. (2017) 'Dehexing postwar West Balkan masculinities: the case of Bosnia, Croatia, and Serbia, 1998 to 2015', *Men and Masculinities*, 20 (2): 154–80.

Edkins, J. (2003) *Trauma and the Memory of Politics*. Cambridge: Cambridge University Press.

Feld, C. (2012) 'Image and disappearance in Argentina: reflections on a photo taken in the basement of ESMA', *Journal of Latin American Cultural Studies*, 21 (2): 313–41.

Gaunt, R. (2011) 'Beyond suffering: aesthetics, politics and post-memory in a photo-essay by Lucila Quieto', *After Image*, 39 (1): 65–69.

Gilloch, G. (2002) *Walter Benjamin: Critical Constellations*. Cambridge: Polity.

Graff-McRae, R. (2010) *Remembering and Forgetting 1916: Commemoration and Conflict in Post-Peace Process Ireland*. Dublin: Irish Academic Press.

Gready, P. (2011) *The Era of Transitional Justice: The Aftermath of the Truth and Reconciliation Commission in South Africa and Beyond*. Abingdon: Routledge.

Halbwachs, M. (1992) *On Collective Memory*, ed. and trans. L. A. Coser. Chicago, IL: University of Chicago Press.

Haugbolle, S. (2010) *War and Memory in Lebanon*. Cambridge: Cambridge University Press.

Hirsch, M. (1997) *Family Frames: Photography, Narrative and Postmemory*. Cambridge, MA: Harvard University Press.

Hirsch, M. (2001) 'Surviving images: Holocaust photographs and the work of postmemory', in B. Zelizer (ed.), *Visual Culture and the Holocaust*. New Brunswick, NJ: Rutgers University Press.

ICTY (International Criminal Tribunal for the former Yugoslavia) (n.d.), 'Achievements'. Available at: www.icty.org/en/about/tribunal/achievements (accessed 3 September 2020).

Image of War Photography Museum (n.d.) 'Because War Belongs in a Museum'. Available at: https://image-of-war-blog.tumblr.com (accessed 2 September 2020).

Irvine, J. A. and Lilly, C. S. (2007) 'Boys must be boys: gender and the Serbian Radical Party, 1991–2000', *Nationalities Papers*, 35: 93–120.

Jacobs, J. (2008) 'Gender and collective memory: women and representation at Auschwitz', *Memory Studies*, 1 (2): 211–25.

Jansen, S. (2002) 'The violence of memories: local narratives of the past after ethnic cleansing in Croatia', *Local History*, 6 (1): 77–94.

Jedlowski, P. (2001) 'Memory and sociology: themes and issues', *Time and Society*, 1: 29–44.

Jelin, E. (2003) *State Repression and the Labors of Memory*. Minneapolis, MN: University of Minnesota Press.

Jenkins, H. (2006) *Confronting the Challenges of Participatory Culture: Media Education for the 21st Century*. Chicago, IL: John D. and Catherine T. MacArthur Foundation.

Levitsky, S. and Murillo, M. V. (2008) 'Argentina: from Kirchner to Kirchner', *Journal of Democracy*, 19 (2): 16–30.

McDowell, S. and Braniff, M. (2014) *Commemoration as Conflict: Space, Memory and Identity in Peace Processes*. Basingstoke: Palgrave MacMillan.

MCHW (Memorial Centre of Homeland War) Vukovar (n.d.) 'Ovčara mass grave'. Available at: www.mcdrvu.hr/en/portfolio_page/mass-grave-ovcara/ (accessed 4 August 2022).

Milicevic, A. (2006) 'Joining the war: masculinity, nationalism and war participation in the Balkans war of secession, 1991–1995', *Nationalities Papers*, 34 (3): 265–87.

Mostov, J. (1995) '"OUR WOMENS"/"THEIR WOMENS": symbolic boundaries, territorial markers, and violence in the Balkans', *Peace and Change*, 20 (4): 515–29.

Neill, W. J. V. (2017) 'Representing the Maze/Long Kesh prison in Northern Ireland: conflict resolution centre and tourist draw or Trojan Horse in a culture war?', in J. Z. Wilson, S. Hodgkinson, J. Piché and Kevin Walby (eds), *The Palgrave Handbook of Prison Tourism*, pp. 241–60. London: Palgrave Macmillan.

Nora, P. (1996) 'Preface to English language edition: from *Lieux de memoire* to Realms of Memory', in P. Nora (ed.) *Realms of Memory: Rethinking the French Past*. New York, NY: Columbia University Press.

Otálvaro-Hormillosa, G. (2013) 'Ex-ESMA', *Performance Research*, 18 (4): 116–23.

Rowlands, I. (2020) 'Emotive new Vukovar father and son monument unveiled', *Total Croatia News* (22 September). Available at: www.total-croatia-news.com/news/46797-vukovar-father-and-son-monument (accessed 22 September 2020).

Sontag, S. (2002 [1979]) *On Photography*. London: Penguin.

Stoler, A. (2008) *Along the Archival Grain: Epistemic Anxieties and Colonial Common Sense*. Princeton, NJ: Princeton University Press.

Sullivan, G. A. (1998) *The Drama of Landscape: Land, Property, and Social Relations in the Early Modern Stage*. Stanford, CA: Stanford University Press.

Trkanjec, Z. (2020) 'Serbian envoy kneels before Ovčara memorial in Vukovar', *Euractiv* (18 November). Available at: www.euractiv.com/section/politics/short_news/serbian-envoy-kneels-before-ovcara-memorial-in-vukovar/ (accessed 18 November 2020).

Vladisavljevic, A. (2019a) 'Croatian journalists mourn veteran photographer Hjvoje Pola', *Balkan Insight* (2 April). Available at: https://

balkaninsight.com/2019/04/02/croatian-journalists-mourn-veteran-photographer-hrvoje-polan/ (accessed 3 September 2020).

Vladisavljevic, A. (2019b) 'Croatian photo exhibition documents wartime detention camps', *Balkan Insight* (18 October). Available at: https://balkaninsight.com/2019/10/18/croatian-photo-exhibition-documents-wartime-detention-camps/ (accessed 3 September 2020).

Vladisavljevic, A. (2020) 'Croatian exhibition celebrates rebels for peace', *Balkan Insight* (15 January). Available at: https://balkaninsight.com/2020/01/15/croatian-exhibition-celebrates-rebels-for-peace/ (accessed 3 September 2020).

Walsh, R. (1977) 'Open letter from a writer to the Military Junta, 24 March 1977', *History Is a Weapon*. Available at: www.historyisaweapon.com/defcon1/walshopenletterargjunta.html (accessed 10 October 2020).

Zelizer, B. (1998) *Remembering to Forget: Holocaust Memory through the Camera's Eye*. Chicago, IL: Chicago University Press.

10

The tears of the mothers: conflict and memory in comparison

Catherine McGlynn

In 2011 a monument was erected in Osh, the largest city in the south of Kyrgyzstan. The monument, a peace memorial with a bell atop a plinth, calling for peace in the world, was unveiled by the city's mayor, Melis Myrzakmatov, on the first anniversary of violence in the city between the Kyrgyz and Uzbek communities. However, the monument (which still stands, albeit without its bell) does not record what those events are and there is no explicit mention of the conflict in the inscription, which has been written in Kyrgyz, Russian and English, but not in Uzbek. This monument and the way it implicitly presents the events it does (not) commemorate is a testament to the multiple ways in which public space can be used to capture and construct memories by those who present official memories and those who view the resulting artefacts.

The purpose of this chapter is to compare the case studies of Northern Ireland and Kyrgyzstan with a view to generating new perspectives on memory and conflict. However, such comparison requires critical engagement with the difficulties in drawing meaningful comparison. The key argument is that while Northern Ireland is undoubtedly caught up in arguments about the legacy of the past and its meaning for the future in ways that have been obstructive for political engagement and development, the level of 'noise' in the debate reminds us that others elsewhere are very limited in their ability to contest the use of different platforms to shape the past into a certain story.

The examination of the way in which memories of the Osh conflict have been formed will involve focus on the physical monuments to the violence, principally the peace memorial mentioned above as well as a statue known as *The Tears of the Mothers*. The other form of memorialisation considered will be the production of two documents. One is the *Report of the Independent International Commission of Inquiry into the Events in Southern Kyrgyzstan in June 2010* and the other is Myrzakmatov's (2011) own account, *Searching for Truth – The Osh Tragedy*. In focusing on these artefacts, key themes of territory, language and insecurity can be presented for comparative analysis.

Comparing and understanding

The use of a comparative approach for understanding Northern Ireland or for using it as an example of phenomena regularly studied within the discipline of comparative political science is well established. Both the causes of the conflict and its transformation by the Good Friday Agreement, interlinked with or separate to Northern Ireland as a case study in consociationalism, have made it a popular choice for inclusion in studies of political violence, political systems and peace processes (see, for example, McGarry, 2001; Tonge, 2014).

As Bara (2009: 45) observes, 'the process of comparison lies at the very heart of analysis'. Comparing events and institutions increases our confidence that we can explain why something has happened and make recommendations for change. It can also lift us out of our assumptions about the inevitability of events such as ethnic conflict and reductive explanations for them as we see the structural and agentic forces that drive seemingly spontaneous violence. However, the messy human world makes for a very imperfect laboratory, and comparing two or more cases in order to explain, assess and predict is fraught with difficulties. There is, for example, the danger of applying concepts across different circumstances to the point where they are stretched beyond their original meaning (Keman, 2014), and the subjectivity of one's own approach in terms of both personal and professional experience means the partial perspective one hopes to challenge by looking elsewhere ends up being superimposed on a profoundly different landscape. In addition, when it comes specifically to the investigation of memory, Forest and Johnson (2011) observe that the construction and contestation of collective memory has most often been explored using other approaches, reflecting an assumption of what can be collected in order to systemise and generalise.

This does not invalidate making comparisons, not least as a ready means of triangulating claims, but it does call for clarity of intention and critical awareness of one's own perspective. And when it comes to using other cases to aid our understanding of social or collective memory in Northern Ireland, we should bear in mind McDaid's (2019) caution; his examination of how the term 'ethnic cleansing' has been utilised in Northern Ireland underlined that importing concepts can sometimes produce very little beyond a very superficial comparison. This also applies to the exportation of Northern Ireland's situation elsewhere.

Kyrgyzstan may not have been as common an option for evaluation compared to conflicts in Lebanon, Israel/Palestine or the former Yugoslavia. However, this is a positive thing in many ways. Arguably, cross-referencing with under-researched points of comparison helps develop a body of knowledge that is beset by various types of selection bias, something that caused Peters (1998) to invoke the classic command from the film *Casablanca* to round up the usual suspects when encouraging us to examine what particular cases we are being offered for consumption by a researcher and why.

One potential point of comparison could be drawn from the regime instituted upon Kyrgyz independence which has been described as having consociational features either when assessing the accommodation of the state's significant Russian minority (Juska, 1999) or the mechanisms for harmonising northern and southern interests (Huskey, 2008). However, such arrangements were fragmentary and generally informal, and a systematic crossover between institutions would be difficult.

Interestingly, researchers specifically concerned with how conflict in southern Kyrgyzstan has been informally remembered and officially memorialised have themselves drawn explicit comparison with the significance of community demarcation of territory and the use of space in Northern Ireland (see Harrowell, 2015; Megoran, 2013). In this arena, the fragmentary and the informal are of utmost importance, and engaging with the mental mapping and opportunities for storytelling of events carries the potential to help us explore what is and is not remembered, and how those pasts shape the present.

The Osh conflict

Kyrgyzstan is one of a number of Central Asian states which emerged as independent entities in 1991 when the USSR broke up. The Tsars had created a land empire over the course of three centuries. The revolution of 1917 led to civil war, and during this period some colonies sought independence. However, the victorious Bolsheviks reincorporated much of this territory and the Tsarist empire was recreated in the boundaries of the new USSR. A contradictory attitude to nationalism (a supposedly bourgeois ideology associated with a phase of historical development that Lenin's vanguard had skipped in the accelerated journey to socialism) was apparent in the USSR's history (Suny, 2005). There was emphasis on both a civic *Homo sovieticus* state identity and the creation of republics around titular nations. These republics were not neatly mapped segments of peoples within borders but came to be seen as belonging to those named national majorities (Bond and Koch, 2010). In Central Asia, this division cut through the Fergana Valley, bringing a large number of Uzbeks into what would become Kyrgyzstan. This meant that Osh, the largest city in the south, was a strongly Uzbek location. Policies that informed the modernisation of the Soviet years eroded the Kyrgyz connection to nomadic lifestyles and formalised the Kyrgyz language.

One of the last tasks of the Soviet Red Army before the USSR disintegrated was deploying to Osh in 1990 to quell a violent conflict between Kyrgyz and Uzbek residents. There was anxiety about how land was being divided between the two communities as state control of resources weakened. Unfounded rumours that Uzbeks had organised themselves into gangs and had murdered their Kyrgyz neighbours set off the formation of groups dedicated to what they saw as defence against this Uzbek threat; this resulted in looting, abduction, rape and murder. The explosion of violence has been attributed to the power vacuum created by the collapse of the old system and the subsequent fears that the Uzbeks would use their superior resources and social capital to make a literal and metaphorical land grab in the Fergana Valley (Bond and Koch, 2010; Tishkov, 1995).

The first president of the newly independent Kyrgyzstan, Askar Akaev, strongly followed the example of President Boris Yeltsin in

Russia in committing to a civic accommodating vision of the nation that the new state would contain, while also following Yeltsin's lead in privileging ethnic ties through rights of return for the Kyrgyz diaspora (Laruelle, 2012). Akaev took charge of a country where the titular national group was numerically the largest but only just outweighed the combined numbers of other ethnic groups, and where the desire for a strong Kyrgyz identity within the state was needed not just to shore up confidence undermined by those demographics but to stop sub-state ties of region and clan standing in the way of an imagined community who could embrace democracy (Huskey, 2003). Kyrgyz cultural roots were drawn back to the mythic warrior Manas, whose powers in repelling invaders and unifying peoples had been captured in oral epic poems since at least the eighteenth century, if not the much longer pedigree (sometimes millennia) claimed for the celebration of his origins and exploits.

Akaev committed himself to democratisation and economic liberalisation and, by association, to building a civic nation, under the auspices of his slogan 'our common home'. His seven principles of Manas were formulated to give him a strong Kyrgyz base and outmanoeuvre overtly nationalist political challenges (Hanks, 2011). However, this included inter-ethnic harmony on the grounds that Manas himself had drawn alliances and personal connections from other communities (Megoran, 2012, 2013). In practical terms, this resulted in policies such as recognising Russian as an official language, setting quotas for the inclusion of different ethnic groups within registered political parties and providing funding for Uzbek higher-education institutions.

Akaev dispensed with democratising impulses once he 'found autocracy more convenient' (McFaul, 2022: 222), especially for his zeal for nepotism, but he was forced from power in the Tulip Revolution of 2005, which brought Kurmanbek Bakiyev to power. This era saw absolutely rampant corruption and another revolution occurred in April 2010, leading to an interim government headed by Roza Otunbayeva, who was determined to restore the primacy of parliament and contain executive power as a means of recommitting to democratisation. However, the government immediately found that fundamental state structures had been hollowed out to the point of not functioning, such had been the capitulation to organised crime networks.

The 2010 revolution provides the background to the violence in Osh that June. Bakiyev was a southern politician who had been deposed by northerners, exacerbating southern fears that the northern capital of Bishkek would either ignore or suppress their political requirements. The weak interim government had actively solicited the armed support of Uzbek leaders in putting down some southerners' attempts to rally around Bakiyev in the cities of Osh and Jalal-Abad. Principal among these leaders was Kadyrjon Batyrov, a politician who had built a power base from within the Uzbek National Cultural Centre that had been created after the 1990 riot. He used this base to mobilise Uzbeks to lobby for inclusion in spheres where they were marginalised, such as public-sector employment (Matveeva *et al.*, 2012). Batyrov rallied his supporters at the People's Friendship University, which he himself had founded, the day after Bakiyev was overthrown and told them now was the time to become more politically engaged. Whether rightly or wrongly, he was subsequently known as the man who had instigated the burning down of Bakiyev's house.

David Gullette and John Heathershaw (2015) argue that Batyrov's actions, both actual and attributed, represented to many Kyrgyz people in the south the overstepping of an implicitly understood boundary that directly impinged upon their sense of sovereignty. There was panic that once again Uzbeks were ready to exploit their financial dominance and numerical superiority in Osh to strike for more power while the state was in flux. The long-held mistrust of possible irredentist intentions on the part of the government in neighbouring Uzbekistan also featured in these anxieties, despite a general lack of active assistance to the Uzbek diaspora in Kyrgyzstan. Bond and Koch (2010) suggest that the authoritarian regime in Uzbekistan viewed Uzbeks in Kyrgyzstan as a possible threat because of their experiences of a living in a relatively liberal and free regime. By this time, Uzbeks were also depicted as a threat because of their association with violent Islamism, most notably through the Islamic Movement of Uzbekistan (Ismailbekova, 2013; Laruelle, 2012).

As in 1990, the escalation of the violence after a period of skirmishes and confrontation was sparked by rumours of a mythic outrage perpetrated by Uzbeks, this time a gang rape of Kyrgyz women in a university dormitory. And as in 1990, rioting broke out and groups organised on both sides, undertaking acts of violence.

By the end of the riots approximately 470 people had been killed, thousands had been injured and sexual violence was a prominent feature of the carnage (KIC, 2011). A key difference between 2010 and 1990 was that this time there was no post-conflict restitution through the justice system. Instead, despite the majority of the victims of violence – including the dead – being Uzbek, it was Uzbeks who found themselves arrested, tried in local courts and imprisoned for crimes committed in Osh and Jalal-Abad. The local state response to the conflict reflected the dominance of Kyrgyz people in the security forces and criminal justice system, echoed throughout the whole public sector of Kyrgyzstan.

Remembering and framing the conflict

Kyrgyzstan's urban architecture had been altered since independence by the introduction of the symbolism of the Kyrgyz nation to the landscape and to the formal realm. The circular emblem on the flag represents the tribes brought together by Manas but it is also the roof of a yurt, the traditional felt dwelling of Kyrgyz nomads. This foregrounding of both a nomadic past and the Manas legend as the root of the modern people has been key to the national story constructed for the new state (Laruelle, 2012).

Manas and his allies began a march across the landscape with statues, usually relatively small but numerous, springing up in parks and other public places. This did not involve the obliteration of Soviet-era iconography, however, and Lenin, Marx and Engels still appear in statue form in both northern and southern cities, alongside buildings full of depictions of the revolutionary Soviet people created by the glory of Bolshevism (all of them notably white and European). A lot of this survival can be attributed to financial pressures and the prohibitive cost of wholesale change, leaving Central Asian states with, in Roy's memorable phrase, 'a washed-out USSR, rusting away, with nobody bothering to repaint it' (Roy, 2000: 163). The importance of the tourist dollar is recognised, and emblems of Soviet nostalgia such as the mural in Osh of Misha, the mascot from the 1980 Moscow Olympics, are marketed to visitors as a key attraction. However, conscious decisions have been made, such as not following

Uzbekistan in changing from Cyrillic to Arabic lettering, or moving rather junking the iconic 'flying Lenin' when a statue symbolising Kyrgyz independence and liberty was erected in 2004. This is suggestive of an accommodation with the past and of an unwillingness to alienate ethnic Russians (Lenin in his new location still received floral tributes on the anniversary of the 1917 revolution).

Before turning to examine the monuments that Myrzakmatov commissioned after the violence, documents that frame the memory of the conflict must be examined as they provide the context for the way in which the violence has been interpreted and understood both at the elite and local level for the Kyrgyz. These documents offer two very different versions of events and were received in very different ways. One is a report by an external body, created at the behest of the government in Bishkek, and the other is by Myrzakmatov. The impact of the first lies in its rejection and the impact of the second in its wider acceptance.

The interim government were very quick to seek the assistance of the international community. The month after the riots, President Otunbayeva announced the formation of the Kyrgyzstan Inquiry Commission (KIC), headed by former Finnish parliamentarian Kimmo Kiljunen, a senior figure in the Organization for Security and Co-operation in Europe, which had provided policing and security in the immediate aftermath of the violence. When Otunbayeva announced the formation of KIC at a press conference in July 2010, she stated that the commission would be rigorous and 'dot all the "i"s'. Crucially, she promised that lessons would be learned for both communities in the south, reflecting an implicit understanding that there was blame and suffering on both sides (Volosevich, 2010). However, as Wilkinson (2015: 418) observes, 'it had already become starkly evident that there were conflicting views about what exactly the lessons to be learnt were, and indeed who should be learning them'.

The report placed the blame firmly on Kyrgyz actors, not just for the violence itself but also the continued sweeping by security forces of Uzbek *malhallas* (neighbourhoods) afterwards in order to continue to use the criminal justice system to persecute Uzbeks. What happened in June 2010 amounted to crimes against humanity, though not genocide (KIC, 2011). The suggested reparation reflected KIC's focus on the consequences of nation-building: 'Kyrgyzstan should take a strong public stand against extreme nationalism and ethnic exclusivity' (KIC, 2011: iv), the commission spelled out. Key recommendations were for the state to revert upon independence to its original name, the Republic of Kyrgyzstan, rather than the title of the Kyrgyz Republic that it still holds, and for official status to be accorded to the Uzbek language.

The government first delayed the report, then issued rebutting commentary on it and, finally, when the popular reaction had escalated to burning the document, literally made Kiljunen *persona non grata*. For those viscerally outraged to the point of arson, it was another recounting of the events of June 2010 that resonated more strongly. The Osh mayor, Melis Myrzakmatov, one of the few of Bakiyev's circle to stay in a position of political power, published a testament entitled *Searching for Truth – The Osh Tragedy* with the telling subtitle *Documents, Facts, Interviews, Appeals and Statements*, signifying his desire to present this as a mirror of an independent inquiry in which 'the author submits to the reader's court all the necessary documents and facts containing analysis' (Myrzakmatov, 2011).

The document then took the signifiers of a formal commission and suggested a dispassionate investigation. However, it was designed to tell a story that linked very recent events to a longer story of connection to and alienation from the land; the main title, *Searching for Truth*, is explicitly connected to Manas, with Myrzakmatov using the quotation 'let each of us seek the truth in our heart, and justice will always triumph in it' (Myrzakmatov, 2011) in explaining why he had named his work so. For a culture that had maintained the importance of oral history even through the Soviet period of suppression (Hardenberg, 2012), this telling of the latest way in which a threatened people had found the collective will to defend their territory carried a lot of emotional power.

This work presented the June 2010 violence as a series of acts of self-defence (Megoran, 2012) in the face of an Uzbek insurgency (which Myrzakmatov always officially presents as a small group of separatists receiving help from over the border, rather than the majority of Uzbeks in Osh) that had to be challenged for the sake of security. Myrzakmatov explains how from his vantage point on the ground in Osh he saw a subversive strategy unfold. The violence was depicted as planned, with Uzbeks clearly striking first and the Kyrgyz having to come together to repel their advance.

Myrzakmatov's document 'has become a popular imagination of the events, drawing images of the fight over control of the land that was originally in Kyrgyz hands'; it tapped directly into the anxiety that Uzbeks were always on the outside pushing and taking at the expense of the Kyrgyz, the rightful heirs of Manas (Gullette and Heathershaw, 2015: 198). The insecurity of Kyrgyzstan as a place on a map has many dimensions to it, from border conflicts with neighbouring Tajikistan to jostling for influence between very large powers such as China, Russia and the US (Ackali, 2005). *Searching for Truth* connected the genuine geo-political weaknesses of the Kyrgyz state to a story of a past where the Kyrgyz as a people have always struggled to hold on to what is rightfully theirs.

It was Myrzakmatov who erected the peace memorial in Osh, along with another commemorative sculpture, *The Tears of the Mothers*, showing an Uzbek and Kyrgyz woman embracing and crying. These memorials are small and not in prominent locations. Forest and Johnson (2011) describe monuments as public goods in that they are so publicly available that one cannot help but be a consumer of them. However, Harrowell's (2015) research into the way Osh residents map out different memories of the city demonstrates that their size and location mean they do not imprint themselves on people's minds, and it is Myrzakmatov's imposing and prominent erection of legendary heroes (including, inevitably, Manas) that has made an impact, reflecting his prescription for quelling further violence through strengthening Kyrgyz national identity, not weakening it as the independent inquiry recommended.

The use of imagery and monuments by Myrzakmatov reminds us that narratives about more recent events are grounded for different groups in Kyrgyzstan in older events and established stories, tied together in the production of remembered histories. Some of the pasts that have been constructed for Osh tell the tale of a multicultural city where communities met to trade and interact, and this was something that Akaev sought to promote in his Osh 3000 events, which were designed to commemorate the supposed three-thousandth anniversary of the founding of the city.

Harrowell's (2015) work found that older residents still mentally mapped onto that past and that they also envisioned Osh through a Soviet prism, which was one of security and prosperity. Megoran (2013) also found that the story of coexistence and peace was one that residents would tell of their 'memory' of the past. However, this vied with different stories that 'remembered' a conflictual past. One was of a beautiful Uzbek city, made ugly by the Soviets and then unsafe by the Kyrgyz. The other was of a site for underlining Uzbek power, where the experience was one of marginalising the weaker Kyrgyz population, thus stymying dreams of national self-determination. Megoran points out that these are not distinct and coherent narratives, and if a story of interdependence and shared space is to be told again, there will have to be some form of reconciliation and dialogue.

Following Halbwachs (1992), Mitchell (2003) argues that the past is socially acquired by emphasising that memorials are not enough – the repetition of commemoration is required to sustain social memories. Therefore, there needs to be an element of the spectacular in monuments and commemorative events. Perhaps this also explains the limited resonance of the Osh memorials for the city's residents. That said, there are commemorations at these places, some of them very high profile. In 2015 the Kyrgyz prime minister Temir Sariev stood with head bowed next to the UN Secretary-General Ban Ki-Moon at the site of *The Tears of the Mothers* (his successor, Antonio Guterres, would attend two years later). At the same time, Kyrgyz president Almazbek Atambaev issued a statement marking the fifth anniversary in which he put the blame firmly on Bakiyev and his supporters (RFE/RL's Kyrgyz Service, 2015), which governments in Bishkek have done right from the immediate aftermath of the violence (Ismailbekova, 2013).

Such elite engagement with the memorial suggests that the priorities of Kyrgyz politicians are the need to present a degree of something in the area of contrition to an international audience while downplaying any acknowledgement of the deeper causes than the last stirrings of a corrupt cadre now overthrown (though it must be noted that Ban Ki-Moon did not play along; his speech at the monument was a plea for justice for Uzbeks still serving long jail terms, including life, as a result of the violence). The choice of *The Tears of the Mothers* for these ceremonies by government officials is important. The two women are equal in physical stature and in their loss. The patterns and clothing symbolise both communities without the need for the use (or deliberate avoidance) of the Uzbek language. The implied equality of this memorial allows the government to co-opt it to tell the story it has from the beginning – that both sides have something to learn from the events.

Recommendations from research for how to break down the estrangement and anxiety in Osh focus very strongly on Kyrgyz insecurity. This does not mean that in criticising the KIC report, there is disagreement that 'the systematic denial of justice to Uzbeks undermines the ability of Kyrgyz leaders to secure the unity and harmony that they have identified as being imperative to avert further violence' (Megoran, 2012: 4).

However, a key theme that emerges is that the mismatch between the perspective of international organisations that nationalism is to be discouraged or successfully tamed into a very capacious vision of the people, and Kyrgyz perceptions that their new state had faltered because the nation, envisioned as the sovereignty of the Kyrgyz people, had not been allowed to thrive (Gullette and Heathershaw, 2015; Wilkinson, 2015). This explains in particular the anger provoked by the commission's support for the promotion of the Uzbek language when a significant anxiety since independence had been about how to raise the proficiency and general usage of Kyrgyz (Pavlenko, 2008).

The alienation of the Kyrgyz by the international reaction has only encouraged a nationalism that is rooted in the need to saturate the state with cultural messages and sideline minorities (Laruelle, 2012). Therefore, acknowledging that states will build nations upon ethno-national cores and finding ways to make that a process that can still be inclusive (Megoran, 2012) is key; this also requires tackling the pernicious issue of corruption, which encourages the use of monoethnic networks to get things done (Wilkinson, 2015). It is, however, difficult to pinpoint the sequencing of events that could make this happen and fix the weaknesses of both state and nation, or the point at which the Kyrgyz would feel secure enough to acquiesce graciously to Uzbek concerns.

Kymlicka's (2004) review of nationalism and national minorities on the other side of the former Soviet Bloc in Europe identified a common trend of minorities being encouraged to throw their lot in with reformers to hasten the democratic consolidation that would allow their demands to be met. However, he argues that many of those movements have never given any indication that they would be genuinely interested in listening to claims for ethnic differentiation.

Drawing comparisons

When reviewing the physical commemoration of the Osh violence and the documentary representations of it, as well as the significant and growing body of research into it, central themes emerge quite readily: the importance of space and territory; the potential for unifying as well as divisive interpretations of the past; the insecurity of the community whose national identity is meant to align with the state; tensions over language; and, finally, the role of the international audience. As already stated, making use of those to illuminate our understanding of how memory is constructed, reproduced and challenged in Northern Ireland needs to be done in a way that does not stretch concepts beyond their meaning or create superficial comparisons without acknowledgement of the specific context in which conflict has emerged.

In particular, despite both cases being beset by ethno-national antagonism, there is no equivalent in Northern Ireland of one of the most significant organising principles of social and political life in Kyrgyzstan, which is membership of a clan, 'an informal social institution in which actual or notional kinship based on blood or marriage forms the central bond among members' (Collins, 2002: 140). Although these Central Asian networks were meant to have been suppressed in the Soviet era, they continued to operate and to influence public and private life. Since independence, clan politics, and the horizontal and vertical ties they create, have remained a key vehicle by which people seek resources and access to services. In Kyrgyzstan the hollowing out of the Bakiyev era meant they became even more important as a means of getting on (Matveeva et al., 2012). The fact that a key cleavage for clan power has been the divide between the north and the south of the state (Bond and Koch, 2010) also explains much of the geography of Kyrgyzstan's political instability.

Clans could be argued to be a soft institution (Pennington, 2009) which influence political decision-making. They carry sanctions if their informal rules are crossed and their existence can confound the understanding of someone trying to interpret how power is expressed and challenged in formal spheres. This all provides a dynamic that militates against the legitimacy of government institutions for which one would have to engage in some mental contortions to find an equivalent in Northern Ireland.

We should also think about key differences in the cases of Kyrgyzstan and Northern Ireland when we consider the potential for future violence. Most notably there is no equivalent of paramilitary organisations in Kyrgyzstan and the Islamic Movement of Uzbekistan is not – despite Kyrgyz fears about the Islamification of Uzbek identity – a nationalist movement, and retains very little support.

Three things stand out when considering the work in this volume and other research into the politics of memory in Northern Ireland in relation to what happened in Osh and the way in which it is being incorporated into different narratives of the history of state and peoples. The first is the difference in the scale of commemoration in Northern Ireland. This may seem obvious given that June 2010 is one event and a relatively recent one, but that is not the point being made here. Even to scale, the commemoration of the violence is very limited and Uzbek communities are not in a position to offer a public alternative to the rather anodyne imagery represented in *The Tears of the Mothers* monument. Instead, they have turned to what Ismailbekova (2013) terms public avoidance.

The very public debate about the legacy of the past in Northern Ireland has, to say the least, generated a lot of antagonism and played a role in political paralysis. However, it does drive forward campaigns that result in tangible outcomes, leading to investigations and inquiries that produce different forms of accountability, both individual and collective. The multiplicity of commemorations also creates the potential for internal division rather than two agreed stories controlled by two ethnic elites, something noted in particular by Brown and Grant's (2016) survey of commemoration in the region.

The second issue to consider is the significance of language. For Kyrgyzstan, the conflict has been one about the official recognition (or not) of languages that are the vernacular for communities and which have played a role in the socio-economic spheres in which different communities dominate (agriculture for the Kyrgyz and business for Uzbeks). For Northern Ireland, the Irish language is, despite interest and education in it, not a language of the day-to-day, and increased visibility or proficiency in it would never be seen as a challenge to the ability of people to communicate with each other in English in Northern Ireland. However, it seems whatever intention there is in seeking recognition for language rights, the emotions generated between and within groups do not vary.

The third issue is that of security and insecurity. One does not want to overdo a comparison by making unionists 'play' the role of the Kyrgyz or vice versa, but the dynamics created by insecurity do suggest a strong parallel in experience, especially with the ideology of loyalism. In Graham's (1997) assessment of how identity is constructed, the emphasis in loyalism is on identifiable people and events in their history, avoiding the difficulty of rooting themselves in contested territory. In addition, the need to preserve dominance, and give no ground because there is no outcome to accommodation other than destruction, has long been an observation made by those seeking to explain strategies and understandings within loyalism (see, for example, Nelson, 1984; Todd, 1987).

For both situations, it would seem that tackling the insecurity of the majority group would offer a place of comfort and confidence whereby the difficult issues of the past could be tackled in a way that allowed people to reshape the significance of events; therefore, the potential to tell different stories in the future is there. However, while anxieties over resources and their allocation, for example, could be addressed through socio-economic policies that promote and share prosperity, these are unlikely to be introduced in the short term in states that cannot or will not prioritise redistributive approaches. In addition, the nature of this insecurity is profoundly existential. This needs to be acknowledged and it cannot be wished away, but it also means that for groups seeking to redefine and differentiate citizenship, a strategy of waiting it out and staying silent is unlikely by itself to produce the conditions for the painful process of genuine dialogue.

References

Ackali, P. (2005) 'Democracy and political stability in Kyrgyzstan', in B. N. Schlyter (ed.), *Prospects for Democracy in Central Asia*, pp. 41–58. Stockholm: Swedish Research Institute in Istanbul.

Bara, J. (2009) 'Methodology', in J. Bara and M. Pennington (eds), *Comparative Politics*, pp. 41–64. London: Sage.

Bond, A. R. and Koch, N. R. (2010) 'Interethnic tensions in Kyrgyzstan: a political geographic perspective', *Eurasian Geography and Economics*, 51 (4): 531–62.

Brown, K. and Grant, A. (2016) 'A lens over conflicted memory: surveying "Troubles" commemoration in Northern Ireland', *Irish Political Studies*, 31 (1): 139–62.

Collins, K. (2002) 'Clans, pacts and politics in Central Asia', *Journal of Democracy*, 13 (3): 137–52.

Graham, B. (1997) 'Ulster: a representation of place yet to be imagined', in P. Shirlow and M. McGovern (eds), *Who Are 'the People'? Unionism, Protestantism and Loyalism in Northern Ireland*, pp. 34–54. London: Pluto.

Gullette, D. and Heathershaw, J. (2015) 'The affective politics of sovereignty: reflecting on the 2010 conflict in Kyrgyzstan', in M. Laruelle and J. Engvall (eds), *Kyrgyzstan: Beyond 'Democracy Island' and 'Failing State': Social and Political Changes in a Post-Soviet Society*, pp. 185–209. Lanham, MD: Lexington Books.

Forest, B. and Johnson, J. (2011) 'Monumental politics: regime type and public memory in post-communist states', *Post-Soviet Affairs*, 27 (3): 269–88, https://doi.org/10.2747/1060-586X.27.3.269.

Keman, H. (2014) 'Comparative research methods', in D. Caramani (ed.), *Comparative Politics*, pp. 47–59. Oxford: Oxford University Press.

Hanks, R. R. (2011) 'Crisis in Kyrgyzstan: conundrums of ethnic conflict, national identity and state cohesion', *Journal of Balkan and Near Eastern Studies*, 13 (2): 177–87.

Harrowell, E. (2015) 'From monuments to mahallas: contrasting memories in the urban landscape of Osh, Kyrgyzstan', *Social and Cultural Geography*, 16 (2): 203–25, https://doi.org/10.1080/14649365.2014.972972.

Halbwachs, M. (1992) *On Collective Memory*, ed. and trans. L. A. Coser. Chicago, IL: University of Chicago Press.

Hardenberg, R. (2012) 'Collective, communicative and cultural memories: examples of local historiography from northern Kyrgyzstan', *Central Asian Survey*, 31 (3): 265–76.

Huskey, E. (2003) 'National identity from scratch: defining Kyrgyzstan's role in world affairs', *Journal of Communist Studies and Transition Politics*, 19 (3): 111–38.

Huskey, E. (2008) 'Foreign policy in a vulnerable state: Kyrgyzstan as military entrepot between the great powers', *China and Eurasia Forum Quarterly*, 6 (4): 5–18.

Ismailbekova, A. (2013) 'Coping strategies: public avoidance, migration, and marriage in the aftermath of the Osh conflict, Fergana Valley', *Nationalities Papers*, 41 (1): 109–27.

Juska, A. (1999) 'Ethno-political transformation in the states of the former USSR', *Ethnic and Racial Studies*, 22 (3): 524–53.

KIC (Kyrgyzstan Inquiry Commission) (2011) *Report of the Independent International Commission of Inquiry into the Events in Southern Kyrgyzstan in June 2010*. Available at: https://reliefweb.int/sites/reliefweb.int/files/resources/Full_Report_490.pdf (accessed 18 April 2018).

Kymlicka, W. (2004) 'Justice and security in the accommodation of minority nationalism', in S. May, T. Modood and J. Squires (eds), *Ethnicity, Nationalism and Minority Rights*, pp. 144–76. Cambridge: Cambridge University Press.

Laruelle, M. (2012) 'The paradigm of nationalism in Kyrgyzstan: evolving narrative, the sovereignty issue, and political agenda', *Communist and Post-Communist Studies*, 45: 39–49.

Matveeva, A., Savin, I. and Faizullaev, B. (2012) 'Kyrgyzstan: tragedy in the south', *Ethnopolitics Papers* no. 17.

McDaid, S. (2019) 'Opportunities and challenges in comparative "Troubles" scholarship' [blog post], *Writing the 'Troubles'* (22 July). Available at: https://writingthetroublesweb.wordpress.com/2019/07/22/comparative-troubles/ (accessed 1 September 2019).

McFaul, M. (2022) 'The fourth wave of democracy and dictatorship: noncooperative transitions in the postcommunist world', *World Politics*, 54 (2): 212–44.

McGarry, J. (ed.) (2001) *Northern Ireland and the Divided World: Post-Agreement Northern Ireland*. Oxford: Oxford University Press.

Megoran, N. (2012) *Averting Violence in Kyrgyzstan: Understanding and Responding to Nationalism*. London: Chatham House.

Megoran, N. (2013) 'Shared space, divided space: narrating ethnic histories of Osh', *Environment and Planning*, 45: 892–907.

Mitchell, K. (2003) 'Monuments, memorials, and the politics of memory', *Urban Geography*, 24 (5): 442–59.

Myrzakmatov, M. (2011) *Searching for Truth – The Osh Tragedy: Documents, Facts, Interviews, Appeals and Statements*. Available at: www.fergananews.com/archive/2011/melis_russ.pdf [in Kyrgyz] (accessed 10 June 2019).

Nelson, S. (1984) *Ulster's Uncertain Defenders: Loyalists and the Northern Ireland Conflict*. Belfast: Appletree Press.

Pavlenko, A. (2008) 'Multilingualism in post-soviet countries: language revival, language removal and sociolinguistic theory', *Bilingual Education and Bilingualism*, 11 (3): 275–314.

Pennington, M. (2009) 'Theory, institution and comparative politics', In J. Bara and M. Pennington (eds) *Comparative Politics*, pp. 13–40. London: Sage.

Peters, B. G. (1998) *Comparative Politics: Theory and Methods*. New York, NY: New York University Press.

RFE/RL's Kyrgyz Service (2015) 'Ban Ki-Moon joins Kyrgyz commemoration of victims of Osh clashes', Radio Free Europe/Radio Liberty (11 June). Available at: www.rferl.org/a/kyrgyzstan-ban-ki-moon-commemoration-osh-victims/27067234.html (accessed 25 September 2019).

Roy, O. (2000) *The New Central Asia: Geopolitics and the Birth of Nations*. New York, NY: IB Tauris.

Suny, R. G. (2005) 'Nation-making among the Ruins of Empire', in Z. Barany and R. G. Moser (eds), *Ethnic Politics After Communism*, pp. 1–13. Ithaca, NY: Cornell University Press.

Tishkov, V. (1995) '"Don't kill me, I'm a Kyrgyz": an anthropological analysis of violence in the Osh ethnic conflict', *Journal of Peace Research*, 3 (2): 133–49.

Todd, J. (1987) 'Two traditions in unionist political culture', *Irish Political Studies*, 2 (1): 1–26.

Tonge, J. (2014) *Comparative Peace Processes*. Cambridge: Polity.

Volosevich, A. (2010) 'Kyrgyzstan: the country cannot do without international investigation', *Fergana News* (21 July). Available at: www.fergananews.com/articles/6668 (accessed 15 March 2018).

Wilkinson, C. (2015) 'Imagining Kyrgyzstan's nationhood and statehood: reactions to the 2010 Osh violence', *Nationalities Papers*, 43 (3): 417–36, https://doi.org/10.1080/00905992.2014.961127.

11

The problem of legacy and remembering the past in Northern Ireland

Graham Spencer

> It is important to keep remembering the names and faces of the people who died, and the unforgiveable circumstances in which they lost their lives, if only to combat the efforts of those who tirelessly seek to whitewash the past.
> (Eilis O'Hanlon, *Belfast Telegraph*, 29 July 2020)

> It can be dangerous to question the stories people tell about themselves because so much of our identity is both shaped by and bound up with our history. That is why dealing with the past, in deciding on which version we want, or on what we want to remember and forget, can become so politically charged
> (Margaret MacMillan, *The Uses and Abuses of History*, 2010)

> If history is an attempt to discover what actually happened, memory is an attempt to recover the experiences of it
> (Susan Neiman, *Learning from the Germans*, 2019)

Three notable points of concern (among others) arise when thinking about the need to re-examine the past (more specifically, the period referred to as the Troubles) in Northern Ireland. The first relates to the problem of selectivity in how the past is conceived and constructed. The second relates to the problem of detaching expectations about how the past will be approached from community and group narratives that stress that past in conflictive and divisive terms. And the third relates to the problem of how the outcomes of any legacy process (a formal system of measures to assist engagement) can help build a future that breaks from the enmity of the past. There is little doubt that a comprehensive process that effectively grapples with legacy issues has to be constructed at government level if it is to

The problem of legacy and remembering the past 223

have any chance of succeeding. Yet, at the same time, envisaging a legacy process ostensibly in political terms is almost certain to make it fail.

By developing a legacy process as an extension of political interests it is obvious that such a process will become a reflection of communal rather than individual priorities and that zero-sum, competitive scenarios will dominate proceedings, as well as outcomes. In that instance, a legacy process will do little more than provide a platform to further reinforce old conflict attitudes and ideologies, with individual needs minimised as communal or group needs are maximised. Because of this, I would argue that any constructive attempt to examine the past should be conceived primarily as a therapeutic project, providing mental health support for individuals, otherwise group and community disputes about responsibility, blame and morality used during the conflict will continue to dictate public attention and reaction.

The structures envisaged as necessary to address the suffering and pain of the Northern Ireland conflict were initially set out in the Consultative Group on the Past (CGP) report in 2009. The report was rejected at its launch across the political divide in Northern Ireland and its recommendations were effectively shelved until the Stormont House Agreement (SHA) of 2014, where it was revitalised in an amended and more hesitant form. The SHA envisaged a legacy process as achievable through four mechanisms: the first, an oral history archive 'to share experiences and narratives related to the Troubles'; the second, a Historical Investigations Unit to conduct 'investigations into outstanding Troubles-related deaths'; the third, an Independent Commission on Information Retrieval that would 'enable victims and survivors to seek and privately receive information about the deaths of their next of kin'; and the fourth, an Implementation and Reconciliation Group to 'oversee themes, archives and information recovery' as well as 'encourage and support other initiatives that contribute to reconciliation, better understanding of the past and reducing sectarianism' (NIO, 2014).

Operating as an adjunct of the oral history archive would be a mental health trauma service designed to support victims and survivors' needs by enabling 'access to advocate-counsellor services if they wish' (NIO, 2014). Some six years after the SHA proposals and after numerous contestations about what legacy design would set out to achieve, a ministerial statement in March 2020 sought to reassure once again that the overall aim would be to 'help the whole of society heal the wounds of the Troubles' in order to 'become better reconciled to our difficult history' (Lewis, 2020).

This chapter sets out to highlight some of the problems that may impact on a legacy process and argues that if the aim of that process is to address the past in ways that help loosen society from the historical grip of conflict, then such an approach as that envisaged by the SHA is highly unlikely to meet that objective. The reasons for this are extensive, and the few that I look at here can only be touched upon in general terms, but they nevertheless relate to a central theme, namely the inability of the political parties to deliver an inclusive legacy process. Parties who cannot agree the cause of the conflict are unlikely to accept a collective or shared responsibility for it. Further, they will lack any common point of reference for what constitutes a victim or a perpetrator and, because of that, have little means by which to agree how such a process will be used to shape a better and more tolerant society.

Outside of those immediate political disputes one might also add that the divisions of collective memory, the disputed nature of truth, the impossibility of social and political reconciliation, and the marginalisation rather than prioritisation of mental health support as further reasons (and ones I want to look at here) why one should remain highly sceptical about the proposed model having beneficial effect. Having elaborated on how current approaches to the above areas are likely to hinder rather than help Northern Ireland better comprehend its troubled history, and how the political landscape is more inclined to intensify rather than defuse attitudes about conflict, the chapter concludes by arguing for an understanding and remembering of the past based on personal transformation and therapeutic intervention.

Collective memory

Presumably, when we talk about 'dealing with' or 'addressing' the past in Northern Ireland, we are talking about the need to understand and remember that past differently (why embark on a process which merely confirms what is already known?). But, if that is the case, what then is the difference in that understanding and remembering that we seek and how can it be achieved when community narratives and collective memories about the myths and divisions of conflict continue to dominate? What seems fairly obvious is that without an inclination to approach the history of the conflict differently, engagement will be used to reassert the attitudes of that conflict and so bring little in the way of re-evaluation or new understanding into the public realm. Surely, if anything new is to come out of a legacy process, it will need to comprehensively address the tendency for communities to think about each other in conflicting terms (negative, dehumanising and divisive) and, foremost, meet the needs of individuals who live with the trauma and pain of conflict. Or, to put it slightly differently, it will need to consider how groups use memories and experiences to remember the past, but in the light of new, alternative, often repressed memories and experiences.

With regard to the role of collective memory in Northern Ireland, it is apparent how this has historically been used as a separation device between communities and influenced by strong identity associations that exist in opposition with each other. Because of this, if we are to better grasp how the conflict is imagined, perpetuated and experienced, we need to give time to better understand how antagonistic outlooks come into play and how each group or community uses negative stereotypes about the other for purposes of internal cohesion and stability. In particular, we need to be attentive to how collective memory generates powerful emotional attachment to images of tragedy in order to maintain identity boundaries and encourage allegiance (MacMillan, 2010: 47–48).

For those like Todorov, collective memory is a deception since it is not memory at all, 'but a variety of discourse used in the public arena' that 'serves to reflect the image that a society, or one of its constituent groups, wishes to give of itself' (Todorov, 2000: 132). Todorov's argument is that memory is personal and based on lived experience, so to generalise and simplify it is to make it little more than a contrivance for propaganda goals. In comparison to this emphasis on collective memory as an illusion, Rieff acknowledges that collective memory has value but that this is metaphorical rather than factual. The effect is symbolic meaning attributed to events that is so strong it provides an assumed historical accuracy and truth which, in reality, is lacking (Rieff, 2016: 35). However, one of Rieff's central points (and of importance for us here) is that collective memory is undesirable because of the tendency for it to be used to advocate war rather than peace, and because of 'the determination to exact revenge rather than commit to the hard work of forgiveness' that it encourages (Rieff, 2016: 39). It is this influence, Rieff notes, that makes collective memory antithetical to reconciliation. Collective memory, from this perspective, relies on using stories about the past not for inclusive and conciliatory purposes, but exclusive and conflictive purposes (Rieff, 2016: 116).

One of the more notable problems with regard to collective memory in addressing a past conflict is the difficulty those who adhere to that memory have in accepting any departure from what is conventionally believed, and no longer to relate to that memory as a 'duty'. In this instance, where memory is used to reinforce group expectations, its main purpose is to act as a 'fabricated narrative in the service of social-ideological needs' (Blustein, 2008: 177). Constructed more as an extension of political and social interest, collective memory, Blustein insists, 'is used and manipulated to strengthen and serve the authority of the ruling powers or to challenge that authority' (Blustein, 2008: 187).

Given this tendency, entering into any legacy process from a position based on defending collective memory clearly poses problems for any new understanding or openness to change. Then, collective memory becomes a resistance to change, especially so when findings or expressions do not confirm what is already believed and known. In that case, new or alternative experiences and perceptions are likely to be seen not only as a distortion, or untruthful, but as an actual threat to communal identity and solidarity, with the measure of what is accepted (and not accepted) relative to the emotional weight of attachment to established narratives. The cost of distancing oneself from the influence of collective memory thus also brings with it the danger of being no longer seen as representative of the community (Blustein, 2008: 193). For that reason, what is generally believed brings with it a pressure for conformity that makes public criticism a dangerous business, and this is particularly the case when criticism starts to bring to light how memory has been used for reasons of corruption, coercion and abuse.

If there are numerous ways to forget and remember the past that come from considering individual accounts in relation to collective narratives (Neiman, 2019: 374), then the possibilities of remembering differently (as well as forgetting differently) will need to reflect this potentially uncomfortable relationship. Indeed, one might argue this is essential if learning about the past is to have any credibility and to move beyond being more than just a confirmation exercise. But, for this to happen, individual memory and experience must be given emphasis, since it is a changed relationship between the individual and collective memory that enables one to move outside the limitations of the past and so to see one's place in the community and society differently.

To get some idea of how collective memory and narratives work, perhaps we might reflect on how the republican movement in Northern Ireland (mostly the Provisional IRA and Sinn Féin) has continued to stress a collective narrative of victimhood and present republican communities as those who have suffered most in the conflict (Spencer, 2015b: 305), even though close to some 60 per cent of Troubles deaths were caused by republicans. This victimhood relies on ignoring or diverting attention from any infliction of pain and suffering (including from the many victims within the Catholic community killed by republicans), with republican leaders insisting that in any legacy process there must be 'no hierarchy of victims' (those leaders are less keen on stressing a comparative 'no hierarchy of perpetrators' approach as a basis for addressing the past).

On the suffering created by republican terrorism Sinn Féin is clear: such victims are the inevitable result of British repression, their misery ultimately a matter of discrimination and brutality imposed by the British state. Given this emphasis, republican responsibility is displaced by British responsibility and it is the British government who must accept the brunt of responsibility for the conflict and the victims created by it. As former Sinn Féin president Gerry Adams put it when talking about a legacy process, the British government 'cannot be the objective facilitator of any truth recovery process', lacks honesty and is unwilling 'to take responsibility for their actions during the conflict' (Sinn Féin, 2009). This gives credence to the view, as one astute commentator in Northern Ireland put it, that 'the removal of politicians and their narrow and constricted political agendas is vital if we are to develop a non-partisan and inclusive legacy process' (Roberts, 2018).

Victim narration has sustained the republican 'struggle' throughout the Troubles, so using it to try and influence how a legacy process might be conducted should come as no surprise. However, this should not distract us from the fact that a shared response to how victims might be treated (which could be seen to exemplify the 'no hierarchy of victims' seen as necessary by Sinn Féin) *has* been put forward but was widely rejected across the political divide in Northern Ireland. It came in the form of a recommendation from the CGP in their 2009 report on dealing with the past, proposing that all victims of the conflict should be awarded £12,000. Though it is unclear how this figure was reached, the aims of the compensation were interesting.

First, by awarding all the same sum and not excluding perpetrators from being victims, the proposal avoided the potential for discriminatory categorisation (the suggested moral equivalence is also why so many rejected the proposal) and indeed avoided the 'no hierarchy of victims' approach that Sinn Féin called for. But secondly, I would suggest, its rejection was also related to the probability of it bringing an end to a 'victim culture' that has been used to serve collective memory and political objectives rather than meet individual needs. Recipients of the money would be officially and formally recognised as having suffered but its acceptance would bring with it a responsibility to no longer express (and perhaps see) oneself as a victim because of that recognition. It risked, to put it another way, drawing a line under the public articulation of victimhood, and with it the dilution of a victim culture in Northern Ireland.

For those who continue to assert victim status as a vital part of collective memory, the rejection of the CGP report, because of one minor section that sought to apply a non-discriminatory response to victims, is understandable since to accept that recommendation is to accept the need for an end to the victimhood narrative and, with it, the end of using blame for ideological reasons to exert pressure on opponents in order to gain future advantage. As Todorov put it: 'victimhood gives you grounds to complain, to protest, to make demands, and others just have to respond, or else cut off relations entirely ... a victim can rely on the recognition and attention that his status provides more or less indefinitely' (Todorov, 2000: 143). Moreover, the reiteration of victimhood means that a 'community can claim convincingly to have been the victim of injustice in the past' so as to make sure it 'acquires an inexhaustible line of credit in the present' (Todorov, 2000: 143), as illustrated by the way republicans repeatedly used victimhood throughout the peace process to try and extract further concessions from the British government (Spencer, 2015b: 305).

It could be argued that the widespread rejection of the CGP report came about because it did not provide a recommendation on victims that offered any obvious or immediate ground for political exploitation. Its framework was constructed on the basis of a very deliberate need to de-politicise approaches to dealing with the past that the political parties could not easily differentiate or use, and so the proposals advocated were rejected precisely because they had managed to avoid the trap of political difference. Stupidly, rather than supporting the report and seeing its recommendations as the basis of a shared approach, the British government effectively shelved it, preferring to give space and credibility to the outrage about compensating victims and so making it harder to resolve the 'victims issue' as a result.

The CGP report, which remains unsurpassed as an overarching attempt to confront the pain and trauma of the conflict (and which was filleted, adapted and re-packaged in the SHA), recommended a four-stranded approach to dealing with the past that would be overseen by a Legacy Commission. Those strands would operate to: (1) facilitate a shared future; (2) investigate and review historical cases from the Troubles; (3) co-ordinate an information recovery process; and (4) look at 'linked or thematic cases emerging from the conflict'. The extensive report also talks about the value of forgiveness and the formation of a reconciliation forum based on the promotion of healthcare services that particularly look at the impact of trauma, suicide and addiction. Though there are dangers in selectively dissecting the CGP report to support alternative agendas, it is interesting that a reconciliation forum is envisaged as response mechanism to address the therapeutic needs of individuals for reconciliatory purposes.

The proposition that therapeutic needs should also be seen in the light of reconciliatory ambition remains consistent with a wider interest in the international arena about the therapeutic being used 'to promote individual well-being and healing through behavioural and attitudinal change as the basis for conflict prevention' (Humphrey,

2005: 205), an interest drawn from the realisation that the trauma of violence and war in societies 'is potentially conflict producing' (Humphrey, 2005: 206). Focus on mental health services and related support is therefore seen as particularly important for addressing conflict because it changes the relationship of victims with their suffering and helps mitigate calls for blame and retaliation in the process (Humphrey, 2005: 217).

With regard to Northern Ireland there is another point worth making here about the importance of mental health support. By 2018, some twenty years after the Good Friday Agreement which marked the end of the conflict, more people had died by suicide than from the entire Troubles period (4,500 compared to an estimated 3,600 murders, bombings and other killings from the Troubles). This comparison between a higher 'post-conflict-related' death rate and a 'conflict-related' death rate lends particular power to a comment made by Dr Iris Elliott of the Mental Health Foundation who, in response to the figures, stressed, 'We cannot achieve a peaceful society in Northern Ireland without peaceful minds' (quoted in McDonald, 2018). This insightful observation highlights how shared aspirations and intentions also depend on mental health and a new relationship with the attitudes and beliefs that enable communal expectations about the past to be widened and challenged.

What seems fairly obvious is that as long as one community continues to claim victimhood and views the other as the reason for that victimhood, there can be no agreed basis for the cause of conflict and so no consensual framework for addressing the consequences of that conflict. Similarly, if an approach that measures the conflict by numbers killed is prioritised, there can be no agreement on responsibility for entering such a process. Since addressing the suffering of individuals through therapeutic rather than political structures is more likely to help individuals move towards alternative ways of understanding suffering that can have a beneficial impact on mental health but that may not be compatible with the priorities of collective memory, a new connection between the external world of the political, achieved through the internal transformation of the individual, is needed if new ways of living are to be found (Bolton, 2017: 187).

The demands of collective memory as self-defence often provide the justification for engagement in conflict. But no such emphasis can be applied to all actors equally when there is no shared sense of responsibility about the actions and consequences of that engagement. Not surprisingly, the ethos of a legacy process designed to promote reconciliation in Northern Ireland finds no agreed moral ground from which to move. This problem is compounded by those who stress legacy as a political process and who see the primary role and function of that process being to serve political agendas and efforts to maintain exclusive positions. Unless individual experience is given precedence over collective positions on actions and events, it is unlikely that the pain of the past can be sensitively encountered, or re-imagined, or moved beyond. And, unless there is a fundamental change of emphasis away from political interference, there will be no new conclusions reached about the past, just more insistence for greater certainties to support divisive political interests.

The potential for reconciliation, given the dominating influence of collective memory for reasons of political interference and influence, is surely minimal. The starting point for addressing the past should be what kind of society is envisaged once a formal process to do that has been concluded. Possible conflicts that may arise from different strands of a legacy process working against rather than with each other, remain another issue of contention (Roberts, 2018), but the central problem of how inclusivity can be made workable brings us directly to another point of concern, and that is how competing notions of morality and truth might be applied by the different communities to deal with the past more inclusively.

Truth

For an inclusive legacy process to find broad social acceptance, there surely needs to be some agreed and shared understanding of what the past means, not just as a timeline or chronology of violence with an emphasis on facts, but as a context by which to interpret the impact of conflict and suffering. This requires some degree of shared moral understanding about how the truth of testimony and information is to be assessed. Different views on the past are likely to prioritise different levels of responsibility for it and, in turn, bring different expectations about blame and reaction. But the concept of inclusiveness as the basis for a process that seeks to remember the past differently, and facilitate new understanding because of an emphasis on respect and collaboration, has to recognise that such inclusivity also requires a new moral order to represent the change sought.

This also brings into play questions about how determinations of right and wrong and good and bad will be reached, as well as how an environment can be created to accommodate opposing judgements and different demands on accountability. As said, the problem with collective memory being used as a context for the reception of testimony or information arises when that testimony or information does not confirm or correspond with the moral credibility of the pre-existing narrative. Then, it tends not to be believed, with exponents of new narratives, who cast doubt on the validity and relevance of old ones, likely to be isolated or made to feel excluded as accepted community voices.

If disputes in relation to dominant narratives are more likely to maintain disparity and division than reduce it, and the basis of that tension is moral difference, then one of the key challenges for those designing a legacy process is how to deal with opposing moral positions of equivalent value within the one process. To get some sense of how difficult this might be, perhaps we should briefly consider how the two different Catholic and Protestant communities in Northern Ireland conceptualise morality differently. More specifically, this means looking at how Catholics and Protestants in Northern Ireland are inclined to measure moral order from different standpoints that draw from religious foundations, with Catholics tending to conceptualise action in communal terms and Protestants tending to conceptualise action in individual terms (O'Malley, 1995: 25). And, while many Catholics are inclined to accept the single moral authority symbolised by the Church (even if they have no congregational attachment, Catholic teaching and values still influence perceptions) with its strong emphasis on society and community, Protestants tend to rely more on 'private judgement' and view the morality of collective narratives with suspicion.

This suspicion among Protestants derives, in particular, from the view that there is a Catholic tendency to avoid moral clarity when it comes to individual action and responsibility and a preference for interpreting each in a wider context of social cause and effect.

One outcome of this distinction is a strong propensity to view responsibility (and so right and wrong) as a tension over authenticity and truth. Such differences provide an interpretive basis by which to discern right and wrong as well as shape cultural values that inform moral order and shape expectations of community, society, identity and difference.

The Catholic emphasis on individual action, seen through a spectrum of moral shades, differs from a Protestant emphasis which tends to exclude social circumstances as the context for action, also has wider ramifications for thinking about conflict. For, if one community is likely to understand conflict in terms of social conditions and circumstances and another community is likely to understand conflict in terms of individual behaviour and decision-making, then any inclusive context for accommodating both these perspectives will need to give attention to the competing notions of right and wrong that inevitably arise.

Elaborating on this distinction by looking at the dominant Presbyterian strand of Protestantism in Northern Ireland, O'Malley notes how such people, influenced by Calvinist Puritanism, tend to believe that 'right and wrong are not only morally indistinguishable, but absolutes'. And that because of this, 'they bring the same inflexible, no-compromise stance to their attitudes on every issue and the same distrust of others – especially Catholics – who do not share their rigidity'. One consequence of such a view, O'Malley contends, is that, 'They mistake their own rigidity for virtue, for standing for principle, for an honesty they are unwilling to impute to others who do not share their unyielding dogmatism' (O'Malley, 1995: 26).

For many Protestants, this demand for clarity creates with it a 'sense of the Catholic propensity to conceal real intentions' (O'Malley, 1995: 26). As one respondent to O'Malley's inquiry into this area put it, 'Honesty and truth and right and wrong have a rather simplistic, straightforward, uncomplicated meaning for Protestants', which stands in contrast to the belief of many Protestants that 'Catholics do not say what they mean' (O'Malley, 1995: 25) because Catholicism is 'a religion of equivocation, where right and wrong are gradations on a theological curve' (O'Malley, 1995: 24), and where, because of this variance, there arises ambiguity which, 'in the eyes of Protestants', is the 'root cause of their distrust of Catholics in general, and of Irish Catholics in particular' (O'Malley, 1995: 23).

There is obvious danger in exaggerating this moral distinction, but considered in the light of the enmity of conflict and how this may relate to reconciliation (Spencer, 2012: 95–139) one can see how divergent notions of truth can become a significant problem for any inclusive legacy process. Given how opposing justifications for violence have been used by terrorist groups in Northern Ireland and how the morality of that violence is perceived more widely within the respective communities (Spencer, 2008: 7–53, 2015a: 67–110), one might reasonably expect opposing ideas about accountability and authenticity (and so truth) to limit how the past is conceived and understood.

This moral antagonism is another reason why reconciliation as a social and communal outcome is highly unlikely and why individual re-imagination of suffering and trauma through therapeutic services is the more constructive and beneficial path. Reconciliation has greater possibility not as a political entity but as a process of individual transformation that evolves from new and alternative ways of thinking and feeling about pain and trauma in ways that may have wider positive implications for social relations. Seeking to use available testimony about past injustices, unresolved crimes and individual stories of suffering as part of a broader social narrative of repair will invariably pose a challenge for memories and narratives that resist change. For example, how will a community react to stories that bring to light how individuals from that community have historically used the 'cover' of militant groupings to coerce, intimidate, torture or abuse residents? Will one-to-one or small-group crimes that resulted in suffering, trauma, depression and cruelty be seen as 'conflict-related'? And most importantly, how will these accounts be used to help better understand the past?

A political emphasis given to a legacy process is at odds with the intimacy of interaction that arises between victim and therapist, where layers of suffering can be carefully unwrapped as part of a process to change how pain is re-lived and experienced. This transformation of the personal is fundamental to reconciliation (with both conflicted areas of the self and others) and more likely to produce positive impact (for those who want it) compared to reconciliation envisaged as a community or social exercise. On this, as Ignatieff points out:

> It is perilous to extrapolate from traumatised individuals to whole societies. It is simply an extravagant metaphor to think of societies coming awake from a nightmare. The only coming awake that makes sense to speak of is one by one, individual by individual in the recesses of their own identities. Nations, properly speaking, cannot be reconciled to other nations, only individuals to individuals. (Quoted in Boraine, 2000: 371–72)

Managing competing notions of truth was a problem that the team tasked with designing the Truth and Reconciliation Commission in South Africa faced. In the end, four conceptualisations were applied: the first, objective or factual truth or forensic truth; the second, personal or narrative truth; the third, social or 'dialogical truth'; and the fourth, healing or restorative truth (Boraine, 2000: 288–91). The attention given to each and how those categorisations were used represented some attempt to accommodate differences in how various groups related to the causes of division and injustice in South Africa, if framed by a common objective to support the development of a new nation after apartheid. Though the eventual success of this project is disputable (Hope, 2018), the expansive use of 'truth' at least reflected different approaches and interpretations of the apartheid problem that gave space for alternative testimonies.

So far, in the case of Northern Ireland, there has been no acknowledgement of how each community is likely to view truth or use that truth as a reference point in relation to the other community. Not surprisingly, this makes 'truth', and the divergent concepts of accountability and authenticity that come from it (and not forgetting there may be at least ten variants of it that each produce different points of focus for understanding; see Baggini, 2018), an inhibitive rather than facilitative influence for rethinking the past in Northern Ireland, and certainly obstructs the likelihood of inclusive outcomes.

Reconciliation

If the aim of reconciliation is to bring about a space where different and opposing views can be treated with mutual respect, it is obvious that this space will need to be inclusive in design and function. Such a space would, generally speaking, seek to encourage independent and exclusive positions to be seen as interdependent, enabling those who engage with it to re-evaluate and loosen the grip of their pain, and invite participants to think more carefully about the possible advantages of a shared future (Lederach, 1997: 27–31). But this need for inclusivity also runs counter to the objectives of party politics, which depends on the exaggeration of difference and division.

Here the emphasis on good/bad, us/them, is about exclusivity, not inclusivity, so to expect political parties to actively create or support an inclusive approach to the past is to expect those parties to act against their own interests and inclinations to tighten (not loosen) polarised attitudes and judgements on which they depend. The likelihood of politicians in Northern Ireland (most, anyway) working to cultivate a sense of sameness, when the environment in which they operate is combative and driven by defensive and offensive tendencies, indicates just how implausible a politics of reconciliation is.

Yet, taking this into account, as well as any potential conflicts of interest that may occur through the different mechanisms proposed by the SHA (such as whether the findings of a historical investigation will undermine the information retrieval process, or how the four strands will be used for convergent rather than divergent ends), there remains an assumption from the current legacy proposals that an overarching ethos of reconciliation will somehow develop and provide a galvanising influence on the need for change.

However, where there are examples of victims and perpetrators coming together to try and bring about some shared (but not reconciled) understanding, it is apparent that a separation between political and personal needs is a vital component in the success of that interaction (Spencer, 2011a: 231). Then, the burden of pain and suffering is re-imagined through a process of 'internalised dialogue' that evolves as a result of non-confrontational interpersonal engagement that helps create distance between the past and the future in order to make the present more tolerable (Spencer, 2011a: 187–98, 285–302).

When transferred outside of the private world into the public sphere, obstructions to this transformation increase (Spencer and Alderdice, 2019), since the expectations of communal responsibility and identity are threatened by gestures or dialogue that might potentially blur the boundaries of certainty by moving towards moderation or re-evaluation (Spencer, 2011b). The very idea of inclusivity is, therefore, a danger to divided communities who use national identity and political ambitions against each other and who see the potential for inclusive interaction as a threat to or dilution of that identity, even if movement in this direction is what is needed to build reconciliation.

This process of 'narrative incorporation', as Dwyer puts it, is one where stories and images of identity are absorbed into a wider narrative that attempts to understand differences between a 'former' and 'new self', and uses equilibrium to try and overcome destructive impulses as the basis for interaction (Dwyer, 1999: 88). On that basis, the real point of reconciliation, Dwyer suggests, is to support 'strategies of narrative revision' (Dwyer, 1999: 96) that strive to position individual experience in a context of shared or collective purpose, so drawing notions of the past and future into an interlocking dynamic (Dwyer, 1999: 83).

Even religious groups who talk about forgiving and remembering in Northern Ireland tend to arrive at different conclusions about how each might be reached, articulating positions on conditionality that reflect divisions in the political process (Spencer, 2012). The proposition, as expressed in the CGP report, that 'both sides must somehow be enabled to reach agreement that there was wrongdoing on both sides' since mutual recognition and admission make 'mutual forgiveness possible' (CGP, 2009: 54) is based on the premise that there is a joint desire to admit wrongdoing (when there is not) and rather overlooks the differences that shape interpretations and expectations about responsibility and accountability. Similarly, the need for actors to have the 'moral stature' to admit 'mistakes in their moral decisions' (Spencer, 2009: 55), and through this admission help to create a new context that others can enter in order to make reconciliation possible, seems highly unlikely.

With the two dominant political parties in Northern Ireland (Sinn Féin and the Democratic Unionist Party) coming to power as a bulwark against the extreme demands and views of the other, there is no possibility of 'mutual understanding' on the past (or anything else) emerging in the near future. Collective memory, for both, remains the articulation of collective identity that draws from a tightly controlled representation of past events and actions that are all too often used to accuse or condemn. Inevitably, the more extreme the political parties, the more extreme their reading of political circumstances and the less likely any impetus for change is. Though some degree of nationally shared understanding about pain may help validate the sense of individual loss felt, as with 9/11 (Herman, 1992: 221), what a collective understanding does not do is provide space for letting individual experiences be felt and understood differently, and so how loss, or pain, may be felt and known differently (Herman, 1992: 177).

Conclusion

While it is important that a legacy process that constructively grapples with the past must have an external and formal dimension where information about structures and purpose can be used to create public anticipations about change, it is argued here that the real basis for that change is transformation of the individual. And that although the political system offers a starting point for implementing structures of engagement, the likelihood of success rests more on personal than political intervention.

Attempts to use a legacy process to primarily serve political agendas will inevitably doom it to failure. For years now the political parties in Northern Ireland have been at loggerheads to agree what or who constitutes a victim, as republicans seek to blur all victims into a category of sameness (their sameness) while unionists object to the very idea of sameness because of the connotations of moral symmetry or equivalence suggested.

Even in August 2020, some months after former Northern Ireland Secretary of State Julian Smith signed legislation for a victim compensation scheme that would be available to those 'injured through no fault of their own in a Troubles-related incident' (NIO, 2020) and that proposed annual payments ranging from £2,000 to £10,000 to such victims for the rest of their lives, republicans objected to the exclusion from the scheme of those injured due to their own actions or who committed serious crimes. For Sinn Féin's Deputy First Minister Michelle O'Neill, such a scheme would exclude thousands of republicans (a unionist argument not made about the many loyalist ex-combatants who would also be excluded) and so would be discriminatory (Young, 2020).

Conducted at the political level, and because of the enduring political divisions in Northern Ireland, it is apparent that there can be no consensus about dealing with the past when no moral equivalence about that past is available. Memory remains contested, and because of that it reflects an inability to contemplate symmetry when it comes to recognition and responsibility. On that basis, the foundations for legacy have not been thoughtfully or sensitively prepared and political articulations continue to reassert conflict attitudes and motivations (Edwards, 2008).

Suggestions that engagement by community or political groups is more about seeking to de-legitimise the position of opponents and that greater attention should be paid to ensuring there is no imbalance in the public articulation of memory also indicates a problem of accessibility (McGrattan, 2020). On three key fronts about how memory is used, how truth is understood and how reconciliation might be achieved, a politically driven legacy process lacks the basis for delivery. Further, proposed structures for engagement offer little prospect for hope, largely because the separate strands inhibit a systematic and coherent approach to ending old conflict narratives and attitudes.

The goal of a shared and more inclusive understanding of the past may seem a commendable ambition, but in lacking a clear impetus to transform underlying divisions and enmities the design of the process does not serve that ambition well. Indeed, because of its divergent construction and the inability of the different strands to consistently support an inclusive ethos, it would appear that the process may well work against the very thing it seeks to bring about, namely reconciliation.

Within much literature on reconciliation, there is little talk about countries, states or different national identities being reconciled. The emphasis for this transformation is on the individual (of the self or with another) who is changed through listening and dialogue (Griswold, 2009; Schlink, 2010), and where the quiet, non-invasive environment of privacy and one-to-one interaction is the foundation for constructive engagement. This environment of intimacy and trust that has the potential to transform one's relationship with accusation, judgement and expectations of revenge is a therapeutic one. It is here, in the private realm, where the most contentious, disabling and non-conforming accounts become permissible, and it is through such personal interaction that the means to achieve a new understanding of trauma and suffering (and, subsequently, how to live with it less destructively or painfully) is possible.

It is through this engagement, to put it slightly differently, that one's relationship with experiences and emotions from the past, and so the past itself, can change. And, though there may be many ways to express one's feelings beyond the therapeutic process (which is not for everyone), it would appear to be the case that until individuals feel free enough to talk about the past in ways which contradict or undermine the narratives of established collective memory, Northern Ireland will not have loosened itself from the destructive clasp of conflict.

References

Baggini, J. (2018) *A Short History of Truth*. London: Quercus.
Blustein, J. (2008) *The Moral Demands of Memory*. Cambridge: Cambridge University Press.
Bolton, D. (2017) *Conflict, Peace and Mental Health*. Manchester: Manchester University Press.
Boraine, A. (2000) *A Country Unmasked*. Oxford: Oxford University Press.
CGP (Consultative Group on the Past) (2009) *Report of the Consultative Group on the Past*. Belfast: CGP. Available at: https://cain.ulster.ac.uk/victims/docs/consultative_group/cgp_230109_report.pdf (accessed 20 March 2020).
Dwyer, S. (1999) 'Reconciliation for realists', *Ethics and International Affairs*, 13: 81–98.
Edwards, A. (2008) 'Drawing a line under the past', *Peace Review*, 20 (2): 209–17.
Griswold, C. L. (2009) 'Forgiveness and narrative', in P. Godobo-Madikzela and C. Van Der Merwe (eds), *Memory, Narrative and Forgiveness*, pp. 98–112. Newcastle: Cambridge Scholars Publishing.
Herman, J. L. (1992) *Trauma and Recovery*. New York, NY: Basic Books.
Hope, C. (2018) *The Café De Move-On Blues*. London: Atlantic Books.
Humphrey, C. (2005) 'Reconciliation and the therapeutic state', *Journal of Intercultural Studies*, 26 (3): 203–20.
Lederach, P. (1997) *Building Peace*. Washington, DC: United States Institute of Peace Press.

Lewis, B. (2020) 'Secretary of State for Northern Ireland, Brandon Lewis MP, oral statement: 18 March 2020: addressing Northern Ireland legacy issues' (Statement UIN HLWS163). London: Northern Ireland Office. Available at: https://questions-statements.parliament.uk/written-statements/detail/2020-03-18/HLWS163 (accessed 20 August 2020).

MacMillan, M. (2010) *The Uses and Abuses of History*. London: Profile Books.

McDonald, H. (2018) 'Northern Ireland suicides outstrip Troubles death toll', *Guardian*, 20 February.

McGrattan, C. (2020) 'Nationalism and dealing with the past in Northern Ireland, 1998–2018: the disarticulation of unionist memory', in P. J. Roche and B. Barton (eds), *The Northern Ireland Question: Perspectives on Nationalism and Unionism*, pp. 225–49. London: Wordzworth Publishing.

Neiman, S. (2019) *Learning from the Germans*. London: Allen Lane.

NIO (Northern Ireland Office) (2014) *The Stormont House Agreement*. Available at: https://assets.publishing.service.gov.uk/government/uploads/system/uploads/attachment_data/file/390672/Stormont_House_Agreement.pdf (accessed 18 August 2020).

NIO (2020) *A Legal Framework for a Troubles-Related Incident Victims' Payment Scheme: Government Response*. Available at: https://assets.publishing.service.gov.uk/government/uploads/system/uploads/attachment_data/file/862650/VP_consultation_govt_response.pdf (accessed 16 March 2020).

O'Malley, P. (1995) 'The question of religion', *Fortnight*, February.

Roberts, T. (2018) 'Refreshingly honest view from loyalism on legacy resolution', *eamonnmallie.com* (22 June). Available at: https://eamonnmallie.com/2018/06/refreshingly-honest-view-from-loyalism-on-legacy-resolution-by-tom-roberts/ (accessed 21 March 2020).

Schlink, B. (2010) *Guilt about the Past*. London: Beautiful Books.

Sinn Féin (2009) 'Consultative Group on the Past report is deeply flawed' (25 March). Available at: https://www.sinfein.ie/contents/15634 (dead link; accessed 15 May 2020).

Spencer, G. (2008) *The State of Loyalism in Northern Ireland*. Basingstoke: Palgrave Macmillan.

Spencer. G. (ed.) (2011a) *Forgiving and Remembering in Northern Ireland*. London: Continuum.

Spencer, G. (2011b) 'Loyalist perspectives on apology, regret and change', in J. W. McAuley and G. Spencer (eds), *Ulster Loyalism after the Good Friday Agreement: History, Identity and Change*, pp. 244–60. Basingstoke: Palgrave Macmillan.

Spencer, G. (2012) *Protestant Identity and Peace in Northern Ireland*. Basingstoke: Palgrave Macmillan.

Spencer, G. (2015a) *From Armed Struggle to Political Struggle*. London: Bloomsbury.

Spencer, G. (2015b) 'Managing the tensions of difference: an interview with Jonathan Powell', in G. Spencer (ed.), *The British and Peace in Northern Ireland*. Cambridge: Cambridge University Press.

Spencer, G. and Alderdice, J. (2019) 'Forgiveness, the individual and the conflict society', in S. Hance (ed.), *Forgiveness in Practice*. London: Jessica Kingsley.

Rieff, D. (2016) *In Praise of Forgetting: Historical Memory and its Ironies*. New Haven, CT: Yale University Press.

Todorov, T. (2000) *Hope and Memory*. Princeton, NJ: Princeton University Press.

Young, D. (2020) 'Sinn Féin's North leader "ignoring rule of law" over case for victims of Troubles', *Irish Independent*, 18 August.

Index

Abercorn Restaurant bombing 85
Adair, Johnny 89, 166
Adams, Gerry 45, 87, 88, 108, 111, 129, 130, 133, 227
agonism 18, 20, 21, 26, 27, 32
Akaev, Askar 207, 208
Aldershot bombing 85
Alliance Party 61
Anderson, Martina 107
Andersonstown News 119
Andy Tyrie Interpretative Centre 157
Anglo-Irish Agreement (1985) 145
Ankersmit, Frank 48
An Phoblacht 119, 126, 127, 131
Argentina 183, 185–188, 197, 198
   Art Memoria Colectivo 183, 191
   the disappeared 189, 191, 196
   ESMA, (the Higher School of Mechanics of the Navy) 187, 189–191
Armenian genocide 43
Arnold, Richard 41
Atambayev, Almazbek 214
Atia, Nadia 99

Bakiyev, Kurmanbek 208, 209
Barkan, Elazar 70
Bar-Tal, Daniel 147, 149
Battle of the Boyne 145

Battle of the Somme 145, 152, 153
Batyrov, Kadyrjon 209
Beattie, Geoffrey 83
Beiner, Guy 73, 84
Bekeris, Eugenia 197
Belfast Telegraph 222
Belfast violence (1920–22) 40, 42, 43
Blair, Tony 64
Bloody Friday 86
Bloody Sunday 65, 85
Bloomfield, Sir Kenneth 57
Blustein, Jeffrey 226
Bombay Street 39
Bonnett, Alastair 99, 112
Bosnia 120
   Srebrenica 48
Bourdieu, Pierre 169, 170, 179
Bradley, Denis 56
   see also Consultative Group on the Past, Eames/Bradley report
Bradley, Karen 66, 67
Brubaker, Rogers 78, 79
Burntollet Bridge 22

Carr, Garrett 113
Carroll, Adrian 86
Carson, Sir Edward 151
Carthy, Matt 132
Cash, John 149

Chauviré, Roger 106
Claudy bomb 86
collective memory 6–9, 11
   comparative approaches 205, 206
   definitions 144, 186, 189
   in Argentina 191
   in Croatia 192
   problems with 225, 226, 230–232, 237, 238, 240
   see also Irish republicans, collective memory and identity
   see also Ulster loyalists, collective memory and identity
Colombia 4
Commemoration 9, 10, 118–121, 126, 173
   Voices of 68 exhibition 27–30
   see also Irish Republican commemoration, Ulster loyalist commemoration
Connerton, Paul 10, 155, 156, 188
Connolly, James 126
Conservative Party 91
Consultative Group on the Past (Eames-Bradley Report) 1, 2, 56, 59, 63, 223, 228, 229, 237
Cosmopolitanism 19–21, 23
Craig, James 151
Croatia 185, 187, 188, 192, 197, 198
   Homeland War of Independence 192, 193, 195
   Vukovar massacre 192–194
   Vukovar memorials 187, 188, 193, 194
Cunningham, John Pat 66
Cyprus 78, 120

Dalton, Des 101, 108
Darby, John 147
Darkley massacre 86
Davies, Jeremy 99
Dawson, Graham 91
Democratic Unionist Party (DUP) 61, 66, 91, 237
Derry Journal 137
Doberti, Paula 197
Doherty, Kieran 127
Dwyer, Susan 237

Eames, Archbishop Robin 56
Economic and Social Research Council (ESRC) 69
Elliott, Dr Iris 230
Empey, Sir Reg 89
Engels, Friedrich 210
English, Richard 83, 168
Enniskillen bomb 145
Ervine, David 26
ethnic conflict 80
ethno-nationalism 79, 172, 216
   see also nationalism
European Union 19, 20
Ex-Prisoners Interpretative Centre (EPIC) 157

Faulkner, Brian 143
Fein, Helen 42
Fianna Fail 103
Fine Gael 103
First World War 151,152
Flags, Identity, Culture and Tradition commission (FICT) 16,32
Foucault, Michel 111
France, class privilege 170

gender, feminist perspectives on memory work 171, 172
   gender equality 165
   gendered memory 195–197
   see also Ulster loyalists, women in loyalism
Gilloch, Graeme 189
Glazer, Peter 97, 98, 100, 112

Index 245

Glennon, Kieran 43
Good Friday Agreement (1998) 15, 23, 58
　constructive ambiguity 17
　prisoner releases 64
Gorman, Tommy 85
Grand Orange Lodge of Ireland 146
Greysteel massacre 89
Guterres, Antonio 214

Haass, Dr Richard 59, 60
　Haass report (2013) 23
Hain, Peter 91
Hart, Peter 41
Haugbolle, Sune 189
Hayes, Maurice 110
He, Yinan 92
Hendron, Joe 89
Herron, Stephen 68
Hillsborough Agreement (2010) 125
historical memory 78, 79, 81, 82
Hobsbawn, Eric 78
Hogan, Henry 132
Horowitz, Donald 80, 120
Howard, Michael 81
Hoxha, Eliza 195, 197
Hughes, Brendan 26
hunger strikes 102, 105–107, 111, 126, 127
Hunt, John 108
Hutching, Denis 66

Ignatieff, Michael 91, 235
imagined communities 81
Implementation and Recovery Group (IRG) 60, 61, 69, 70, 72, 138, 223
Independent Commission on Information Recovery (ICIR) 60, 61, 67, 68, 223
Iraq 120
　Battle of Fallujah 52
　pogrom against Jews in Baghdad 42

Ireland, Easter Rising 104, 105, 124, 126
　government 61, 63
　home rule crisis 82
　partition 40
　Second Dáil 109
　War of Independence 106, 126
Irish Independent 43
Irish National Liberation Army (INLA) 86, 87
Irish News 119
Irish republicans, collective memory and identity 44–47, 51, 79, 83, 97, 98, 101–112, 123, 160
　Commemoration 121, 122, 124–135, 138
　dissident republicans 101, 107, 108, 111, 113, 135–137
Irish Republican Army (IRA) 44, 63, 85–89, 105, 108, 111, 130, 131, 133, 227
　border campaign 104, 105
　Continuity IRA 108, 109
　Official IRA 85
　on the runs 64
　New IRA 112
　Real IRA 112
Irish Republican News 45
Irish Republican Socialist Party (IRSP) 87
Irish Times 88, 143
Israel 120

Judt, Tony 90
Justice 62–65, 67

Kearney, Declan 128, 132, 137
Kearney, Richard 104
Keightley, Emily 99, 100
Kelly, Gerry 129, 132, 134, 136
Kennedy, Liam 50
Kiljunen, Kimmo 211, 212
Kirchner, Cristina 190, 191
Kosovo 45, 195

Kyrgyzstan 204, 206, 216, 217
  The (2010) revolution 209
  The Tulip Revolution 208
  violence (1990) 207
  violence (2010) 209–212
Kyrgyzstan Inquiry Commission
  (KIC) 211,212, 215

Lebanon 186
legacy 1–3, 16, 26, 56–59,
  222,223, 227–229, 231, 238,
  239
Lenin, Vladimir 207, 210, 211
Lewis, Brandon 2, 3, 224
Loach, Ken 110
Longley, Michael 113
Lowenthal, David 103

McAlister, Dr Siobhan 112
McAuley, James W. 85
McDonald, Mary Lou 128, 129, 135
Mac Ginty, Roger 147
McGlinchey, Dominic 87
McGrattan, Cillian 80, 91, 239
McGuinness, Martin 108, 111,
  129, 131–133, 136
McIntyre, Anthony 111
McKee, Lyra 112, 113
MacMillan, Margaret 222
McVeigh, Jim 126
Martin, Declan 132
Marquez, Gabriel Garcia 4, 5
Marx, Karl 98, 210
May, Theresa 66
Maze/Long Kesh 105, 106, 185,
  187, 199
Meehan, Martin 45
memory activism 25, 100
memory studies 18
Menem, Carlos 190, 191
Mental Health Foundation 230
Mladic, Ratko 48
mnemonic imagination 99, 100
Moloney, Ed 26
Moon, Ban-ki 214
Morrison, Danny 52, 111

Mouffe, Chantal 18, 19
Muro, Diego 100, 102
Murphy, Conor 45
Murray, Sean 44
Myrzakmatov, Melis 204,
  211–213

Nagle, John 83
nationalism 19, 83, 207, 215
  Basque nationalism 100
  Irish nationalism 101
  see also ethno-nationalism
National Museums Northern
  Ireland (NMNI) 14, 27, 30,
  31
Neiman, Susan 222
Nerve Centre, Derry/Londonderry
  29
Netherlands Institute for War
  Documentation (NIOD) 48,
  49
Nocher, David 86
Nora, Pierre 185
North Atlantic Treaty
  Organisation (NATO) 19
Northern Ireland, civil rights
  movement 22, 23, 27, 125
  cross-community programmes
    177
  economy 15
  paramilitaries 84
  peace process 15, 17, 27, 63,
    64, 93, 123, 125, 165
  political murals 168, 169
  social segregation 83
  welfare reform 60, 61
Northern Ireland Community
  Relations Council 30
Northern Ireland Executive 59, 91
Northern Ireland Office (NIO) 16,
  59
Northern Ireland Victims
  Commission 58

Ó'Caoláin, Caoimhghín 126, 127
O'Donnell, Ruan 107

Index 247

O'Faolain, Sean 113
O'Hanlon, Eilis 222
O'Neill, Leona 113
O'Neill, Michelle 135, 238
O'Neill, Terence 22
O'Malley, Padraig 232, 233
Oral History Archive (OHA) 68, 69
Orange Standard 146
O'Rawe, Richard 105, 111
Organization for Security and Co-operation in Europe (OSCE) 211
Orwell, George 83
O'Shea, Sinéad 113
O'Sullivan, Meghan 59, 60
Otunbayeva, Roza 208, 211

Palestine 120
parallel processing 47–49, 51
Passerini, Luisa 81
Patterson, Henry 73
Patterson, Owen 59
Pearse, Pádraig 104, 126
People's Democracy 22
Perrin, Jorge Gonzalez 183
Pickering, Michael 99, 100
Polan, Hrvoje 196, 197
Police Ombudsman 59
Police Service of Northern Ireland (PSNI) 123
  Historical Enquiries Team (HET) 59, 63
  Historical Investigations Unit (HIU) 60–62, 65, 223
Pollak, Andy 110
populist politics 20
Prager, Jeffrey 150
Progressive Unionist Party (PUP) 168
Purple Standard 153, 157, 160
Purvis, Dawn 168

Queens's University Belfast 22
Quieto, Lucila 195–197

radical nostalgia 97–100
Red Hand Commando 147
Renewable Heat Incentive scandal 16, 61
Republican Sinn Féin 101, 108, 109
Rieff, David 72, 73, 82, 91, 225, 226
Roberts, Tom 68
Robinson, Peter 61
Royal Irish Regiment (RIR) 128
Royal Ulster Constabulary (RUC) 22, 38, 128
RTE 22
Runia, Eelco 47
Russia, collapse of USSR 207
  Moscow Olympics 210
  pogroms against Jews 41, 42
Ryan, Mick 104, 105

Sands, Bobby 106, 107, 111
Santayana, George 81, 82
Saoradh 112
Sariyev, Temir 214
Second World War 19
sectarianism 85–90
Shankill bomb 88
Shankill Butchers 86
Shankill Defence Association 39
Shirlow, Peter 63, 65
Siege of Derry 145
Sigerson, George 101
Sinn Féin 45, 64, 66, 87, 101, 106–108, 111, 123, 124, 128, 227, 228
Social Democratic and Labour Party (SDLP) 61
social forgetting 83, 84
Soldier F 65
Sontag, Susan 78, 185
South Africa, Truth and Reconciliation Commission 235
Smith, Anthony D 79
Smith, Julian 238

Spain, US veterans of the International Brigades 100
St Andrews Agreement (2006) 93
Stewart, A.T.Q 71
Stormont Assembly 16
Stormont House Agreement (2014) 16, 23, 61, 68, 71, 138, 223, 224
Sullivan, Garrett 194

Thompson, Judith 66
Todd, Jennifer 167
Todorov, Tzvetan 225, 228
Tóibín, Colm 105
Townshend, Charles 105, 106
Troubles 37, 38
 Internment 40
 Troubles tourism 103, 177, 178
 violence (1969) 38–40, 44, 45
 (1972) 85, 86
truth and reconciliation 67–75, 235, 239
Turkey, violence against minorities 42
 see also Armenian genocide

Ulster Defence Association (UDA) 89, 147, 154, 157, 168, 173
 Ulster Freedom Fighters (UFF) 64,89
 Ulster Young Militants (UYM) 147, 167
Ulster Defence Regiment (UDR) 128
Ulster Defence Union 154
Ulster Division (36th) 151–153
Ulster loyalists 39, 79, 83, 85, 88
 collective memory and identity 145–150, 155, 156, 159–161, 218
 commemoration 151–153, 173
 opposition to Home Rule 151, 154
 women in loyalism 166–170, 174–180
Ulster Museum 27,28
Ulster Special Constabulary (B-Specials) 39, 145
Ulster Unionist Party (UUP) 39
Ulster Volunteer Force (UVF) 64, 68, 86, 147, 153, 154, 156, 157, 168
Unionist Voice 150
United Nations (UN) 19, 48
United Kingdom, Brexit 16, 103
 British Army 39, 129, 130
 government 2, 61, 63, 93
University of Liverpool, Institute of Irish Studies 29,30
Uzbekistan 209

victims 57–60, 238
Villiers, Theresa 60
visual memory 186, 187, 189, 191, 193, 196–199

Walsh, Rudolfo 183
Wilson, Robin 93
Wilson, Sammy 66
Woodward, Shaun 59
Wright, Billy 166
Wright, Frank 82, 90
Wright, Patrick 99

Yeltsin, Boris 207, 208
Yugoslavia 40, 41, 78, 79
 International Criminal Tribunal for the former Yugoslavia (ICTY) 193, 194
 Yugoslav National Army 194

EU authorised representative for GPSR:
Easy Access System Europe, Mustamäe tee 50,
10621 Tallinn, Estonia
gpsr.requests@easproject.com

www.ingramcontent.com/pod-product-compliance
Lightning Source LLC
Chambersburg PA
CBHW051608230426
43668CB00013B/2027